Mastering OpenVPN

Master building and integrating secure private
networks using OpenVPN

Eric F Crist

Jan Just Keijser

BIRMINGHAM - MUMBAI

Mastering OpenVPN

First published: August 2015

Production reference: 1260815

Published by Packt Publishing Ltd.
Livery Place
35 Livery Street
Birmingham B3 2PB, UK.

ISBN 978-1-78355-313-6

www.packtpub.com

Credits

Authors
Eric F Crist

Jan Just Keijser

Reviewers
Stefan Agner

Emmanuel Bretelle

Michael A Cossenas

Guillaume Destuynder

Commissioning Editor
Amarabha Banerjee

Acquisition Editors
Richard Brookes-Bland

Larissa Pinto

Content Development Editor
Pooja Nair

Technical Editor
Mitali Somaiya

Copy Editors
Roshni Banerjee

Rashmi Sawant

Project Coordinator
Judie Jose

Proofreader
Safis Editing

Indexer
Hemangini Bari

Graphics
Sheetal Aute

Production Coordinator
Nitesh Thakur

Cover Work
Nitesh Thakur

About the Authors

Eric F Crist is an IT professional with experience in hardware and software systems integration. With a few others, he has had a key role in building the OpenVPN community to what it is today. He works in research and development as a principal computer system specialist for St. Jude Medical. His role involves system engineering, configuration management, and cyber security analysis for products related to the Cardiovascular Ablation Technology division.

You can find him online at the Freenode and EFNet IRC networks as `ecrist`. He calls the Twin Cities, Minnesota, his home and lives with his wife, DeeDee, his son, Lance, and his daughter, Taylor.

Jan Just Keijser is an open source professional from Utrecht, the Netherlands. He has a wide range of experience in IT, ranging from providing user support, system administration, and systems programming to network programming. He has worked for various IT companies since 1989. He has been working mainly on Unix/Linux platforms since 1995. He was an active USENET contributor in the early 1990s.

Currently, he is employed as a senior scientific programmer in Amsterdam, the Netherlands, at Nikhef, the institute for subatomic physics from the Dutch Foundation for Fundamental Research on Matter (FOM). He is working on multi-core and many-core computing systems, grid computing, as well as smartcard applications. His open source interests include all types of virtual private networking, including IPSec, PPTP, and of course, OpenVPN. In 2004, he discovered OpenVPN and has been using it ever since.

His first book was *OpenVPN 2 Cookbook, Packt Publishing*.

About the Reviewers

Stefan Agner completed his bachelor's degree in information technology from the Lucerne University of Applied Sciences and Arts in 2009 and has worked in the field of embedded systems as a software engineer since then. He focuses on driver development and system programming and prefers to work with the open source software stack. Currently, he is working to upstream Linux support for the ARM-based Freescale Vybrid SoC for his employer, Toradex AG.

He describes himself as an open source enthusiast who works with Linux and other free software not only in his professional life as a software engineer, but also in his spare time. At several smaller companies, he successfully deployed and managed OpenVPN as the primary VPN solution. For his private IT infrastructure, he runs OpernWrt-powered routers, which serve as OpenVPN servers. He also likes to blog about technical stuff, such as fascinating projects and interesting problems he comes across.

Emmanuel Bretelle has 10 years of experience in devops, systems, and network administration. He has leveraged OpenVPN, its plugin capabilities, and cross-platform compatibility to help connect employees across the globe to corporate networks.

He has also developed and open sourced two OpenVPN plugins: openvpn-mysql-auth and openvpn-ldap-auth.

When not fiddling around with new technology or automating his way out, he enjoys traveling and chilling out.

Michael A Cossenas is a Linux/network administrator from Athens, Greece.

He has been working as a network security specialist for Digital Sima, a company specializing in LAN/WAN networking. He is now employed as a subcontractor for IBM Greece and manages 50 plus SUSE-based Linux servers as one of their customers.

His first experience with Linux was way back in 1998, using RedHat 5.2. Since then, he has worked on various open source projects, including Zimbra, DRBD, KVM, and Postfix.

He is also an OpenVPN forum moderator.

He works as a subcontractor for IBM Greece in the SO (Strategic Outsourcing) department.

I would like to thank my family (my wife, Froso, my son, Antony, and my daughter, Kate) for supporting me in difficult times.

www.PacktPub.com

Support files, eBooks, discount offers, and more

For support files and downloads related to your book, please visit www.PacktPub.com.

Did you know that Packt offers eBook versions of every book published, with PDF and ePub files available? You can upgrade to the eBook version at www.PacktPub.com and as a print book customer, you are entitled to a discount on the eBook copy. Get in touch with us at service@packtpub.com for more details.

At www.PacktPub.com, you can also read a collection of free technical articles, sign up for a range of free newsletters and receive exclusive discounts and offers on Packt books and eBooks.

https://www2.packtpub.com/books/subscription/packtlib

Do you need instant solutions to your IT questions? PacktLib is Packt's online digital book library. Here, you can search, access, and read Packt's entire library of books.

Why subscribe?

- Fully searchable across every book published by Packt
- Copy and paste, print, and bookmark content
- On demand and accessible via a web browser

Free access for Packt account holders

If you have an account with Packt at www.PacktPub.com, you can use this to access PacktLib today and view 9 entirely free books. Simply use your login credentials for immediate access.

Table of Contents

Preface

Privacy and security on the Internet and in private networks is a growing concern and is increasingly common in the news, where there are breaches of each. Virtual private networks (VPN) were created out of a need for secured communications. The most popular and widely used open source VPN software today is OpenVPN. *Mastering OpenVPN* aims to educate you on deployment, troubleshooting, and configuration of OpenVPN and provide solid use cases for various scenarios.

What this book covers

Chapter 1, Introduction to OpenVPN, discusses the various types of Virtual Private Networks and some of their various strengths and weaknesses. PPTP, OpenVPN, IPSec, and other protocols are also discussed in this chapter.

Chapter 2, Point-to-point Mode, covers the OpenVPN roots, point-to-point mode, and the initially only supported mode. It also covers the tap mode in a bridged scenario and an uncommon configuration.

Chapter 3, PKIs and Certificates, explains the complex concept of X.509 certificates and PKIs with examples and a demonstration of a couple of utilities. It also covers how to create a certificate chain and deploy that chain to their VPN.

Chapter 4, Client/Server Mode with tun Devices, walks you through the most common deployment mode, a tun or routed, and its setup. It also discusses the passing of client-backed routes along with IPv4 and IPv6.

Chapter 5, Advanced Deployment Scenarios in tun Mode, covers policy-based routing and configuring OpenVPN to integrate your VPN clients with the rest of the LAN. Complex examples of tun mode are examined, showing that they are appropriate even in advanced scenarios.

Chapter 6, Client/Server Mode with tap Devices, discusses the often misused and less commonly deployed tap or bridged mode VPNs. Solid examples of broadcast and OSI layer 2 traffic are demonstrated in this chapter.

Chapter 7, Scripting and Plugins, helps you gain an understanding of the methods to extent the VPN, including authentication, routing, and protocol enhancements. This chapter helps an administrator create a local experience for a worker or a user on the move.

Chapter 8, Using OpenVPN on Mobile Devices and Home Routers, helps you learn how to use home router OSes and features to deploy OpenVPN. We understand that it's not just enterprise or commercial users looking to protect their privacy and data. Increasingly, home users desire to deploy secure connections to their home resources.

Chapter 9, Troubleshooting and Tuning, will help you become an expert in your OpenVPN deployment by learning how to troubleshoot problems and bugs. The ability to identify issues creates a solid and reliable installation and confidence in your users.

Chapter 10, Future Directions, gives you a brief history and lengthier discussion of the future direction of OpenVPN, and the mindset of the developers is revealed. It also helps you understand the reasoning and history behind the various decisions behind features and bugs.

What you need for this book

You should have the following entities for a complete experience of reading and following *Mastering OpenVPN*:

- A Unix, Linux, or Mac OS X system
- A Windows system
- A server (Windows or Linux, whichever is preferred, Linux or FreeBSD suggested)
- A solid understanding (101 or 201 level) of networking (UDP and TCP over IP)

An IRC client or a web browser is also helpful. When you run into trouble or have too many questions, pop in to #openvpn on irc.freenode.net, and look for @janjust or @ecrist. We look forward to talking to you!

Who this book is for

This book is really designed for anyone looking to deploy a VPN solution to any private or enterprise network. OpenVPN can be used for point-to-point tunnels, intra-network connections, and road warriors. The concepts covered in this book can be applied generally across more than just OpenVPN deployments, with the exception of configuration argument specifics.

Conventions

In this book, you will find a number of styles of text that distinguish between different kinds of information. Here are some examples of these styles, and an explanation of their meaning.

Code words in text, database table names, folder names, filenames, file extensions, pathnames, dummy URLs, user input, and Twitter handles are shown as follows: "You can specify a message digest as parameter to the --auth option."

A block of code is set as follows:

```
proto udp
port 1194
dev tun
server 10.200.0.0 255.255.255.0
```

When we wish to draw your attention to a particular part of a code block, the relevant lines or items are set in bold:

```
proto udp
port 1194
dev tun
server 10.200.0.0 255.255.255.0
```

Any command-line input or output is written as follows:

```
#  mkdir -p /etc/openvpn/movpn
```

Note that first character (the prompt) is used to indicate a root-shell (#) or a user shell ($).

New terms and **important words** are shown in bold. Words that you see on the screen, in menus or dialog boxes for example, appear in the text like this: "Launch the OpenVPN GUI application, select the configuration `basic-udp-client` and click on **Connect**."

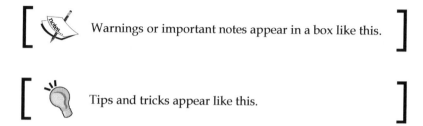

> Warnings or important notes appear in a box like this.

> Tips and tricks appear like this.

Reader feedback

Feedback from our readers is always welcome. Let us know what you think about this book—what you liked or may have disliked. Reader feedback is important for us to develop titles that you really get the most out of.

To send us general feedback, simply send an e-mail to `feedback@packtpub.com`, and mention the book title via the subject of your message.

If there is a topic that you have expertise in and you are interested in either writing or contributing to a book, see our author guide on `www.packtpub.com/authors`.

Customer support

Now that you are the proud owner of a Packt book, we have a number of things to help you to get the most from your purchase.

Downloading the example code

You can download the example code files for all Packt books you have purchased from your account at `http://www.packtpub.com`. If you purchased this book elsewhere, you can visit `http://www.packtpub.com/support` and register to have the files e-mailed directly to you.

Errata

Although we have taken every care to ensure the accuracy of our content, mistakes do happen. If you find a mistake in one of our books—maybe a mistake in the text or the code—we would be grateful if you would report this to us. By doing so, you can save other readers from frustration and help us improve subsequent versions of this book. If you find any errata, please report them by visiting http://www.packtpub.com/submit-errata, selecting your book, clicking on the **errata submission form** link, and entering the details of your errata. Once your errata are verified, your submission will be accepted and the errata will be uploaded on our website, or added to any list of existing errata, under the Errata section of that title.

To view the previously submitted errata, go to https://www.packtpub.com/books/content/support and enter the name of the book in the search field. The required information will appear under the **Errata** section.

Piracy

Piracy of copyright material on the Internet is an ongoing problem across all media. At Packt, we take the protection of our copyright and licenses very seriously. If you come across any illegal copies of our works, in any form, on the Internet, please provide us with the location address or website name immediately so that we can pursue a remedy.

Please contact us at copyright@packtpub.com with a link to the suspected pirated material.

We appreciate your help in protecting our authors, and our ability to bring you valuable content.

Questions

You can contact us at questions@packtpub.com if you are having a problem with any aspect of the book, and we will do our best to address it.

1
Introduction to OpenVPN

The Internet in modern society is as ubiquitous as any public utility. When someone buys a home or moves into a new apartment, or a business moves into a new space, an Internet service is the first utility on the list to be ordered, followed by power, heat, trash, and maybe (but not likely) a land line or telephone service. You could even argue that the modern qualifier isn't even necessary. With programs such as One Laptop per Child, coupled with efforts by the likes of Facebook and Google, so-called third-world nations have the Internet where there is no running water, sewers, or even telephone services.

When you have such a wide-reaching service with so many individuals, at a certain point it will be necessary to secure and protect the data transmitted on that network. With most crowds and heavy concentrations of people, there is a more nefarious element looking to take advantage of those with less knowledge. **Virtual Private Networks (VPNs)** were created out of a greater need for secured communication across an otherwise unprotected infrastructure. The original large-scale network, ARPANET, had very little (if any) protection and authentication and all other nodes were inherently trusted. The network landscapes today are very different and even many casual, nontechnical users are aware of the lack of security of their connections.

Government agencies have long been targets for intelligence. For thousands of years, methods and procedures have been slowly perfected and tuned to protect sensitive information from enemies and other prying eyes. Initially, wax-sealed letters carried by trusted individuals meant you and the receiver could trust a message had arrived safely and untampered. As time and technology have progressed, it became easier to intercept those messages, read or alter them, and send them along their way.

World War II saw some of the greatest advances in cryptography and secure communications. From devices such as the German Enigma machine to the Navajo Code Talkers, communicating securely between troops and command was a never-ending arms race. Today, governments and militaries aren't the only groups with a desire for privacy. Corporations want to maintain data integrity and protection for **payment card industry (PCI)** standards to protect consumers. Family members want to discuss family matters over private channels, where the community at large isn't able to eavesdrop. Others wish to break through the national firewalls meant to oversee the populous and restrict content deemed controversial or against party politics.

Every day, most people use a VPN or have a use for a VPN, whether they realize it at the time or not. Many different VPN technologies exist, both from commercial vendors and as open source projects. One of the most popular pieces of open source VPN software is OpenVPN. The goal of this book is to make you an OpenVPN master; you will learn not just the technology behind it, but the reasoning, logic, and logistics of everything involved. While this book will mention and touch on the commercial offering from OpenVPN Technologies, Inc., Access Server, the primary focus will be on the open source/community version of OpenVPN.

What is a VPN?

Put simply, a VPN allows an administrator to create a "local" network between multiple computers on varying network segments. In some instances, those machines can be on the same LAN, they can be distant from each other across the vast Internet, or they can even be connected across a multitude of connection media such as wireless uplinks, satellite, dial-up-networking, and so on. The *P* in VPN comes from the added protection to make that virtual network private. Network traffic that is flowing over a VPN is often referred to as *inside the (VPN) tunnel*, compared to all the other traffic that is *outside the tunnel*.

In the following figure, network traffic is shown as it traditionally traverses across multiple network segments and the general Internet. Here, this traffic is relatively open to inspection and analysis. Though protected protocols such as HTTPS and SSH are less vulnerable, they are still identifiable; if an attacker is snooping network traffic, they can still see what type of connection is made from which computer to which server.

When a VPN is used, the traffic *inside* the tunnel is no longer identifiable.

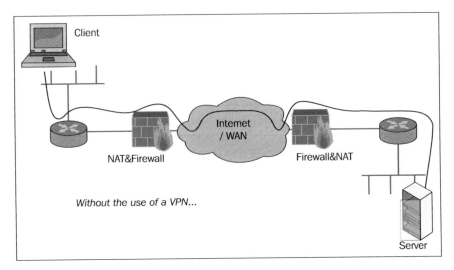

The traffic within a VPN can be anything you would send over a local or wide-area network: web traffic, e-mail, text, graphics, and so on. Examples of some applications include the following:

- Automated Teller Machines: ATMs may use a VPN to connect more securely to banking systems.
- Open / Free Wi-Fi: With the proliferation of free or open wireless networks, everyday users can utilize a VPN to protect the entirety of their Internet browsing.
- Corporate networks: Corporations and other organizations may use a VPN to connect multiple office locations or even entire data centers.
- GeoIP / Location-based services: Some websites serve data based on geographic location by using GeoIP databases and other records. A VPN can allow you to "bounce" through another machine in a location closer to the content you really want. Internet video services such as Hulu, YouTube, and Netflix are common examples of this.

- Bypassing censorship / Political freedom: Some regimes, such as North Korea or China, have extraordinarily restrictive censorship rules. The "Great Firewall of China" is one extreme example. The lockdowns of Internet access during political uprisings such as the "Arab Spring" attempt to contain and control reports outside the conflict. VPNs can aid in getting outside those restrictive rules to the greater Internet.

Here is an example of the traffic within a VPN. While the VPN itself is routed across the Internet like in the preceding figure, devices along the network path only see VPN traffic; those devices are completely unaware of what is being transmitted inside the private tunnel. Protected protocols, such as HTTPS and SSH, will still be protected inside the tunnel from other VPN users, but will be additionally unidentifiable from outside the tunnel. A VPN not only encrypts the traffic within, it hides and protects individual data streams from those outside the tunnel.

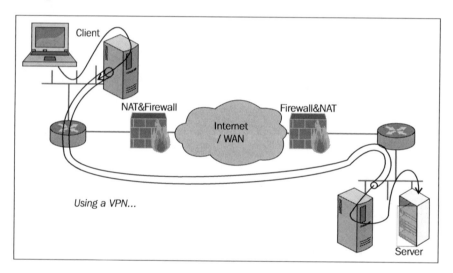

It should be noted that the preceding figure shows both the strengths and one of the greatest threats of VPN technologies. The VPN tunnel is *dug* through routers and firewalls on both sides. Thus, all the network traffic that is flowing via the VPN tunnel is bypassing the regular network defenses, unless special measures are taken to police the VPN traffic.

Most VPN implementations utilize some form of encryption and, additionally, authentication. The encryption of the VPN ensures that other parties that may be monitoring traffic between systems cannot decode and further analyze otherwise sensitive data. Authentication has two components, each in a different context.

First, there is user or system authentication that ensures those connecting to the service are authorized. This type of authentication may be in the form of per-user certificates, or a username/password combination. Further, rules specific to a given user can be negotiated such as specific routes, firewall rules, or other scripts and utilities. Typically, these are unique to a single instance, though even that can be configurable (when OpenVPN is used, see `--duplicate-cn`).

The second component of authentication is added protection to the communication stream. In this case, a method of signing each packet sent is established. Each system verifies the VPN packets it receives are properly signed before decrypting the payload. By authenticating packets that are already encrypted, a system can save processing time by not even decrypting packets that do not meet the authentication rules. In the end, this prevents a very real potential **Denial of Service (DoS)** attack, as well as thwarting **Man in the Middle (MITM)** attacks, *assuming the signing keys are kept secure*!

Types of VPNs

There are many VPN products available on the market, both commercial and open source. Almost all of these VPN products can be separated into the following four categories:

- PPTP-protocol based VPNs
- IPSec-protocol based VPNs
- SSL-based VPNs
- OpenVPN

Some people argue that OpenVPN is also an SSL-based VPN, as it uses an SSL or TLS-like protocol to establish a secure connection. However, we have created a separate category for OpenVPN, as it is different from almost every other SSL-based VPN solution.

We will now go into more detail about each of the four types of VPNs:

PPTP

One of the oldest VPN protocols is the **Point-to-Point Tunneling Protocol (PPTP)** developed by Microsoft and Ascend in 1999. It is officially registered as RFC2637 (see `https://www.ietf.org/rfc/rfc2637.txt` for the full standard). The PPTP client has been included in Windows ever since 1995 and is still included in most operating systems.

Nowadays, the PPTP protocol is considered fundamentally insecure, as the strength of the security of the connection is directly related to the strength of the authentication mechanism chosen (for example, the password). Thus, an insecure password leads to an insecure VPN connection. Most PPTP setups use the MS-CHAPv2 protocol for encrypting passwords, and it is this protocol which is fundamentally broken. The security of the PPTP protocol, including the Microsoft MS-CHAPv2 extensions, has been discussed in the article available at `https://www.schneier.com/paper-pptpv2.html`.

It is also possible to use X.509 certificates for securing a PPTP connection, which does lead to a fairly secure connection. However, not all PPTP clients support EAP-TLS, which is needed to allow the use of X.509 certificates.

PPTP uses two channels, a control channel for setting up the connection and another channel for data transport. The control channel is initiated over TCP port 1723. The data channel uses the **General Routing Encapsulation (GRE)** protocol, which is IP protocol 47. For comparison, "regular" TCP/IP traffic is done using IP protocol 6 (TCP) and 17 (UDP).

PPTP clients are available on almost all operating systems, ranging from Windows to Linux and Unix derivatives to iOS and Android devices.

IPSec

The IPSec standard is the official IEEE/IETF standard for IP security. It is officially registered as RFC2411 (see `https://www.ietf.org/rfc/rfc2411.txt` for the full standard). IPSec is also built into the IPv6 standard.

IPSec operates at layer 2 and 3 of the OSI model of the network stack. It introduces the concept of security policies, which makes it extremely flexible and powerful, but also notoriously hard to configure and troubleshoot. Security policies allow an administrator to encrypt traffic between two endpoints based on many parameters, such as the source and destination IP address, as well as the source and destination TCP or UDP ports.

IPSec can be configured to use pre-shared keys or X.509 certificates to secure the VPN connection. Additionally, it uses either X.509 certificates, one-time passwords, or username/password protocols to authenticate the VPN connection.

There are two modes of operation in IPSec: *tunneling mode* and *transport mode*. Transport mode is used most often in combination with the **Level 2 Tunneling Protocol (L2TP)**. This L2TP protocol performs the user authentication as described in the preceding section. The IPSec clients built into most operating systems usually perform IPSec+L2TP, although it is also possible to set up an *IPSec-only* connection. The IPSec VPN client built into Microsoft Windows uses IPSec+L2TP by default, but it is possible to disable or bypass it. However, this involves cryptic commands and security policy changes.

Like PPTP, IPSec also uses two channels: a control channel for setting up the connection and one for data transport. The control channel is initiated over UDP port 500 or 4500. The data channel uses the **Encapsulated Security Payload (ESP)** protocol, which is IP protocol 50. For comparison, "regular" TCP/IP traffic is done using IP protocol 6 (TCP) and 17 (UDP). The integrity of IPSec packets is ensured using **Hash-based Message Authentication Code (HMAC)**, which is the same method that OpenVPN uses.

One of the main disadvantages of IPSec is that many vendors have implemented extensions to the standard, which makes it hard (if not impossible) to connect two IPSec endpoints from different vendors.

IPSec software is included in almost all operating systems, as well as firewall, router, and switch firmware.

SSL-based VPNs

The most commonly used VPNs nowadays are SSL-based VPNs, which are based on the SSL/TLS protocol. SSL-based VPNs are often called client-less VPNs or web-based VPNs, although there are some vendors that provide separate client software, such as Cisco AnyConnect and Microsoft SSTP. Most SSL-based VPNs use the same network protocol as is used for secure website (HTTPS), while OpenVPN uses a custom format for encrypting and signing data traffic. This is the main reason why OpenVPN is listed as a separate VPN category.

There is no well-defined standard for SSL-based VPNs, but most use the SSL/TLS protocol to set up and secure the connection. The connection is secured in most cases by using X.509 certificates, with one-time password or username/password protocols for authenticating the connection. SSL-based VPNs are very similar to the connections used to secure websites (HTTPS) and the same protocol and channel (TCP and port 443) is often used.

Even though SSL-based VPNs are often called web-based or client-less, there are quite a few vendors that use a *browser plugin* or ActiveX control to "enhance" the VPN connection. This makes the VPN noninteroperable with unsupported browsers or operating systems.

OpenVPN

OpenVPN is often called an SSL-based VPN, as it uses the SSL/TLS protocol to secure the connection. However, OpenVPN also uses HMAC in combination with a digest (or hashing) algorithm for ensuring the integrity of the packets delivered. It can be configured to use pre-shared keys as well as X.509 certificates. These features are not typically offered by other SSL-based VPNs.

Furthermore, OpenVPN uses a virtual network adapter (a tun or tap device) as an interface between the user-level OpenVPN software and the operating system. In general, any operating system that has support for a tun/tap device can run OpenVPN. This currently includes Linux, Free/Open/NetBSD, Solaris, AIX, Windows, and Mac OS, as well as iOS/Android devices. For all these platforms, client software needs to be installed, which sets OpenVPN apart from client-less or web-based VPNs.

The OpenVPN protocol is not defined in an RFC standard, but the protocol is publicly available because OpenVPN is a piece of open source software. The fact that it is open source actually makes OpenVPN more secure than closed-source VPNs, as the code is continually inspected by different people. Also, there is very little chance of secret backdoors being built into OpenVPN.

OpenVPN has the notion of a control channel and a data channel, both of which are encrypted and secured differently. However, all traffic passes over a single UDP or TCP connection. The control channel is encrypted and secured using SSL/TLS, the data channel is encrypted using a custom encryption protocol.

The default protocol and port for OpenVPN is UDP and port 1194. Before IANA granted OpenVPN an official port assignment, older clients (2.0-beta16 and older) defaulted to port 5000.

Comparison of VPNs

Each of the different VPN technologies has its own characteristics, advantages, and disadvantages. Even though this book is about OpenVPN, there are use-cases where, for example, an IPSec-based VPN is more suitable, depending on the requirement of the users.

Advantages and disadvantages of PPTP

The main advantage of PPTP-based VPNs is that the VPN client software is built into most operating systems. Also, the startup time for configuring and initializing a PPTP VPN connection is quite short.

Disadvantages of PPTP-based VPNs are the lack of security and the lack of configuration options on both the client and server side. Furthermore, the EAP-TLS extension that enables the use of X.509 certificates is fully supported only on Microsoft Windows, although a patch exists for the open source pppd package to enable EAP-TLS support. The pppd package is included in almost every Linux distribution. Also, if one must resort to using EAP-TLS, then the ease of setting up a PPTP VPN is greatly diminished. This is because EAP-TLS requires setting up a public key infrastructure, just like IPSec and OpenVPN.

Another major disadvantage of PPTP is the use of the GRE protocol, which does not integrate well with NAT'ing devices.

Advantages and disadvantages of IPSec

Advantages of the IPSec protocol are its strong security, good support from different vendors and platforms, including xDSL and Wi-Fi routers, as well as the ability to use fine-grained security policies to control the flow of traffic.

The downsides of IPSec are that it is notoriously difficult to configure and troubleshoot, different IPSec implementations from different vendors do not play nicely together, and IPSec does not integrate well with NAT'ted networks. Most notably, it is not recommended, and sometimes not even possible, to run an IPSec server that is on a NAT'ted network.

Advantages and disadvantages of SSL-based VPNs

SSL-based VPNs, or web-based VPNs, have the advantage of there being no or very little client software involved. This makes installation and initialization on the client side very easy.

The disadvantage of a web-based VPN is that it is often not a *full-blown* VPN and allows access to a single server or set of servers. Also, it is harder to share local data with the remote site or server.

Advantages and disadvantages of OpenVPN

Advantages of OpenVPN are its ease of deployment, its configurability, and the ability to deploy OpenVPN in restricted networks, including NAT'ted networks. Also, OpenVPN includes security features that are as strong as IPSec-based solutions, including hardware token security and support for different user authentication mechanisms.

Disadvantages of OpenVPN are its current lack of scalability and its dependence on the installation of client-side software. Another disadvantage is the lack of a GUI for configuration and management. Notably the tap interface driver for Microsoft Windows has often caused deployment issues when a new version of Windows is released.

History of OpenVPN

OpenVPN was originally written by James Yonan with an initial release, Version 0.90, in 2001 under the GPL. The initial release allowed users to create a simple point-to-point VPN over UDP using the Blowfish cipher and, optionally, the SHA1 HMAC signature. With Version 1.0, TLS-based authentication and key exchange was added along with a `man` page.

Improvements for OpenVPN 1.x included better TLS support, replay protection, and porting to other operating systems. Some ports included OpenBSD, Mac OS, and better packaging for RedHat. Prior to Version 1.1.1, the tun device had to be configured manually outside OpenVPN. This release added the `--ifconfig` option, which automatically configured the tun device, greatly simplifying the overall configuration.

The 1.x series was relatively crude compared to the current OpenVPN Version, 2.3.8, as would be expected of a new project. One primary hurdle was the integration of OpenSSL. As OpenSSL was notorious for its poor or completely absent documentation, the developer had to go directly to the source code to integrate the project with OpenVPN. License changes were also required early on to allow the more-specific GNU Public Licensed code to link against the non-GPL OpenSSL library. Those issues were worked out and feature additions were prominently present in the change log throughout the 1.x series.

Some notable updates in the 1.x series include:

- 2001.05.13 (0.90): This was the initial release
- 2002.03.23 (1.0): This allowed TLS authentication and key exchange

- 2002.04.09 (1.1.0): This had a OpenBSD port and OpenSSL linking
- 2002.04.22 (1.1.1): This had the `--ifconfig` option
- 2002.05.22 (1.2.0): This had configuration files (instead of just command-line options, `pthread` support, and a Solaris port)
- 2002.07.10 (1.3.0): This had better FreeBSD support and logging improvements
- 2002.10.23 (1.3.2): This had initial IPv6 support and more FreeBSD improvements
- 2003.05.07 (1.4.0): This included MTU features
- 2003.07.24 (1.5-beta1): This had TCP support
- 2003.11.03 (1.5-beta13): This had support for configuration parameters `--http-proxy`, `--redirect-gateway`, and `--crl-verify`
- 2004.02.01 (1.6-beta5): This had the SOCKS5 proxy and IPv6 on FreeBSD
- 2004.05.09 (1.6.0): This is the final 1.x release

OpenVPN 2.0 has seen great advances from the 1.x releases. With 2.0, effort was put in to provide multiclient server instances, improved threading, and a better Windows tun/tap adapter. Development for 2.0 overlapped 1.x for over a year, with initial test releases for 2.0 dating back to November 2003 and the final 1.x release not arriving until May 9, 2004. When it was finally released, 2.0 saw 29 test releases, 20 beta releases, and 21 release candidates over a year and a half of effort (November 2003 to April 2005).

Some key features of the 2.0 release, in comparison to 1.6.0, are as follows:

- It allows a server instance to accept connections from multiple clients
- It enables the server-side `config` option `push` to clients (`--push`/`--pull`)
- It allows username/password authentication
- It supports `chroot` and the downgrading of daemon privileges (`--user`/`--group`/`--chroot`)
- It supports client connect scripts
- It has a management interface
- The inception of Easy-RSA

Development from 2.0 to 2.0.9 mostly consisted of bug fixes and corrections for a few security vulnerabilities. Apart from some sporadic contributions from a few others, OpenVPN was primarily developed by James up to and into the 2.1 release. 2.0.9 remained a stagnant official release from October 2006 until Version 2.1.0 in December 2009.

OpenVPN 2.1 was the first major release with a notable amount of code written by someone other than James Yonan. Alon Bar-Lev has many significant contributions dating back to 2.1-beta3 with many patches for cryptography support and corrections. Considered the first real community release, 2.1 saw much work in the core code base involving the management interface and network addressing. Some notable release notes include the following:

- 2005.11.12 (2.1-beta7): The `ca`, `cert`, `key`, and `dh` files could be specified inline in the configuration file.
- 2006.01.03 (2.1-beta8): The `--topology` subnet was added.
- 2006.02.16 (2.1-beta9): Port sharing was allowed so that OpenVPN and HTTPS could share a port.
- 2008.09.10 (2.1_rc10): Warn if the common 192.168.0.0/24 or 192.168.1.0/24 subnets are used. `--server-bridge` was added for DHCP proxy support.
- 2010.08.09 (2.1.2): It had a Python-based Windows build system, with improved handling of AUTH_FAIL for the management interface.
- 2010.11.09 (2.1.4): This was the final release of the 2.1 series.

In August 2008, there had been no official release since 2.0.9. Additionally, there was very little community support apart from the mailing list. There was interest in building a community and Krzee King and Eric Crist pushed to build one around the project. Initially, all effort was directed at supporting users.

As the group of individuals supporting OpenVPN grew, it attracted folks who could write good code. Contact was made with OpenVPN Inc., with the goal to not only provide better levels of support for OpenVPN, but to also build and extend the software James had written, but the efforts of the cooperation were rebuffed.

Talks began on **Internet Relay Chat (IRC)** which is a communication tool preferred by many developers for porting the project so that advancements could be made. Development began; some members managed IRC and helped on the mailing lists. Others built a source repository, wiki, and a web forum. The average usage was roughly 2 posts per day on the forum and about 8 users on IRC.

In early 2009, OpenVPN technologies hired Samuli Seppänen to help build and interact with the open source community. Samuli has been instrumental in forging a solid relationship between the corporation and the enthusiasts and volunteers. A strong community has been built around the project. Today, the forum averages 16 posts per day (more than 35,000 messages in total), and IRC fluctuates between 150 and 250 users on any given day.

OpenVPN 2.2 was the first release after the switch to a more community-oriented development model. After hashing out a development model and a direction, the community wanted to move with the project and work started right away.

Initially, for OpenVPN 2.2, James was still in overall control of what was merged into the main source tree, as the tree was still managed using subversion at OpenVPN Technologies. Later, the source tree was migrated to GIT and the roles reversed, where James' changes were accepted and merged into the open source project tree.

The notable changes in OpenVPN 2.2 were:

- SOCKS plaintext authentication
- Improved platform support for `--topology` subnet
- The tap mode on Solaris
- Windows build compiled with `ENABLE_PASSWORD_SAVE` enabled
- Windows IPv6 tun support
- Client certificates could be omitted with behavior similar to a web browser (`--client-cert-not-required`)
- Client certificates could now indicate a separate username instead of using the certificate common name (--x509-username-field)
- Support was removed for Windows 2000 and earlier
- 2011.04.26 Version 2.2.0 was released
- 2011.07.06 Version 2.2.1 was released with minor changes, mostly build/install related
- 2011.12.22 Version 2.2.2 was released with Windows tap driver changes

OpenVPN 2.3 is the beginning of a major turn in build structure within OpenVPN. The end goal, in a nutshell, is to create a more extensible and plugin-friendly source. With the build for mobile platforms such as Android and iOS already requiring a ground-up rewrite, James and other developers cleaned up older code in favor of more compact and normalized functions. Those rewrites are done in C++, as opposed to the current C language used.

While listed in the change log of past revisions, IPv6 support, both as a payload as well as for transit in OpenVPN, did not really mature until the 2.3 release. The vast majority of the IPv6 contributions were a result of hard work by Gert Döring.

Another important feature of the 2.3 release was the addition of PolarSSL support. PolarSSL is an alternative cryptographic library to OpenSSL and OpenVPN can now be built against either library. This topic is discussed in greater detail later in this chapter.

The list of improvements and additions for the 2.3 release is vast, but the highlights are as follows (the full change log is at https://community.openvpn.net/openvpn/ wiki/ChangesInOpenvpn23):

- Cross-platform IPv6 support (transit AND payload)
- New plugin API
- Support for building against PolarSSL, and ground work for other potential alternatives
- Clients can now inform the server of LZO support, and the server can automatically disable LZO for that client
- Workaround for local routing conflicts (--client-nat)
- A new --crl-verify directory mode, files named as common names disable certificates as if they were revoked
- Certificate UTF-8 support for certificate fields
- Project split for various subprojects:
    - OpenVPN core project
    - tap-windows
    - Easy-RSA
    - OpenVPN build system
- Kill client connections from the management interface

Version 2.3.8 was most recent release at the time of writing.

OpenVPN packages

There are several OpenVPN packages available on the Internet:

- The open source or community version of OpenVPN
- OpenVPN Access Server, the closed-source commercial offering by OpenVPN Inc.
- The mobile platform versions of OpenVPN for both Android and iOS (part of the code is closed-source, as a requirement of Apple)

The open source (community) version

Open source versions of OpenVPN are made available as each release is published. The community has resources to build binary packages for multiple platforms, including both 32-bit and 64-bit Windows clients. The currently available download options are available at `http://openvpn.net/index.php/download/community-downloads.html`.

Some operating system package maintainers track development and make snapshot releases available. FreeBSD, for example, has a security/openvpn-devel port that tracks weekly tarball snapshots from OpenVPN development. If you'd like to run the latest and greatest bleeding-edge version of OpenVPN, look at your package maintainer first. Otherwise, you can always build directly from source.

The community version of OpenVPN can act both as a VPN server and as a VPN client. There is no separate *client-only* version.

The closed source (commercial) Access Server

OpenVPN Technologies, Inc. offers a commercial version of OpenVPN called Access Server. Compared to the open source project, Access Server offers many features and deployment options that may appeal to some organizations. Access Server is a paid product, but a trial with two license keys enabled is available from the website.

Software packages, virtual appliances, and cloud services are all available from OpenVPN Technologies, Inc. at `https://openvpn.net/index.php/access-server/overview.html`.

OpenVPN Access Server includes its own OpenVPN client, OpenVPN Connect, for both Windows and Mac OS. This client software generally works only with OpenVPN Access Server. It is also possible to use the community version of OpenVPN as a client for an OpenVPN Access Server.

The mobile platform (mixed) OpenVPN/ OpenVPN Connect

For mobile devices, such as iPhones/iPads and Android devices, OpenVPN Technologies, Inc., provides a special OpenVPN Connect Client. OpenVPN Technologies, Inc., and James specifically put a lot of effort and legal wrangling with the likes of Google and Apple to get access to a usable VPN API on each platform.

Due to the nature of Apple's NDA, currently, the source for OpenVPN Connect is unavailable and cannot be shared publicly. The iOS OpenVPN Connection client can be downloaded from the Apple App Store at `https://itunes.apple.com/us/app/ openvpn-connect/id590379981?mt=8`.

There are Android clients written by a few developers, but the officially supported version is OpenVPN for Android, written by Arne Schwabe, which can be found at `https://play.google.com/store/apps/details?id=de.blinkt.openvpn&hl=en`.

OpenVPN Connect, written by OpenVPN Technologies, Inc., is also available. You can download the Android OpenVPN Connect client at `https://play.google. com/store/apps/details?id=net.openvpn.openvpn&hl=en`.

One serious advantage of OpenVPN Connect is that it supports / is supported by both the community version of OpenVPN, as well as the closed-source OpenVPN Access Server. If you have a need to access both types of servers, OpenVPN Connect is recommended.

Other platforms

There are some hardware vendors attempting to integrate support for OpenVPN within their devices. Some offer firmware versions for the VoIP phones that include an older version of OpenVPN. Other firmware projects, such as DD-WRT for Linksys routers, as well as other projects such as FreeNAS, pfSense, and others, also integrate OpenVPN.

OpenVPN internals

The design of OpenVPN is not extensively documented, but most of the internals of OpenVPN can be discovered by looking at the source code.

The tun/tap driver

One of the basic building blocks of OpenVPN is the tun/tap driver. The concept of the tun/tap driver comes from the Unix/Linux world, where it is often natively available as part of the operating system. This is a virtual network adapter that is treated by the operating system as either a point-to-point adapter (*tun-style*) for IP-only traffic or as a full virtual Ethernet adapter for all types of traffic (*tap-style*). At the backend of this adapter is an application, such as OpenVPN, to process the incoming and outgoing traffic. Linux, Free/Open/NetBSD, Solaris and Mac OS include a tun kernel driver, which is capable of both tun-style and tap-style operations. Recently, a similar driver was added to AIX, which is IBM's Unix derivative.

For Microsoft Windows, a special NDIS driver was written by James Yonan, called the TAP-WIN32 adapter. At the moment, the NDIS5 and NDIS6 versions of the driver are available, supporting Windows XP through Windows 8.1. The development of this adapter is now officially separated from the main OpenVPN development, but OpenVPN continues to rely heavily on it.

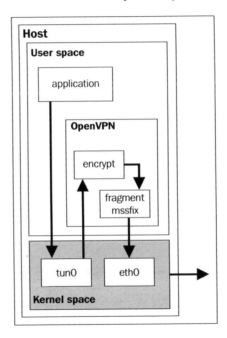

The flow of traffic from a user application via OpenVPN is depicted in the preceding diagram. In the diagram, the application is sending traffic to an address that is reachable via the OpenVPN tunnel. The steps are as follows:

1. The application hands over the packet to the operating system.
2. The OS decides using *normal* routing rules that the packet needs to be routed via the VPN.
3. The packet is then forwarded to the kernel tun device.
4. The kernel tun device forwards the packets to the (user-space) OpenVPN process.
5. The OpenVPN process encrypts and signs the packet, fragments it if necessary, and then hands it over to the kernel again to send it to the address of the remote VPN endpoint.
6. The kernel picks up the encrypted packet and forwards it to the remote VPN endpoint, where the same process is reversed.

It can also be seen in this diagram that the performance of OpenVPN will always be less than that of a regular network connection. For most applications, the performance loss is minimal and/or acceptable. However, for speeds greater than 1GBps, there is a performance bottleneck, both in terms of bandwidth and latency.

It should be noted that the performance of the Windows driver is much lower than the performance of the native tun/tap adapters found in other operating systems. This is true even with the most recent NDIS6 implementation of the TAP-Win32 driver. For a single OpenVPN client, the impact is fairly small. For a large-scale OpenVPN server that serves many clients, this can easily cause performance issues. This is one of the main reasons that the open source community normally recommends the use of a Unix- or Linux-based host as the OpenVPN server.

The UDP and TCP modes

OpenVPN currently supports two ways to communicate between endpoints: using UDP packets or using TCP packets. UDP is a connectionless or lossy protocol; if a packet is dropped in transit, then the network stack does not transparently correct this. TCP packets are a connection-oriented protocol; packets are sent and delivered using a handshake protocol, ensuring the delivery of each packet to the other side.

Both modes of communication have their advantages and disadvantages. It actually depends on the type of traffic that is sent *over* the VPN tunnel to determine which mode of communication is best. Using a TCP-based application over a TCP-based VPN can result in double performance loss, especially if the underlying network connection is bad. In that case, a re-transmittance of lost packets is done for packets lost both inside and outside the tunnel, leading to a double performance hit. This is explained nicely in the article *Why TCP over TCP is a Bad Idea* at `http://sites.inka.de/~W1011/devel/tcp-tcp.html`.

However, it can be similarly argued that sending UDP over UDP is also not a good idea. If an application using UDP for its traffic is susceptible to message deletion or packet reordering attacks, then an underlying encrypted TCP connection will enhance the security of such applications even more than an underlying UDP-based VPN. If the bulk of traffic over the VPN is UDP-based then it is sometimes better to use a TCP connection between VPN endpoints.

When choosing between UDP or TCP transport, the general rule of thumb is as follows: *if UDP (mode udp) works for you, then use it; if not, then try TCP (mode tcp-server and mode tcp-client)*. Some switches and routers do not forward UDP traffic correctly, which can be an issue especially if multiple OpenVPN clients are connected to the same switch or router. Similarly, the performance of OpenVPN over TCP can be severely affected by the choice of **Internet Service Providers** (**ISPs**): some ISPs use odd MTU sizes or packet fragmenting rules, resulting in extremely poor performance of OpenVPN-over-TCP compared to nonencrypted TCP traffic.

The encryption protocol

It has been said that OpenVPN implements TLS over UDP. This is more or less true, but the way OpenVPN uses TLS is different from the way a web browser uses it. Thus, when OpenVPN is run over TCP (using port 443 is a common method to duck firewalls), the traffic is distinguishable from normal TLS traffic. A firewall that uses **Deep Packet Inspection** (**DPI**) can easily filter out OpenVPN traffic.

The main difference between OpenVPN-TLS and browser-TLS is the way packets are signed. OpenVPN offers features to protect against DoS attacks by signing the control channel packets using a special static key (`--tls-auth ta.key 0|1`). Data channel packets, which are sent over the same UDP or TCP connection, are signed completely differently and are very readily distinguished from HTTPS traffic. The OpenVPN website (`http://openvpn.net`) depicts how packets are encrypted for UDP transport, which is illustrated below.

The same mechanism is used for TCP transport (`http://openvpn.net/index.php/open-source/documentation/security-overview.html`).

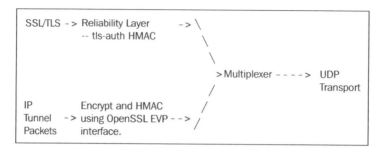

This is also the main reason why *port-sharing*, where OpenVPN and a secure web server share the same IP address and port number, can actually work.

The control and data channels

OpenVPN uses two virtual channels to communicate between the client and server:

- A TLS control channel to exchange configuration information and cipher material between the client and server. This channel is used mostly when the VPN connection is started, as well as for exchanging new encryption keying material. This keying material is renewed after a certain period (based on the `--reneg-sec`, `--reneg-bytes`, or `--reneg-pkts` options).
- A data channel over which the encrypted payload is exchanged.

The exception to this is the older pre-shared key point-to-point mode, in which only the data channel is used.

Encryption and authentication (signing) for the control channel and the data channel are determined differently. The control channel is initiated using a TLS-style protocol, similar to how a secure website connection is initiated. During control channel initialization, the encryption cipher and hashing algorithm are negotiated between the client and server.

Encryption and authentication algorithms for the data channel are not negotiable, but they are set in both the client and server configuration files for OpenVPN. The current default settings are Blowfish as the encryption cipher and SHA1 as the hashing algorithm. The ability to also negotiate cipher and hashing algorithms for the data channel are high on the wish list of the development team, but this requires an extensive change to the code.

Ciphers and hashing algorithms

OpenVPN supports a wide range of encryption ciphers and hashing algorithms. The ciphers are used to encrypt the payload, while the HMAC function makes use of a digest or hashing algorithm to authenticate incoming packets. As OpenVPN uses a control channel and a data channel, there are two sets of ciphers and hashing algorithms that can be configured.

The control channel cipher and hashing algorithms are normally negotiated at startup. The list of available combinations of ciphers and hashing algorithms can be displayed using the following command:

```
$ openvpn --show-tls
```

The available TLS Ciphers listed in order of preference:

```
TLS-ECDHE-RSA-WITH-AES-256-GCM-SHA384

TLS-ECDHE-ECDSA-WITH-AES-256-GCM-SHA384

TLS-ECDHE-RSA-WITH-AES-256-CBC-SHA384

TLS-ECDHE-ECDSA-WITH-AES-256-CBC-SHA384

TLS-ECDHE-RSA-WITH-AES-256-CBC-SHA

TLS-ECDHE-ECDSA-WITH-AES-256-CBC-SHA

TLS-DHE-DSS-WITH-AES-256-GCM-SHA384

TLS-DHE-RSA-WITH-AES-256-GCM-SHA384

TLS-DHE-RSA-WITH-AES-256-CBC-SHA256

TLS-DHE-DSS-WITH-AES-256-CBC-SHA256

TLS-DHE-RSA-WITH-AES-256-CBC-SHA

TLS-DHE-DSS-WITH-AES-256-CBC-SHA

TLS-DHE-RSA-WITH-CAMELLIA-256-CBC-SHA

TLS-DHE-DSS-WITH-CAMELLIA-256-CBC-SHA

TLS-ECDH-RSA-WITH-AES-256-GCM-SHA384

[...]
```

This output was retrieved on a CentOS 6 host using the OpenSSL 1.0.1e library.

The available combinations depend largely on the exact version of the SSL library used. You can specify a list of `tls-ciphers` in the OpenVPN configuration file in a manner that is very similar to configuring the Apache `mod_ssl` module:

```
tls-cipher  TLS-ECDHE-RSA-WITH-AES-256-GCM-SHA384
: TLS-ECDHE-ECDSA-
            WITH-AES-256-CBC-SHA384
: TLS-ECDH-RSA-WITH-AES-256-GCM-
            SHA384
```

List all ciphers on a single line; the preceding output was modified for readability.

For the data channel, the encryption cipher and hashing algorithm are controlled using the `--cipher` and `--auth` options. If the cipher and authentication algorithm are not specified, then the default values of `bf-cbc` and `sha1` are used, respectively.

To retrieve the list of available encryption ciphers, use the following command:

```
$ openvpn --show-ciphers
```

The following ciphers and cipher modes are available for use with OpenVPN. Each cipher shown here may be used as a parameter to the `--cipher` option. The default key size is shown regardless of, whether or not it can be changed with the `--keysize` directive. Using a CBC mode is recommended. In a static key mode, only a CBC mode is allowed:

```
[...]
BF-CBC 128 bit default key (variable)
BF-CFB 128 bit default key (variable) (TLS client/server mode)
BF-OFB 128 bit default key (variable) (TLS client/server mode)
[...]
AES-128-CBC 128 bit default key (fixed)
AES-128-OFB 128 bit default key (fixed) (TLS client/server mode)
AES-128-CFB 128 bit default key (fixed) (TLS client/server mode)
AES-192-CBC 192 bit default key (fixed)
AES-192-OFB 192 bit default key (fixed) (TLS client/server mode)
AES-192-CFB 192 bit default key (fixed) (TLS client/server mode)
AES-256-CBC 256 bit default key (fixed)
AES-256-OFB 256 bit default key (fixed) (TLS client/server mode)
AES-256-CFB 256 bit default key (fixed) (TLS client/server mode)
[...]
```

In this output, only the most commonly-used ciphers are shown. The list of available ciphers again depends on the exact version of the underlying crypto library. However, in most cases, the Blowfish (BF-*) and AES (AES-*) ciphers should be available.

Similarly, for the authentication (HMAC-signing) algorithms, we use the following command to list all the available options:

```
$ openvpn --show-digests
```

The following message digests are available for use with OpenVPN. A message digest is used in conjunction with the HMAC function to authenticate received packets. You can specify a message digest as a parameter to the --auth option:

```
[...]
SHA 160 bit digest size
SHA1 160 bit digest size
[...]
ecdsa-with-SHA1 160 bit digest size
[...]
SHA256 256 bit digest size
SHA384 384 bit digest size
SHA512 512 bit digest size
SHA224 224 bit digest size
```

In this output, only the most commonly-used digests or hashing algorithms are shown. The list of available digests depends on the exact version of the underlying crypto library. In most cases, the SHA-1 and SHA-2 family of hashing algorithms should be available.

OpenSSL versus PolarSSL

Starting with OpenVPN 2.3, support for a new SSL library has been added. The PolarSSL library (http://polarssl.org) can be compiled in instead of the default OpenSSL library. The main reason for adding a second library was to ensure the independence of the underlying encryption libraries and to ensure that no copyright issues would arise, as the OpenSSL copyright license is different from the one that OpenVPN uses.

Summary

In this chapter, we started out by explaining what a VPN is. We then discussed some examples of different types of VPN protocols, including PPTP, IPSec, and OpenVPN. After a brief overview of the history of OpenVPN, we proceeded to dive deeper into the techniques used in OpenVPN. These techniques include the tun/tap adapter and the encryption and packet signing algorithms used.

After this introduction to VPNs and OpenVPN itself, it is now time to learn more about OpenVPN. In the next chapter, we will start with the most basic method of using OpenVPN, the point-to-point mode using pre-shared keys. As we progress throughout this book, you will gain a more in-depth knowledge of how to use OpenVPN in a wide variety of configurations.

2
Point-to-point Mode

At first, point-to-point mode using pre-shared keys was the only available option when using OpenVPN. Nowadays, there are multiple ways to use OpenVPN, but point-to-point mode still has its uses. The term *point-to-point mode using pre-shared keys* is often abbreviated to **pre-shared keys**.

In point-to-point mode, OpenVPN is configured using pre-shared secret keys for predefined endpoints, and only a single endpoint can connect to a *server* instance at a time. The term *server* can be considered misleading, as both endpoints are more or less equal when it comes to functionality. The endpoint that initiates the connection is considered the *client*, the other endpoint is considered as the *server*.

We will start off with a demonstration of a very basic example. After that, we will discuss more features that OpenVPN provides. We will look at the following topics:

- TCP protocol and different ports
- TAP mode
- OpenVPN secret keys
- Routing
- Complete setup, including IPv6
- An IP-less setup
- Three-way routing
- Bridged TAP adapters on both ends
- Combining point-to-point mode with certificates

Pros and cons of the key mode

The main use case for using pre-shared key mode is to connect two remote networks, for example, a main office and a remote office of a small company. As soon as more than three users or endpoints are required, it is far easier to use client/server mode, as described in *Chapter 4, Client/Server Mode with tun Devices*. An example of how to connect three sites together using pre-shared keys is given later in this chapter, and it will become clear why pre-shared key mode does not scale well beyond three sites or users.

The main advantages of using pre-shared key mode are as follows:

- It is very easy to set up
- There is no need for **public key infrastructure** (**PKI**) or X.509 certificates
- Can run on limited hardware, such as Linux-based switches or routers

The disadvantages of using pre-shared key mode are:

- As the name *point-to-point* indicates, only two endpoints can be used by a single connection. Therefore, this mode does not scale well.
- Some GUI wrappers for OpenVPN (for example, GNOME NetworkManager) do not support pre-shared keys. The same applies to the Android and iOS clients.
- The secret key must be copied to the remote endpoint using a secure channel, for example, using SSH. This can sometimes be a security risk.
- It is not possible to encrypt the secret key using a passphrase, like is possible when using X.509 public/private keys.
- It is considered slightly less secure, as the security depends entirely on the security and strength of the pre-shared secret key. Also, there is no **perfect forwarding secrecy** (**PFS**) in this mode. Without PFS, an attacker may record all encrypted VPN traffic. If the attacker manages to break the encryption at some point, then *all* recorded VPN traffic can be decrypted. With PFS, it is not possible to decrypt *old* data.

It is important to realize that OpenVPN actually operates differently when using pre-shared keys compared to using certificates and a client/server setup. The code paths that are followed within OpenVPN are actually quite different, for example, no control channel negotiation is needed. The average end user will not see these differences, but it is important to know these differences when troubleshooting is needed for an OpenVPN connection. Also, when reading an OpenVPN log file with verbosity set to high (that is, anything higher than 5), the output of a pre-shared key connection will look quite different compared to the output of a certificate-based connection.

Unless stated otherwise, the examples in this chapter are all based on endpoints running CentOS 6 64bit. The version of the OpenVPN software installed is v2.3.2, taken from the CentOS-EPEL repository.

The first example

Let's look at our very first example:

1. The simplest and shortest example for connecting two computers using OpenVPN is to start the first endpoint in the *listening* mode, using fixed IP addresses and a tun style network:

```
[root@server] # openvpn \
    --ifconfig 10.200.0.1 10.200.0.2 \
    --dev tun
```

2. Next, launch the OpenVPN *client*:

```
[root@client] # openvpn \
    --ifconfig 10.200.0.2 10.200.0.1 \
    --dev tun \
    --remote openvpnserver.example.com
```

3. In a different terminal window, list the network device:

```
[root@client] # ip addr show tun0
```

```
7: tun0: <POINTOPOINT,MULTICAST,NOARP,UP,LOWER_UP> mtu 1500
    qdisc pfifo_fast state UNKNOWN group default
    qlen 100 link/none
```

```
        inet 10.200.0.2 peer 10.200.0.1/32 scope global tun0
           valid_lft forever preferred_lft forever
```

The following screenshots shows how a connection is established:

```
                        root@centos6-kvm:/etc/openvpn/movpn                          [_][□][x]

File  Edit  View  Search  Terminal  Help
[root@centos6-kvm movpn]# openvpn --ifconfig 10.200.0.2 10.200.0.1 --dev tun --remote openvpnserver.example.com
Mon Sep  8 18:27:29 2014 OpenVPN 2.3.2 x86_64-redhat-linux-gnu [SSL (OpenSSL)] [LZO] [EPOLL] [PKCS11] [eurephia]
[MH] [IPv6] built on Sep 12 2013
Mon Sep  8 18:27:29 2014 ******* WARNING *******: all encryption and authentication features disabled -- all data
will be tunnelled as cleartext
Mon Sep  8 18:27:29 2014 TUN/TAP device tun0 opened
Mon Sep  8 18:27:29 2014 do_ifconfig, tt->ipv6=0, tt->did_ifconfig_ipv6_setup=0
Mon Sep  8 18:27:29 2014 /sbin/ip link set dev tun0 up mtu 1500
Mon Sep  8 18:27:29 2014 /sbin/ip addr add dev tun0 local 10.200.0.2 peer 10.200.0.1
Mon Sep  8 18:27:29 2014 UDPv4 link local (bound): [undef]
Mon Sep  8 18:27:29 2014 UDPv4 link remote: [AF_INET]192.168.122.1:1194
Mon Sep  8 18:27:39 2014 Peer Connection Initiated with [AF_INET]192.168.122.1:1194
Mon Sep  8 18:27:40 2014 Initialization Sequence Completed
```

4. We can now ping the OpenVPN endpoints from either end, provided that the firewall and SELinux rules allow this.

The connection log shows some interesting details. The OpenVPN version on the client-side is `2.3.2 x86_64-redhat-linux-gnu`. This verifies that we are running v2.3.2 on a 64 bit version of a RedHat Linux derivative.

The connection log shows a warning:

Mon Sep 8 18:27:29 2014 ******* WARNING *******: all encryption and authentication features disabled -- all data will be tunnelled as cleartext

This warning is printed as no secret key was specified to encrypt the connection with, which makes this example not very secure.

- The Linux device `tun0` is opened for the connection. We specified `--dev tun`, which tells OpenVPN to open the first available `tun` adapter. If a second OpenVPN connection is now started the next instance will use `tun1`.

- The Linux `iproute2` `/sbin/ip` command is used to set up the `tun0` network adapter. The IP address specified is assigned, along with a default **maximum transfer unit (MTU)** of 1500 bytes.

- By default, OpenVPN will use UDP port 1194 to establish a connection. If the TCP protocol is required, then the command-line arguments on both ends are slightly different (This is shown in the following section).

- From the timestamps printed at the beginning of each line, it can be seen that it takes 10 seconds to establish the initial connection.

If the following message is printed, then the connection was completed successfully. We will see in later examples, however, that this does not necessarily mean that the VPN is functioning properly.

```
Mon Sep  8 18:27:40 2014 Initialization Sequence Completed
```

TCP protocol and different ports

The default protocol that OpenVPN uses is UDP, as it is generally more suitable for VPN connections. However, if the TCP protocol is required, then the preceding example needs to be modified only slightly:

On the listening end, start the OpenVPN server instance:

```
[root@server] # openvpn \
    --ifconfig 10.200.0.1 10.200.0.2 \
    --dev tun \
    --proto tcp-server
```

On the *client* side, the code is as follows:

```
[root@client] # openvpn \
    --ifconfig 10.200.0.2 10.200.0.1 \
     --dev tun \
    --proto tcp-client \
    --remote openvpnserver.example.com
```

OpenVPN will now connect over TCP port 1194. It is also possible to override the port number using the `--port` parameter, for example, `--port 5000`.

The TAP mode

If non-TCP/IP traffic needs to be passed over the VPN tunnel (for example, legacy AppleTalk or IPX traffic), then a *tap* device is required. The *tap* device provides an interface to pass full Ethernet frames over the VPN tunnel. The overhead when passing full Ethernet frames is negligible. The IP assignment for a *tap* device is different from a tun device, as a *tap* device acts as a *regular* network adapter, which needs to be assigned a single IP address and a netmask.

The previous example is now modified. On the listening end, start the OpenVPN server process:

```
[root@server] # openvpn \
    --ifconfig 10.200.0.1 255.255.255.0 \
    --dev tap
```

On the *client* side, the code is as follows:

```
[root@client] # openvpn \
    --ifconfig 10.200.0.2 255.255.255.0 \
    --dev tap \
    --remote openvpnserver.example.com
```

Again, we list the network device configuration:

```
[root@client] # ip addr show tap0
8: tap0: <BROADCAST,MULTICAST,UP,LOWER_UP> mtu 1500
   qdisc pfifo_fast state UNKNOWN group default qlen 100
   link/ether 6e:ea:0e:47:a3:d8 brd ff:ff:ff:ff:ff:ff
    inet 10.200.0.2/24 brd 10.200.0.255 scope global tap0
       valid_lft forever preferred_lft forever
    inet6 fe80::6cea:eff:fe47:a3d8/64 scope link
       valid_lft forever preferred_lft forever
```

Compare it to the configuration from the very first example.

The topology subnet

OpenVPN 2.1 and later support a new topology, a topology subnet for assigning IP addresses in tun-style networks, which is very similar to the IP addresses used in tap-style networks. When using `--topology subnet`, a single IP address and netmask are assigned to the tun interface, with no peer address specified.

While it does not make a lot of sense to use this topology mode for a dedicated point-to-point link, it is possible to use this topology option to make the tun style point-to-point setup almost exactly the same as the corresponding tap style setup. To use this new topology mode, use the setup described next.

On the listening end, start:

```
[root@server] # openvpn \
    --ifconfig 10.200.0.1 255.255.255.0 \
    --dev tun \
    --topology subnet
```

On the client side, the code is as follows:

```
[root@client] # openvpn \
    --ifconfig 10.200.0.2 255.255.255.0 \
    --dev tun \
    --topology subnet \
    --remote openvpnserver.example.com
```

The `--ifconfig` line is now the same as for the tap example. The only other change is the addition of `--topology subnet` on both ends.

The cleartext tunnel

The previous example does not use any encryption ciphers or authentication keys; hence, you get the following warning:

```
Mon Sep 8 18:27:29 2014 ****** WARNING ******: all encryption and
authentication features disabled -- all data will be tunnelled as
cleartext
```

However, a cleartext tunnel does have its uses. In a trusted environment where security is handled at a different level (for example, using a dedicated fiber optic cable), a cleartext tunnel offers better performance over an encrypted tunnel, and it is easier to monitor the flow of traffic over the tunnel.

Also, if you know beforehand that all traffic that will pass over the tunnel is encrypted itself (for example, all traffic is strictly HTTPS), then a cleartext tunnel can be used to avoid double encryption, which can sometimes cause a performance degradation. Especially when running OpenVPN on small or embedded hardware (for example, a Raspberry Pi or even some Arduino boards), encryption introduces a high penalty on performance.

A cleartext tunnel can be set up using the examples given in the previous section. If no secret key is specified, then encryption and authentication (HMAC signing) is automatically disabled. It is also possible to explicitly disable them:

On the listening end, start:

```
[root@server] # openvpn \
    --ifconfig 10.200.0.1 10.200.0.2 \
    --dev tun \
    --cipher none --auth none
```

On the client side, the code is as follows:

```
[root@client] # openvpn \
    --ifconfig 10.200.0.2 10.200.0.1 \
     --dev tun \
    --cipher none --auth none \
    --remote openvpnserver.example.com
```

After the connection is established, we can verify that the contents are indeed sent in cleartext using the `tcpdump` command (or equivalent, for example, Wireshark):

1. Start the connection.

2. Start `tcpdump` and listen on the *regular* network interface, not the tunnel interface itself, and filter out the OpenVPN packets (UDP port 1194) using the following command:

   ```
   [root@server] # tcpdump -l -w - eth0 udp port 1194 | strings
   ```

3. Now, send some text across the tunnel using, for example, nc (netcat):

   ○ On the Server side:

   ```
   $ nc -l -p 31000
   ```

   ○ On the Client side:

   ```
   $ nc 10.200.0.1 31000
   hello from openvpn client
   goodbye
   ```

4. The `tcpdump` output should now show something like this:

```
tcpdump: listening on eth0, link-type EN10MB (Ethernet), capture
size 65535 bytes
V~hello from openvpn client
5goodbye
```

The characters shown in the form of text messages are artifacts from the OpenVPN packet encapsulation.

OpenVPN secret keys

To secure the OpenVPN connection, a secret key is needed. First, we will generate such a key. Then, it needs to be copied to the remote endpoint using a secure channel (example SCP:

```
$ openvpn --genkey --secret secret.key
```

Note that it is not necessary to run this command as root (hence the prompt $). The resulting secret key file has the following format:

```
#
# 2048 bit OpenVPN static key
#
-----BEGIN OpenVPN Static key V1-----
1393ae687606c1f7d465d70227bf63e8
8963e9d1401450002d073d6eab1bffde
b06d1a33cc5c45d4a667016339e921d3
3ac36b1a949eb52e9217e41e4b035a7b
987ddfa9d6766d3b5e4c952dc27f518d
12ccff6b2f0966284382ddc0f62b824a
f576f0982beec9d6a4728d0788499a75
0fd7055ef681404fd463d9862d3a40a9
31fca7d87997c70c07b8303a1b85f1ff
76aa7790e7c341353d2b4ea5049b11a2
51346e7dd39fc1f1e53ae57c46cf60c8
24db00a871262fee78050a9df6a57322
0bb0d980b6cf1be90a2f304f99fb9cde
```

```
7cdf72d20e7dee555c7c99950aa4d8e6

86a020c3a63125fb99d56181ff4ca20c

d6711eab15a4d6faf706f2601eb6 61b7
-----END OpenVPN Static key V1-----
```

After publishing the key here, it is no longer secret.

The `openvpn --genkey` command generates a 2048 bit key, or 256 bytes of random data. Those 256 bytes are listed in hexadecimal format in the `secret.key` file, but not all 256 bytes are currently used (as we will see later on).

The secret key is used by OpenVPN for both encrypting and authenticating (signing) each packet. The default encryption cipher is the Blowfish cipher (`BF-CBC`) and the default HMAC algorithm is `SHA1`. The Blowfish cipher used 128 bit encryption, whereas the key used for the SHA1 algorithm is 160 bits.

If OpenVPN is started with increased debugging output (`--verb 7` or higher), the keys used are printed upon startup:

On the listening end (server), start the OpenVPN daemon:

```
[root@server] # openvpn \
    --ifconfig 10.200.0.1 10.200.0.2 \
    --dev tun \
    --secret secret.key \
    --verb 7
```

On the client side, the command is as follows:

```
[root@client] # openvpn \
    --ifconfig 10.200.0.2 10.200.0.1 \
    --dev tun \
    --secret secret.key \
    --remote openvpnserver.example.com
```

The server-side log output will contain lines of the form:

```
Static Encrypt: Cipher 'BF-CBC' initialized with 128 bit key
Static Encrypt: CIPHER KEY: 1393ae68 7606c1f7 d465d702 27bf63e8
Static Encrypt: CIPHER block_size=8 iv_size=8
Static Encrypt: Using 160 bit message hash 'SHA1' for
```

```
                    HMAC authentication
Static Encrypt: HMAC KEY: 987ddfa9 d6766d3b 5e4c952d c27f518d 12ccff6b
Static Encrypt: HMAC size=20 block_size=20


Static Decrypt: Cipher 'BF-CBC' initialized with 128 bit key
Static Decrypt: CIPHER KEY: 1393ae68 7606c1f7 d465d702 27bf63e8
Static Decrypt: CIPHER block_size=8 iv_size=8
Static Decrypt: Using 160 bit message hash 'SHA1' for
                    HMAC authentication
Static Decrypt: HMAC KEY: 987ddfa9 d6766d3b 5e4c952d c27f518d 12ccff6b
Static Decrypt: HMAC size=20 block_size=20
```

The BF-CBC cipher key is 1393 ae68 7606 c1f7 d465 d702 27bf 63e8, which is exactly the first line of the OpenVPN secret key file.

The SHA1 HMAC key is 987d dfa9 d676 6d3b 5e4c 952d c27f 518d 12cc ff6b, which can also be found in the secret key file starting at the fifth line.

Note that the same keys are used for encrypting and decrypting the data, as well as for authenticating the data. In the next section, we will see how we can use different keys for encrypting and decrypting and authentication.

Using multiple keys

OpenVPN supports the use of *directional* keys, that is, different keys are used for incoming versus outgoing data. This further enhances security. By adding a *direction* flag to the --secret parameter, we can specify that different keys are to be used. The *direction* flag needs to be set to 0 on one end, and to 1 on the other end:

On the listening end (server), start:

```
[root@server] # openvpn \
    --ifconfig 10.200.0.1 10.200.0.2 \
    --dev tun \
    --secret secret.key 0\
    --verb 7
```

On the client side, the code is as follows:

```
[root@client] # openvpn \
    --ifconfig 10.200.0.2 10.200.0.1 \
    --dev tun \
    --secret secret.key 1\
    --remote openvpnserver.example.com \
    --verb 7
```

The server-side log output will now contain lines of the form:

```
Static Encrypt: CIPHER KEY: 1393ae68 7606c1f7 d465d702 27bf63e8
Static Encrypt: HMAC KEY:   987ddfa9 d6766d3b 5e4c952d c27f518d
                            12ccff6b

Static Decrypt: CIPHER KEY: 31fca7d8 7997c70c 07b8303a 1b85f1ff
Static Decrypt: HMAC KEY:   0bb0d980 b6cf1be9 0a2f304f 99fb9cde
                            7cdf72d2
```

The encryption CIPHER and HMAC keys are now clearly different from the decryption CIPHER and HMAC keys. Furthermore, each of these keys can be found in the OpenVPN secret.key file:

- Encryption CIPHER KEY starts at 1 line, 128 bits or 16 bytes long
- Encryption HMAC KEY starts at 5 line, 160 bits or 20 bytes long
- Decryption CIPHER KEY starts at 9 line, 128 bits or 16 bytes long
- Decryption HMAC KEY starts at 13 line, 160 bits or 20 bytes long

Also, the log output on the client side shows that the keys are reversed:

```
Static Encrypt: CIPHER KEY: 31fca7d8 7997c70c 07b8303a 1b85f1ff
Static Encrypt: HMAC KEY:   0bb0d980 b6cf1be9 0a2f304f 99fb9cde
                            7cdf72d2
Static Decrypt: CIPHER KEY: 1393ae68 7606c1f7 d465d702 27bf63e8
Static Decrypt: HMAC KEY:   987ddfa9 d6766d3b 5e4c952d c27f518d
                            12ccff6b
```

This is necessary for the VPN tunnel to function, as the keys that are needed on the server side to *encrypt* the data are needed on the client side to *decrypt* the data and vice versa.

Using different encryption and authentication algorithms

OpenVPN supports many different encryption and authentication (HMAC signing) algorithms. The size of the keys used in each encryption cipher and HMAC algorithm varies, with a current maximum of 256 bits for the ciphers (for example, AES256) and 512 bits for the HMAC key (for example, SHA512). The OpenVPN static key is 2048 bits long, which is large enough for a 512 bit cipher and a 512 bit HMAC key.

If we specify both AES256 as encryption cipher and SHA512 as an authentication algorithm, then we see that the keys used grow in size:

On the listening end (server), start:

```
[root@server] # openvpn \
    --ifconfig 10.200.0.1 10.200.0.2 \
    --dev tun \
    --secret secret.key 0\
    --cipher AES256 --auth SHA512 \
    --verb 7
```

On the client side, the code is as follows:

```
[root@client] # openvpn \
    --ifconfig 10.200.0.2 10.200.0.1 \
    --dev tun \
    --secret secret.key 1\
    --cipher AES256 --auth SHA512 \
    --remote openvpnserver.example.com \
    --verb 7
```

The server-side log output now contains the following lines:

```
Static Encrypt: Cipher 'AES-256-CBC' initialized with 256 bit key
Static Encrypt: CIPHER KEY: 1393ae68 7606c1f7 d465d702 27bf63e8
                            8963e9d1 40145000 2d073d6e ab1bffde
Static Encrypt: CIPHER block_size=16 iv_size=16
Static Encrypt: Using 512 bit message hash 'SHA512' for
```

```
                        HMAC authentication
Static Encrypt: HMAC KEY:    987ddfa9 d6766d3b 5e4c952d c27f518d
                             12ccff6b 2f096628 4382ddc0 f62b824a
                             f576f098 2beec9d6 a4728d07 88499a75
                             0fd7055e f681404f d463d986 2d3a40a9
Static Encrypt: HMAC size=64 block_size=64


Static Decrypt: Cipher 'AES-256-CBC' initialized with 256 bit key
Static Decrypt: CIPHER KEY: 31fca7d8 7997c70c 07b8303a 1b85f1ff
                            76aa7790 e7c34135 3d2b4ea5 049b11a2
Static Decrypt: CIPHER block_size=16 iv_size=16
Static Decrypt: Using 512 bit message hash 'SHA512' for
                HMAC authentication
Static Decrypt: HMAC KEY:    0bb0d980 b6cf1be9 0a2f304f 99fb9cde
                             7cdf72d2 0e7dee55 5c7c9995 0aa4d8e6
                             86a020c3 a63125fb 99d56181 ff4ca20c
                             d6711eab 15a4d6fa f706f260 1eb661b7
```

This log can be matched against the `secret.key` file:

- The encryption `CIPHER KEY` now matches the first 2 lines of the file
- The encryption `HMAC KEY` now matches lines 5-8 of the file

It can be matched similarly for the decryption keys.

 The VPN tunnel is functioning just as before, but now with stronger encryption and authentication in place. If even stronger ciphers or HMAC algorithms are introduced in the future, the OpenVPN static key format will have to be updated.

Routing

As stated before, the main use case for point-to-point style networks is to connect two remote networks over a secure tunnel. In the previous example, the secure tunnel was established, but no network routes were added.

For the next example, consider the following network layout:

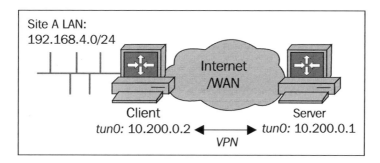

The client-side network **192.168.4.0/24** (with netmask 255.255.255.0) needs to be routed over the VPN tunnel to the server.

On the listening end (server), we start:

```
[root@server] # openvpn \
    --ifconfig 10.200.0.1 10.200.0.2 \
    --dev tun \
    --secret secret.key 0\
    --route 192.168.4.0 255.255.255.0 \
    --daemon --log /var/log/movpn-02-server.log
```

On the client side, the code is as follows:

```
[root@client] # openvpn \
    --ifconfig 10.200.0.2 10.200.0.1 \
    --dev tun \
    --secret secret.key 1\
    --remote openvpnserver.example.com \
    --daemon --log /var/log/movpn-02-client.log
```

On the server side, a *route* statement was added to tell OpenVPN that the network **192.168.4.0/24** is found at the other end of the tunnel. OpenVPN itself will do very little with it, but it will issue the appropriate system /sbin/route or /sbin/ ip route command to configure the system routing tables. Instead of using the OpenVPN --route statement, we can also use the following command:

```
[root@server] # route add -net 192.168.4.0/24 gw 10.200.0.2
```

After the VPN connection has been established, we can alternatively use the `iproute2` command:

```
[root@server] # ip route add 192.168.4.0/24 via 10.200.0.2
```

The second line of statements added in this example instructs OpenVPN to daemonize itself (that is, run silently in the background) and to log all messages to the file `/var/log/movpn-02-server.log`.

Similarly, the same `daemon+log` statement is added on the client side.

> The `--log` statement truncates the `log` file each time OpenVPN starts. If you want to append to the previous `log` file, use the following command:
>
> `--log-append /var/log/movpn-02-server.log`

At this point, the example is not yet fully functional. If we ping a host on the client-side LAN from the VPN server, then we will not receive any response. This has little to do with OpenVPN itself, but mostly with TCP/IP routing. Most of the questions asked on the OpenVPN-users mailing list and OpenVPN internet forum are actually routing questions.

The reason that no response is received from the client-side LAN is two-fold:

- IP Forwarding or routing needs to be enabled on the OpenVPN client. For each operating system, this is achieved in a different manner. On Linux, it is usually sufficient to add or change a line to the file `/etc/sysctl.cnf` and reboot. The following line needs to be altered:

  `net.ipv4.ip_forward = 1`

- It is possible to avoid a reboot by issuing the following command:

  `# sysctl -p`

- We also need to make sure that there is a route back to the OpenVPN server on the client LAN. This can be done by adding a route to the LAN gateway, or by adding a static route to each of the machines on the client LAN. In this example, we add a route on a Linux machine that is attached to the client-side LAN:

  `# route add -net 10.200.0.0/24 gw 192.168.4.100`

  Here, `192.168.4.100` is the LAN IP address of the OpenVPN client.

Routes added this way are *not* persistent and will disappear after a reboot. Adding routes in a persistent manner is distribution-dependent.

Now, the example is functioning as expected. From the OpenVPN server, we can ping the LAN IPs of machines on the client-side LAN and vice versa:

```
$ ping -c 2 192.168.4.100
PING 192.168.4.100 (192.168.4.100) 56(84) bytes of data.
64 bytes from 192.168.4.100: icmp_seq=1 ttl=64 time=5.97 ms
64 bytes from 192.168.4.100: icmp_seq=2 ttl=64 time=4.22 ms

$ ping -c 2 192.168.4.10
PING 192.168.4.10 (192.168.4.10) 56(84) bytes of data.
64 bytes from 192.168.4.10: icmp_seq=1 ttl=63 time=7.37 ms
64 bytes from 192.168.4.10: icmp_seq=2 ttl=63 time=6.09 ms
```

Configuration files versus the command line

As you can see from the previous example, the command-line arguments to OpenVPN can quickly become lengthy and complex. It is also possible (and advisable) to use configuration files to store commonly used options for the OpenVPN. In general, each option can be specified on the command line using the following command:

```
--<some option> <option-arguments>
```

It can also be specified in a configuration file using `<some option> <option-arguments>`, that is, remove the two dashes in front of the command-line argument.

The configuration file is specified on the command-line using the `--config <path>` option. Almost all options specified in a configuration file are treated as if they were specified on the command line. As we will see later in this book, it is possible to store certificates and private key files inline inside a configuration file. It is not easily possible to do the same using command-line arguments.

It is also possible to mix configuration files and command-line arguments. This makes it easy to store commonly used options in a configuration file, which can be overridden using command-line arguments.

Not all configuration options can be overridden. Some options can be specified multiple times (notably, remote <remote-host>). In those cases, the *first* occurrence is usually tried first.

The server-side command line from the previous example can be converted into the following configuration file:

```
ifconfig 10.200.0.1 10.200.0.2
dev tun
secret secret.key 0
route 192.168.4.0 255.255.255.0

daemon
log /var/log/movpn-02-server.log
```

If this configuration file is stored as movpn-02-01-server.conf, then the command to launch the listener becomes:

```
[root@server] # openvpn --config movpn-02-01-server.conf
```

Note that the order of the command-line arguments is important. All options specified before the --config <path> option are overridden by the options specified inside the configuration file. All options specified after the --config option overrule the options in the configuration file (with a few exceptions, as noted earlier).

The complete setup

Based on the previous examples, we can now construct a complete *production-level* setup using configuration files, including routing, logging, IPv6 support, as well as a few other *production* features that OpenVPN offers.

Consider the following network layout:

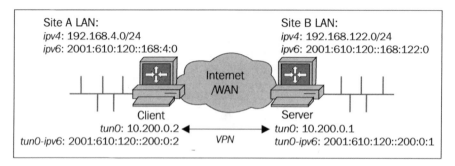

For the server, we create the following configuration file `movpn-02-02-server.conf`:

```
dev tun
proto udp
local   openvpnserver.example.com
lport   1234
remote openvpnclient.example.com
rport   4321

secret secret.key 0
ifconfig 10.200.0.1 10.200.0.2
route 192.168.4.0 255.255.255.0

tun-ipv6
ifconfig-ipv6 2001:610:120::200:0:1 2001:610:120::200:0:2

user   nobody
groupnobody  # use 'group nogroup' on Debian/Ubuntu
persist-tun
persist-key
keepalive 10 60
ping-timer-rem

verb 3
daemon
log-append /var/log/openvpn.log
```

For the client, we create the file `movpn-02-02-client.conf`:

```
dev tun
proto udp
local   openvpnclient.example.com
lport   4321
remote openvpnserver.example.com
rport   1234

secret secret.key 1
ifconfig 10.200.0.2 10.200.0.1
route 192.168.122.0 255.255.255.0

tun-ipv6
ifconfig-ipv6 2001:610:120::200:0:2 2001:610:120::200:0:1
```

```
user   nobody
group nobodygroup nobody  # use 'group nogroup' on Debian/Ubuntu
persist-tun
persist-key
keepalive 10 60
ping-timer-rem

verb 3
daemon
log-append /var/log/openvpn.log
```

The client and server configuration files are very similar, except for the mirrored addresses and mirrored key direction.

There are some new options introduced in these configuration files:

- While `proto udp` is the default protocol, it is wise to explicitly list it in the configuration file to avoid any confusion.

- `local <IP>` is the local IPv4 address on which OpenVPN will listen for incoming connections. If this address is not specified, OpenVPN will listen on address 0.0.0.0, which means all interfaces.

- `lport` is the local port that OpenVPN will listen on. The default value is 1194, but any valid and available port number can be used.

- `remote <IP>` is the remote IPv4 address from which the OpenVPN server process will accept incoming connections. If this address is not specified, OpenVPN will accept incoming connections from all addresses.

- `rport` is the remote port that OpenVPN will connect to. Normally, this is specified using `port` but when a different local port is used, it is handier to explicitly specify `rport`.

- `tun-ipv6` instructs OpenVPN to create a tunnel capable of passing IPv6 traffic.

- `ifconfig-ipv6` configures the local and remote IPv6 endpoints. For this example, the last three numbers of the IPv6 address match the IPv4 endpoints.

- `user nobody` and `group nobody` instruct OpenVPN to drop to UNIX user `nobody` and group it after the connection has come up. This further enhances security, as an attack on the tunnel will less likely result in a root exploit. Note that on Debian/Ubuntu, the group `nogroup` is used.

- `persist-tun` and `persist-key` instruct OpenVPN to not reopen the tun device or generate new keying material whenever the tunnel is restarted. These options are particularly useful in combination with `user nobody`, as the user `nobody` normally does not have the access rights to open a new tun interface.

- `keep-alive 10 60` and `ping-timer-rem` are useful options to make sure that the VPN connection remains up, even if there is no traffic flowing over the tunnel.

Instead of specifying a very lengthy command line to launch ends of the tunnel, we can now start both ends using the following commands:

```
[root@server] # openvpn --config movpn-02-02-server.conf
```

```
[root@client] # openvpn --config movpn-02-02-client.conf
```

Check the `openvpn.log` files on both ends for the magic sentence:

```
Thu Sep 11 13:21:51 2014 Initialization Sequence Completed
```

Finally, we verify that we can reach the other end of the tunnel using both `ping` and `ping6`:

```
# remote IPv4 LAN address
$ ping -c 2 192.168.4.100
PING 192.168.4.100 (192.168.4.100) 56(84) bytes of data.
64 bytes from 192.168.4.100: icmp_seq=1 ttl=64 time=3 ms
64 bytes from 192.168.4.100: icmp_seq=2 ttl=64 time=5 ms
# remote IPv6 tunnel address
$ ping6 -c 2 2001:610:120::200:0:2
PING 2001:610:120::200:0:2(2001:610:120::200:0:2) 56 data bytes
64 bytes from 2001:610:120::200:0:2: icmp_seq=1 ttl=64 time=4 ms
64 bytes from 2001:610:120::200:0:2: icmp_seq=2 ttl=64 time=4 ms
# remote IPv6 LAN address
$ ping6 -c 2 2001:610:120::168:4:100
PING 2001:610:120::168:4:100(2001:610:120::168:4:100) 56 data byte
64 bytes from 2001:610:120::168:4:100: icmp_seq=1 ttl=64 time=6 ms
64 bytes from 2001:610:120::168:4:100: icmp_seq=2 ttl=64 time=3 ms
```

Note that in order to get routing to work that we now need IP forwarding on both ends, as well as the return route for the computers on the LAN segment. On the client-side LAN, we need routes similar to the following:

```
# route add -net 10.200.0.0/24     gw 192.168.4.100
# route add -net 192.168.122.0/24 gw 192.168.4.100
```

Here, 192.168.4.100 is the LAN address of the OpenVPN client.

On the server-side LAN, we need the following:

```
# route add -net 10.200.0.0/24   gw 192.168.122.1
# route add -net 192.168.4.0/24 gw 192.168.122.1
```

Here 192.168.122.1 is the LAN address of the OpenVPN server.

 Currently, it is required to always specify an IPv4 address using `ifconfig`, even if the tunnel is IPv6-only. This shortcoming will be addressed in OpenVPN 2.4+IP-less setup.

Advanced IP-less setup

The capability of OpenVPN to allow user-defined scripts to be run when the VPN connection is started allows for some advanced setups. In this example, we will use a custom up script to create an OpenVPN tunnel, without assigning IP addresses to the endpoints of the tunnel. In a routed network setup, this ensures that the tunnel endpoints can never be reached themselves, which adds some security and can also make the routing tables a bit shorter.

This script has only been tested on Linux systems, as it requires some network interface configuration that is not available on other platforms. We use the same network layout as in the previous example, but without the IPv6 addressing:

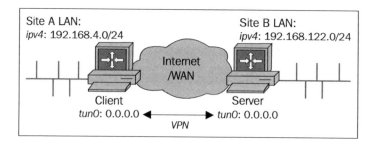

For the server, we create the following configuration file movpn-02-03-server.
conf:

```
dev tun
secret secret.key
ifconfig-noexec

up /etc/openvpn/up.sh
script-security 2
verb 3

daemon
log-append /var/log/openvpn.log
```

Here's the accompanying up.sh script:

```
#!/bin/bash
/sbin/ifconfig $1 0.0.0.0 up
/sbin/ip route add 192.168.4.0/24 dev $1
```

Here, the network 192.168.4.0/24 is the client-side LAN that we want to reach from
the server-side LAN. For the client, we create the file movpn-02-03-client.conf:

```
dev tun
secret secret.key
ifconfig-noexec
remote openvpnserver.example.com

up /etc/openvpn/up.sh
script-security 2
verb 3
daemon
log-append /var/log/openvpn.log
```

Here's the accompanying up.sh script:

```
#!/bin/bash
/sbin/ifconfig $1 0.0.0.0 up
/sbin/ip route add 192.168.122.0/24 dev $1
```

Make sure the up.sh scripts are executable (chmod a+x up.sh) before starting the
VPN connection.

Launch both ends of the tunnel:

```
[root@server]# openvpn --config movpn-02-03-server.conf
```

```
[root@client]# openvpn --config movpn-02-03-client.conf
```

Check the `openvpn.log` files on both ends for the magic sentence:

```
Thu Sep 11 15:57:51 2014 Initialization Sequence Completed
```

Check the addresses assigned to the `tun0` interface:

```
$ ifconfig tun0
tun0      Link encap:UNSPEC  HWaddr 00-00-00-00-00-00-00-00-00-00-00-00-
00-00-00-00
          UP POINTOPOINT RUNNING NOARP MULTICAST  MTU:1500  Metric:1
          RX packets:6 errors:0 dropped:0 overruns:0 frame:0
          TX packets:6 errors:0 dropped:0 overruns:0 carrier:0
          collisions:0 txqueuelen:100
          RX bytes:504 (504.0 b)   TX bytes:504 (504.0 b)
```

Alternatively, you can use a more modern `iproute2` command:

```
$ ip addr show dev tun0
```

The interface is up but does not have an IP address. Next, we want to verify the routing table:

```
$ /sbin/ip route show
[...]
192.168.4.0/24 dev tun0   scope link
[...]
```

The right route is present, so finally we verify that we can ping a host on the client-side LAN:

```
[root@centos6-kvm ~]# ping -c 2 192.168.4.10
PING 192.168.4.10 (192.168.4.10) 56(84) bytes of data.
64 bytes from 192.168.4.10: icmp_seq=1 ttl=62 time=5 ms
64 bytes from 192.168.4.10: icmp_seq=2 ttl=62 time=5 ms
```

Three-way routing

As stated in the introduction, point-to-point networks are an excellent choice when connecting a small number of endpoints. In this example, we will show how to connect three sites together using point-to-point tunnels. It will also show how quickly the configuration of such a setup can become very complex.

Consider the following network layout:

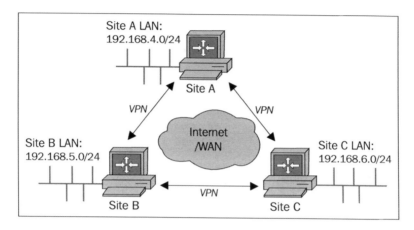

We will create three tunnels between the sites and set up redundant routes. That way, if one of the tunnels goes down, all the sites will remain visible to each other. However, this is at the cost of a performance penalty. Let's assume that the link between site A and site B goes down. The backup route goes from site A to site C to site B, so now traffic from site A to site B has to make an extra hop.

First, we create three secret keys:

```
$ openvpn --genkey --secret AtoB.key
$ openvpn --genkey --secret AtoC.key
$ openvpn --genkey --secret BtoC.key
```

Then, we transfer these keys to all endpoints over a secure channel (for example, using scp).

Next, we create six configuration files: three listener or server configurations, and three client configurations.

First, create the server config file BtoA.conf:

```
dev tun
proto udp
port  1194
remote siteA
secret AtoB.key 0
ifconfig 10.200.0.1 10.200.0.2
route 192.168.4.0 255.255.255.0 vpn_gateway 5
route 192.168.6.0 255.255.255.0 vpn_gateway 10
route-delay
keepalive 10 60
verb 3
daemon
log-append /var/log/openvpn-BtoA.log
```

Next, create CtoA.conf as follows:

```
dev tun
proto udp
port  1195
remote siteAsecret AtoC.key 0
ifconfig 10.200.0.5 10.200.0.6
route 192.168.4.0 255.255.255.0 vpn_gateway 5
route 192.168.5.0 255.255.255.0 vpn_gateway 10
route-delay
keepalive 10 60
verb 3
daemon
log-append /var/log/openvpn-CtoA.log
```

Then, create the last server configuration file BtoC.confuse:

```
dev tun
proto udp
port  1196
remote siteC
secret BtoC.key 0
ifconfig 10.200.0.9 10.200.0.10
route 192.168.4.0 255.255.255.0 vpn_gateway 10
```

```
route 192.168.6.0 255.255.255.0 vpn_gateway 5
route-delay
keepalive 10 60
verb 3
daemon
log-append /var/log/openvpn-BtoC.log
```

Now we create the client (connector) configuration file AtoB.conf:

```
dev tun
proto udp
port  1194
remote siteB
secret AtoB.key 1
ifconfig 10.200.0.2 10.200.0.1
route 192.168.5.0 255.255.255.0 vpn_gateway 5
route 192.168.6.0 255.255.255.0 vpn_gateway 10
route-delay
keepalive 10 60
verb 3
daemon
log-append /var/log/openvpn-AtoB.log
```

Next, we create the client configuration file AtoC.conf:

```
dev tun
proto udp
port  1195
remote siteC
secret AtoC.key 1
ifconfig 10.200.0.6 10.200.0.5
route 192.168.5.0 255.255.255.0 vpn_gateway 10
route 192.168.6.0 255.255.255.0 vpn_gateway 5
route-delay
keepalive 10 60
verb 3
daemon
log-append /var/log/openvpn-AtoC.log
```

Finally, we create the client configuration file CtoB.conf:

```
dev tun
proto udp
port  1196
remote siteB
```

```
secret BtoC.key 1
ifconfig 10.200.0.10 10.200.0.9
route 192.168.4.0 255.255.255.0 vpn_gateway 10
route 192.168.5.0 255.255.255.0 vpn_gateway 5
route-delay
keepalive 10 60
verb 3
daemon
log-append /var/log/openvpn-CtoB.log
```

Start each server and connect its corresponding client:

```
[siteB]# openvpn --config BtoA.conf
```

```
[siteA]# openvpn --config AtoB.conf
```

Check the log file on both sides of the tunnel, and verify that routing is (partially) working before proceeding to the next site:

```
[siteB]$ openvpn --config BtoC.conf
```
```
[siteC]$ openvpn --config CtoB.conf
```

and finally:

```
[siteC]$ openvpn --config CtoA.conf
```
```
[siteA]$ openvpn --config AtoC.conf
```

At this point, all routes should be present, including the redundant routes. For example, site A has two routes to site B (LAN 192.168.5.0/24), as can be seen from the routing table:

```
[siteA]$ ip route show
[...]
192.168.5.0/24 via 10.200.0.1 dev tun0  metric 5
192.168.5.0/24 via 10.200.0.5 dev tun1  metric 10
[...]
```

We can observe the following from this table:

- One via the *direct* tunnel to site B. This route has the lowest metric.
- One via an indirect tunnel: first to site C and then onward to site B. This route has a higher metric and is not chosen until the first route is down.

This setup has the advantage that if one tunnel fails, then after 60 seconds the connection and its corresponding routes are dropped. The backup route to the other network then automatically takes over and all three sites can reach each other again. After the original tunnel comes back up, the routes with the higher metric take precedence again and the original situation is restored.

A downside of this configuration is that during those 60 seconds all traffic is lost. A routing protocol such as RIPv2 or OSPF might help discover the failing routes much faster, resulting in less network downtime.

Route, net_gateway, vpn_gateway, and metrics

The following configuration statements are vital in this setup. The word vpn_gateway is a special OpenVPN keyword and it specifies the VPN remote endpoint address. Normally, this keyword does not have to be specified, *unless* it is also necessary to specify the metric for this route.

The syntax and options for the route directive is:

```
route <network> <netmask> vpn_gateway <metric>
```

Here, gateway can either be explicitly set as an IPv4 address, or the special keywords vpn_gateway or net_gateway can be used. If no gateway and no metric are specified, then vpn_gateway is used.

The keyword net_gateway is useful to specify a subnet that should explicitly not be routed via the VPN. In *Chapter 4, Client/Server Mode with tun Devices*, a more detailed explanation of the route options will be given.

The metric has a default metric that can be set using the following command:

route-metric m

This then applies to all routes. If one wishes to overrule the metric for a particular route (as we have done in this example), then it is required to specify the gateway (vpn_gateway in our case), followed by the metric for that particular route.

The configuration statement route-delay is required here to ensure that the routes are added after all connections are available. Without it the routes might be added too soon, resulting in a failure to add a route to one of the remote subnets.

Bridged tap adapter on both ends

Another advanced use case of a dedicated point-to-point VPN is to bridge two remote network segments together. OpenVPN allows you to bridge two network segments with the same IP address range together to form a single transparent network segment. It is generally not advisable to do this, as the performance of such a bridged network will not be optimal. In some cases, it is unavoidable. Normally, it would be better to assign different subnets to both ends, but sometimes special software is tied to a specific IP address and there is no alternative but to have the same subnet on both ends.

Consider the following network layout:

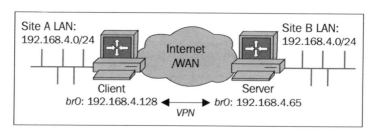

At the client-side, the network **192.168.4.0/24** is in use—with the OpenVPN client found at **192.168.4.128**. At the server side, the same subnet is in use—with the OpenVPN server found at **192.168.4.65**. The goal is to bridge the two networks together, so that all machines on both ends can see each other transparently.

In dev tap mode OpenVPN will create a new or open an existing tap adapter. On most modern operating systems, a tap adapter behaves just like a regular network adapter and if the operating system supports adapter bridging then the tap adapter can be bridged with another network adapter in the system. This is known to work on Linux, Free/Open/NetBSD, and Microsoft Windows. On Linux, the bridge-utils package needs be installed for this example to work.

In this example, the tap adapter is bridged with the LAN interface of both the OpenVPN client and server. In order to be able to do this, the tap adapter is created in a persistent state *before* the VPN connection is initialized:

```
# openvpn --mktun --dev tap0
Thu Sep 11 16:57:30 2014 TUN/TAP device tap0 opened
Thu Sep 11 16:57:30 2014 Persist state set to: ON
```

Then, the bridge is created and initialized. On the client side execute the following commands:

```
# brctl addbr br0
# brctl addif br0 eth0
# brctl addif br0 tap0
# ifconfig eth0 0.0.0.0 up
# ifconfig tap0 0.0.0.0 up
# ifconfig br0 192.168.4.128 netmask 255.255.255.0 up
```

Check the status of the bridge and its associated adapters before continuing. Also, make sure that LAN access is still possible:

```
# brctl show
bridge name     bridge id               STP enabled     interfaces
br0             8000.5c260a307224       no              eth0
                                                        tap0

# ifconfig -a
br0       Link encap:Ethernet  HWaddr 5C:26:0A:30:72:24
          inet addr:192.168.4.128  Bcast:192.168.4.255
          Mask:255.255.255.0
          UP BROADCAST RUNNING MULTICAST  MTU:1500  Metric:1
          RX packets:4 errors:0 dropped:0 overruns:0 frame:0
          TX packets:10 errors:0 dropped:0 overruns:0 carrier:0
          collisions:0 txqueuelen:0
          RX bytes:244 (244.0 b)  TX bytes:732 (732.0 b)


eth0      Link encap:Ethernet  HWaddr 5C:26:0A:30:72:24
          UP BROADCAST RUNNING MULTICAST  MTU:1500  Metric:1
          RX packets:2087 errors:0 dropped:0 overruns:0 frame:0
          TX packets:2427 errors:0 dropped:0 overruns:0 carrier:0
          collisions:0 txqueuelen:1000
          RX bytes:203516 (198.7 KiB)  TX bytes:231571 (226.1 KiB)
          Interrupt:20 Memory:f5400000-f5420000


tap0      Link encap:Ethernet  HWaddr CA:85:1E:AE:AF:59
```

```
UP BROADCAST RUNNING MULTICAST  MTU:1500  Metric:1
RX packets:0 errors:0 dropped:0 overruns:0 frame:0
TX packets:0 errors:0 dropped:11 overruns:0 carrier:0
collisions:0 txqueuelen:100
RX bytes:0 (0.0 b)  TX bytes:0 (0.0 b)
# ping -c 2 192.168.4.10
```

The output should be similar for the server side; with bridge IP address **192.168.4.65**.

Next, we create the configuration file `movpn-02-05.conf`, which can be the same on both sides:

```
dev tap0
secret secret.key
verb 3
daemon
log-append /var/log/openvpn.log
```

> In the configuration file, the full name of the device `tap0` is used. If the `0` is omitted, then OpenVPN will open a new tap adapter and the bridge will not function.

Next, we start the client and the server:

```
[root@server] # openvpn --config movpn-02-05.conf \
    --remote openvpnclient.example.com
```

```
[root@client] # openvpn --config movpn-02-05.conf \
    --remote openvpnserver.example.com
```

After the initialization sequence has been completed, the network segments are bridged. Verify this by pinging a host on the remote end.

It is also useful to watch the traffic flowing over the tunnel. The downside of a bridged network is that all (broadcast) traffic generated on one end is copied to the other end. This can result in poor network performance. If there is a lot of network *background noise*, then this will show up in a `tcpdump` on the `tap0` interface:

```
17:19:57.280459 72:24:b4:f0:16:81 > 01:80:c2:00:00:00, 802.3, length 52:
LLC, dsap STP (0x42) Individual, ssap STP (0x42) Command, ctrl 0x03: STP
802.1d, Config, Flags [none], bridge-id 8000.52:54:00:6e:cd:0b.8003,
length 35
```

```
17:19:59.280486 72:24:b4:f0:16:81 > 01:80:c2:00:00:00, 802.3, length 52:
LLC, dsap STP (0x42) Individual, ssap STP (0x42) Command, ctrl 0x03: STP
802.1d, Config, Flags [none], bridge-id 8000.52:54:00:6e:cd:0b.8003,
length 35


17:20:00.112516 52:54:00:6e:cd:0b > 98:4f:ee:00:7d:e1, ethertype ARP
(0x0806), length 42: Request who-has 192.168.122.23 tell 192.168.122.1,
length 28


17:20:01.112534 52:54:00:6e:cd:0b > 98:4f:ee:00:7d:e1, ethertype ARP
(0x0806), length 42: Request who-has 192.168.122.23 tell 192.168.122.1,
length 28


17:20:01.280468 72:24:b4:f0:16:81 > 01:80:c2:00:00:00, 802.3, length 52:
LLC, dsap STP (0x42) Individual, ssap STP (0x42) Command, ctrl 0x03: STP
802.1d, Config, Flags [none], bridge-id 8000.52:54:00:6e:cd:0b.8003,
length 35


17:20:02.112524 52:54:00:6e:cd:0b > 98:4f:ee:00:7d:e1, ethertype ARP
(0x0806), length 42: Request who-has 192.168.122.23 tell 192.168.122.1,
length 28


17:20:04.161591 98:4f:ee:00:7d:e1 > ff:ff:ff:ff:ff:ff, ethertype ARP
(0x0806), length 60: Request who-has 192.168.4.100 tell 192.168.4.10,
length 46


17:20:05.153670 98:4f:ee:00:7d:e1 > ff:ff:ff:ff:ff:ff, ethertype ARP
(0x0806), length 60: Request who-has 192.168.4.100 tell 192.168.4.10,
length 46
```

The output of this `tcpdump` capture showed that the Spanning Tree Protocol was enabled on the bridge on the server side by issuing the following command:

```
# brctl stp br0 off
```

This traffic was stopped, resulting in much less *noise* over the bridge.

> Turn off STP on a network bridge only if you know what you are doing. In this case, there is no risk of loops as there is only one bridge and there are only two devices connected.

The ARP requests that are seen in the `tcpdump` capture cannot easily be suppressed. However, these requests are very small and should not result in a large performance hit. On a high-latency line, however, these requests will become a bottleneck.

Removing the bridges

If the bridge is no longer needed, it is best to remove the network bridge and the persistent `tap0` devices:

```
# ifconfig br0 down
# brctl delif br0 tap0
# brctl delif br0 eth0
# brctl delbr br0
# openvpn --rmtun --dev tap0
Thu Sep 11 18:55:22 2014 TUN/TAP device tap0 opened
Thu Sep 11 18:55:22 2014 Persist state set to: OFF
```

Remember to bring the `eth0` network interface back online.

Combining point-to-point mode with certificates

For the next example, we borrow some bits from *Chapter 3, PKIs and Certificates*. In client/server mode, OpenVPN is configured using a **Public Key Infrastructure (PKI)**, with X.509 certificates and private keys. It is also possible to use X.509 certificates and private keys to set up a point-to-point tunnel. The advantage of using X.509 certificates over pre-shared keys is that it offers **Perfect Forwarding Secrecy (PFS)**, which greatly enhances the security of your VPN data. Without PFS, if an attacker manages to break the encryption at some point, then all previously recorded VPN traffic can be decrypted. With PFS, it is not possible to decrypt *old* data.

In order to set up a point-to-point tunnel using certificates, we must first copy over the CA certificate and the certificate/private key pair for both endpoints:

```
[root@server] # mkdir -p /etc/openvpn/movpn
[root@server] # chmod 700 /etc/openvpn/movpn
[root@server] # cd /etc/openvpn/movpn
[root@server] # PKI=<PKI_DIR>/ssladmin/active
[root@server] # cp -a $PKI/ca.crt movpn-ca.crt
```

```
[root@server] # cp -a $PKI/Mastering_OpenVPN_Server.crt server.crt
[root@server] # cp -a $PKI/Mastering_OpenVPN_Server.key server.key
```

and

```
[root@client] # mkdir -p /etc/openvpn/movpn
[root@client] # chmod 700 /etc/openvpn/movpn
[root@client] # cd /etc/openvpn/movpn
[root@client] # PKI=<PKI_DIR>/ssladmin/active
[root@client] # cp -a $PKI/ca.crt movpn-ca.crt
[root@client] # cp -a $PKI/client1.crt client1.crt
[root@client] # cp -a $PKI/client1.key client1.key
```

On the server side, we also need to generate a Diffie-Hellman parameter file that is required for VPN session keys. The session keys are ephemeral or temporary keys and are generated when the connection between client and server is first set up.

To generate a Diffie-Hellman parameter file, execute the following commands:

```
[root@server] # cd /etc/openvpn/movpn
[root@server] # openssl dhparam -out dh2048.pem 2048
```

We are now ready to set up the OpenVPN configuration files. On the server side, create the following configuration file, and save it as `movpn-02-06-server.conf`:

```
proto udp
port 1194
dev tun
tls-server
ifconfig 10.200.0.1 10.200.0.2
tls-auth /etc/openvpn/movpn/ta.key 0
dh        /etc/openvpn/movpn/dh2048.pem
ca        /etc/openvpn/movpn/movpn-ca.crt
cert      /etc/openvpn/movpn/server.crt
key       /etc/openvpn/movpn/server.key
persist-key
persist-tun
keepalive 10 60
user  nobody
group nobody
```

```
# use 'group nogroup' on Debian/Ubuntu
verb 3
daemon
log-append /var/log/openvpn.log
```

On the client side, create the configuration file `movpn-02-06-client.conf`:

```
port 1194
dev tun
tls-client
ifconfig 10.200.0.2 10.200.0.1
remote openvpnserver.example.com
remote-cert-tls server
tls-auth /etc/openvpn/movpn/ta.key 1
ca        /etc/openvpn/movpn/movpn-ca.crt
cert      /etc/openvpn/movpn/client1.crt
key       /etc/openvpn/movpn/client1.key
persist-key
persist-tun
keepalive 10 60
user   nobody
group nobody
# use 'group nogroup' on Debian/Ubuntu
verb 3
daemon
log-append /var/log/openvpn.log
```

Next, we start the client and the server:

```
[root@server] # openvpn --config movpn-02-06-server.conf


[root@client] # openvpn --config movpn-02-06-client.conf
```

After the initialization sequence has been completed, we will see that the tunnel created has the same properties as a tunnel created with pre-shared keys.

Summary

Point-to-point was the only supported configuration in the initial versions of OpenVPN. In this chapter, we started off with a very basic point-to-point example. We introduced more features of OpenVPN, and saw that there are good reasons to use this mode in a production environment. In the last use case, bridged TAP adapters are used on both client and server side.

This is the only chapter in which point-to-point mode is explained. In the next chapter, we will properly set up the certificates needed for using the *other* mode of OpenVPN, the client/server model.

3
PKIs and Certificates

Primarily, OpenVPN uses X.509 certificates for client authentication and VPN traffic encryption, though this support can be disabled. Looking at the mailing list and IRC channel history, setup and maintenance of the **Private Key Infrastructure (PKI)** for X.509 certificates is a difficult concept, and can be a cumbersome task.

The OpenSSL binary has all the tools required to manually manage a PKI, but the command options are complicated and, if not automated, can be prone to error. It is recommended that organizations or individuals use a script or other package to manage their PKI. Not only does this limit errors, but also rules and other general criteria can be better adhered to.

Two open source projects exist that are expressly written to work well with OpenVPN implementations. Easy-RSA is a long-standing project that has always been tied closely with the OpenVPN project. Originally written along-side OpenVPN, its initial purpose was to build a **Certificate Authority (CA)** and its requisite components. Today, this project is still maintained alongside the OpenVPN project, though they are technically separate.

Another project, ssl-admin, is a Perl script written to fill perceived gaps in the Easy-RSA code. The two projects approach the PKI management tasks differently, and both have a unique solution. The ssl-admin project is an interactive script providing menus and user feedback, while Easy-RSA is primarily a batch utility.

Today, both the Easy-RSA and ssl-admin projects are maintained by Eric Crist. Josh Cepek joined, and has written most of the initial v3.0 Easy-RSA code. The goal is to eventually merge the two projects and retain all the functionalities of both.

An overview of PKI

PKI is generally a hierarchical organization of encryption certificate and key pairs. Typically, as used with most websites, the top of the hierarchy is the CA. This is the *root* of the entire tree, and trust is rooted at this level. If the root is trusted, all the key pairs underlying will also be trusted. From the root-level CA, there can be client certificates, server certificates, sub-CAs, and **certificate revocation lists** (CRLs). Under each sub-CA, this list of possibilities repeats.

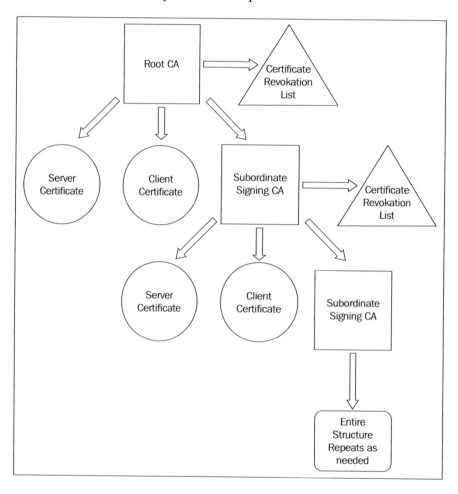

To use a PKI to its full potential, the users and systems need to trust the root CA, and any intermediate CAs in the chain. With most modern web browsers, the browser authors or vendors have vetted and approved a large list of root-level certificate authorities to trust by default. These authorities are generally commercial vendors such as VeriSign, Go Daddy, Comodo, Trend Micro, various government entities, and many others.

Due to this preapproved list for browsers, the vast majority of Internet users are completely unaware of how PKI works. As a result, new users to OpenVPN, and any software that requires a PKI, find configuring and managing a hurdle—both conceptually and technically. In the case of public websites, verification of a third-party site by a trusted authority is needed. In the context of OpenVPN, however, there is generally a single entity within an organization that is implicitly trusted, the IT department. OpenVPN is typically used within a single organization, and trust for such is inherent. Easy-RSA and ssl-admin were both written to help both novice and advanced users better manage their PKI.

With a single point-to-point link, it often doesn't make sense to involve the complexity of PKI to protect a tunnel; pre-shared keys are sufficient. However, when many users are involved, there is much more potential for lost and stolen keys and employee turnover. With a properly configured PKI, it is a relatively simple matter to revoke a lost certificate, or that of a departing employee. A new one is just as easily generated and redeployed.

Using both Easy-RSA and ssl-admin, we will create a simple PKI with a CA, a server certificate, some client certificates, and a certificate revocation list. Additionally, we will use these utilities to generate **Diffie-Hellman (DH)** parameters, which will be used and discussed in later chapters.

The OpenVPN PKI flow is as follows:

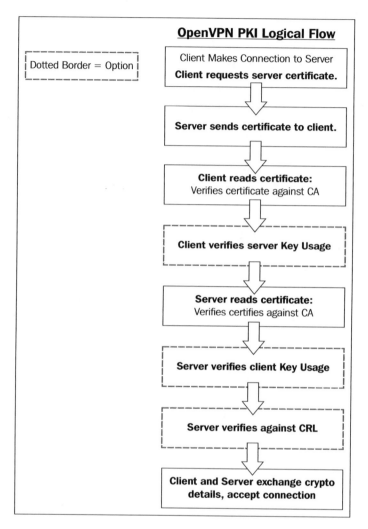

PKI using Easy-RSA

At the time this chapter was written, Easy-RSA 2.2.2 was officially the latest release, alongside v3.0.0-rc2. Since the v3.0 series is nearing release, this section will focus on that version. Releases for Easy-RSA can be found at `https://github.com/OpenVPN/ easy-rsa/releases`.

This exercise will demonstrate how to build a CA from scratch. Upgrading from Easy-RSA 2.2 is not covered here. After downloading the Easy-RSA package, decompress the files, and you should find a directory (in our case, `EasyRSA-3.0.0-rc2`):

```
ecrist@computer:~/Downloads-> tar -xzvf EasyRSA-3.0.0-rc2.tgz
x EasyRSA-3.0.0-rc2/
x EasyRSA-3.0.0-rc2/x509-types/
x EasyRSA-3.0.0-rc2/x509-types/server
x EasyRSA-3.0.0-rc2/x509-types/ca
x EasyRSA-3.0.0-rc2/x509-types/COMMON
x EasyRSA-3.0.0-rc2/x509-types/client
x EasyRSA-3.0.0-rc2/openssl-1.0.cnf
x EasyRSA-3.0.0-rc2/ChangeLog
x EasyRSA-3.0.0-rc2/Licensing/
x EasyRSA-3.0.0-rc2/Licensing/gpl-2.0.txt
x EasyRSA-3.0.0-rc2/COPYING
x EasyRSA-3.0.0-rc2/KNOWN_ISSUES
x EasyRSA-3.0.0-rc2/doc/
x EasyRSA-3.0.0-rc2/doc/Hacking.md
x EasyRSA-3.0.0-rc2/doc/EasyRSA-Upgrade-Notes.md
x EasyRSA-3.0.0-rc2/doc/EasyRSA-Readme.md
x EasyRSA-3.0.0-rc2/doc/EasyRSA-Advanced.md
x EasyRSA-3.0.0-rc2/doc/Intro-To-PKI.md
x EasyRSA-3.0.0-rc2/README.quickstart.md
x EasyRSA-3.0.0-rc2/vars.example
x EasyRSA-3.0.0-rc2/easyrsa
```

Once this is extracted, copy the `vars.example` file to `vars`. It is recommended that you set the Easy-RSA working directory. Line 45 of `vars` defines `EASYRSA` to `$PWD` (present working directory) by default. This can be problematic, particularly if you're using Easy-RSA to manage multiple certificate authorities. Uncomment this line, and change it to something sensible for your environment, such as `/usr/local/etc/easy-rsa`.

When Easy-RSA is initialized, everything within the EASYRSA directory will be deleted. Be careful about what you define here. The EASYRSA directory is where the certificate store resides. This is *not* where the executables and variables are.

You'll likely want to set the organizational fields, which are the following variables:

- EASYRSA_REQ_COUNTRY
- EASYRSA_REQ_PROVICE
- EASYRSA_REQ_CITY
- EASYRSA_REQ_ORG
- EASYRSA_REQ_EMAIL
- EASYRSA_REQ_OU

The values are used as defaults for all certificate requests generated, including the root CA. Make sure those lines are uncommented in the file. No other changes to vars are needed.

If your defined EASYRSA directory does not exist, create it now and copy the openssl-1.0.cnf file from the package distribution to your new directory. For our examples, we have put the EASYRSA certificate store in /usr/local/etc/easy-rsa:

```
ecrist@computer:~/Downloads/EasyRSA-3.0.0-rc2-> mkdir -p /usr/local/etc/
easy-rsa
ecrist@computer:~/Downloads/EasyRSA-3.0.0-rc2-> cp openssl-1.0.cnf /usr/
local/etc/easy-rsa
ecrist@computer:~/Downloads/EasyRSA-3.0.0-rc2-> cp -R x509-types /usr/
local/etc/easy-rsa/
```

Next, we are ready to initialize the Easy-RSA PKI:

```
ecrist@computer:~/Downloads/EasyRSA-3.0.0-rc2-> ./easyrsa init-pki
```

Note that we are using Easy-RSA configuration from ./vars.

```
init-pki complete; you may now create a CA or requests.
Your newly created PKI dir is: /usr/local/etc/easy-rsa/pki
```

In this case, the initialization process cleans out the contents of, in this case, the pki directory, and creates the private and reqs subdirectories.

You can have multiple vars files for managing multiple CAs, and have all those nested in the same EASYRSA root directory. To do this, you have to change the EASYRSA_PKI variable for each CA.

Building the CA

The `build-ca` subcommand first generates a **Certificate Signing Request (CSR)**, and subsequently self-signs that request.

To build the root certificate authority certificate/key pair, run the `build-ca` command:

```
ecrist@computer:~/Downloads/EasyRSA-3.0.0-rc2-> ./easyrsa build-ca


Note: using Easy-RSA configuration from: ./vars

Generating a 2048 bit RSA private key

.......+++

............+++

writing new private key to '/usr/local/etc/easy-rsa/pki/private/ca.key'

Enter PEM pass phrase:

Verifying - Enter PEM pass phrase:

-----
```

You are about to be asked to enter information that will be incorporated into your certificate request. What you are about to enter is what is called a Distinguished Name or a DN. There are quite a few fields but you can leave some blank; some fields will have a default value defined, If you enter '.', the field will be left blank.

```
-----

Common Name (eg: your user, host, or server name) [Easy-RSA CA]:Mastering
OpenVPN
```

> Spaces should not be used in the Common Name field. This will cause problems in Easy-RSA as well as potentially with CCDs, common-name-as-username, and other cases. Make sure there is a trailing forward slash (/) after the path or some subcommands (`gen-crl` and others) will not function.

```
CA creation complete and you may now import and sign cert requests.

Your new CA certificate file for publishing is at:

/usr/local/etc/easy-rsa/pki/ca.crt
```

When self-signing, the CA constraint is set to true and key usage parameters are defined, allowing this new certificate to sign other certificates, including the **Certificate Revocation List** (CRL). This information can be verified using the `openssl` command-line utility:

```
ecrist@computer:~/Downloads/EasyRSA-3.0.0-rc2-> openssl x509 -in /usr/
local/etc/easy-rsa/pki/ca.crt -text -noout
Certificate:
    Data:
        Version: 3 (0x2)
        Serial Number:
            89:39:42:bb:f3:6b:a9:f6
        Signature Algorithm: sha256WithRSAEncryption
        Issuer: CN=Mastering OpenVPN
        Validity
            Not Before: Oct  1 15:02:44 2014 GMT
            Not After : Sep 28 15:02:44 2024 GMT
        Subject: CN=Mastering OpenVPN
        Subject Public Key Info:
            Public Key Algorithm: rsaEncryption
            RSA Public Key: (2048 bit)
                Modulus (2048 bit):

                    ...

                Exponent: 65537 (0x10001)
        X509v3 extensions:
            X509v3 Subject Key Identifier:
                69:6C:A3:85:63:61:09:DE:8F:7D:38:F7:A2:CB:
1C:31:75:90:34:93
            X509v3 Authority Key Identifier:
                keyid:69:6C:A3:85:63:61:09:DE:8F:7D:38:F7:A2:CB:
1C:31:75:90:34:93
                DirName:/CN=Mastering OpenVPN
                serial:89:39:42:BB:F3:6B:A9:F6

            X509v3 Basic Constraints:
                CA:TRUE
            X509v3 Key Usage:
```

```
            Certificate Sign, CRL Sign
     Signature Algorithm: sha256WithRSAEncryption

      . . .
```

In the output from `openssl`, we see the `x509v3 Basic Constraints` as well as the `x509v3 Key Usage` parameters. Your CA is now ready to begin signing client and server certificates.

Certificate revocation list

The `gen-crl` subcommand generates a CRL. Although, at this point, we only have a CA certificate, it is recommended to generate an empty CRL. This allows you to stage your OpenVPN configuration with the file, and will not require a restart later. OpenVPN will log errors if a nonexistent CRL is listed in its configuration, but the file can be replaced on the fly, as it is re-read on every client connection.

```
ecrist@computer:~/Downloads/EasyRSA-3.0.0-rc2-> ./easyrsa gen-crl


Note: using Easy-RSA configuration from: ./vars

Using configuration from /usr/local/etc/easy-rsa/openssl-1.0.cnf

Enter pass phrase for /usr/local/etc/easy-rsa/pki/private/ca.key:


An updated CRL has been created.

CRL file: /usr/local/etc/easy-rsa/pki/crl.pem
```

We can verify the CRL using the `openssl crl` command:

```
ecrist@computer:~/Downloads/EasyRSA-3.0.0-rc2-> openssl crl -noout -text
-in /usr/local/etc/easy-rsa/pki/crl.pem
Certificate Revocation List (CRL):
        Version 2 (0x1)
        Signature Algorithm: sha256WithRSAEncryption
        Issuer: /CN=Mastering OpenVPN
        Last Update: Oct  1 15:50:46 2014 GMT
        Next Update: Mar 30 15:50:46 2015 GMT
        CRL extensions:
            X509v3 Authority Key Identifier:
```

```
                    keyid:69:6C:A3:85:63:61:09:DE:8F:7D:38:F7:A2:CB:
1C:31:75:90:34:93

                    DirName:/CN=Mastering OpenVPN

                    serial:89:39:42:BB:F3:6B:A9:F6


No Revoked Certificates.
    Signature Algorithm: sha256WithRSAEncryption

        . . .
```

Server certificates

OpenVPN can make use of the x509 key usage parameters, ensuring clients connect with valid client certificates, and the clients can ensure a server is authorized to be a server. This prevents one of your client certificates from being used as a server in a **Man-In-The-Middle (MITM)** attack. Without this constraint, it is possible for any certificate signed by the VPN CA to be used to impersonate a client or server. Because the rogue certificate resides within the same PKI, the certificate itself is still valid, and will pass the generic PKI checks.

Easy-RSA supports signing certificates with the server key usage parameter using the build-server-full subcommand.

```
ecrist@computer:~/EasyRSA-3.0.0-rc2-> ./easyrsa build-server-full movpn-
server


Note: using Easy-RSA configuration from: ./vars

Generating a 2048 bit RSA private key

. . . . . . . . . . . .+++

. . . . . . . . . . . . . . . . . . . . . . . . . . .+++

writing new private key to '/usr/local/etc/easy-rsa/pki/private/movpn-
server.key'

Enter PEM pass phrase:

Verifying - Enter PEM pass phrase:

-----

Using configuration from /usr/local/etc/easy-rsa/openssl-1.0.cnf

Enter pass phrase for /usr/local/etc/easy-rsa/pki/private/ca.key:

Check that the request matches the signature

Signature ok
```

```
The Subject's Distinguished Name is as follows
commonName              :PRINTABLE:'movpn-server'
Certificate is to be certified until Oct 18 19:15:31 2024 GMT (3650 days)


Write out database with 1 new entries
Data Base Updated
```

We can verify the server certificate with the `openssl` command:

```
ecrist@computer:~/EasyRSA-3.0.0-rc2-> openssl x509 -noout -text -in /usr/
local/etc/easy-rsa/pki/issued/movpn-server.crt
Certificate:
    Data:
        Version: 3 (0x2)
        Serial Number: 1 (0x1)
    Signature Algorithm: sha256WithRSAEncryption
        Issuer: CN=Mastering OpenVPN
        Validity
            Not Before: Oct 21 19:15:31 2014 GMT
            Not After : Oct 18 19:15:31 2024 GMT
        Subject: CN=movpn-server
        Subject Public Key Info:
            Public Key Algorithm: rsaEncryption
                Public-Key: (2048 bit)
                Modulus:
                    ...
                Exponent: 65537 (0x10001)
        X509v3 extensions:
            X509v3 Basic Constraints:
                CA:FALSE
            X509v3 Subject Key Identifier:
                11:AD:47:E2:1C:87:91:3B:C0:A1:53:F5:77:A7:2F:9F:0B:0F:5D
:9E
            X509v3 Authority Key Identifier:
```

```
E4:81:A0
                  keyid:F0:AF:20:ED:6F:A7:47:0F:C7:F2:B0:EC:CF:8B:30:09:02:

                  DirName:/CN=Mastering OpenVPN
                  serial:84:9E:B9:14:2B:62:B4:50


          X509v3 Extended Key Usage:
              TLS Web Server Authentication
          X509v3 Key Usage:
              Digital Signature, Key Encipherment
    Signature Algorithm: sha256WithRSAEncryption
          ...
```

Note the x509v3 key usage section, and their identification of `TLS Web Server Authentication`. This is what current versions of OpenVPN looks for when remote certificate types are specified.

Client certificates

Just like server certificates, clients can be authenticated using client-specific certificates. With this method, each client can be required to have a unique certificate. The certificate **Common Name (CN)** can be used to determine other parameters to be pushed on a given connection via `client-connect` scripts or the `client-config-dir` option. As of OpenVPN 2.3.7, there is still support for `-client-cert-not-required`. There has been talk of removing this support from a future release. `client-cert-not-required` allows a client to connect without a unique (or any) predefined certificate, much as a web browser would connect to a web server.

The `easyrsa` command is used to build a client certificate in much the same way we built the server certificate:

```
ecrist@computer:~/EasyRSA-3.0.0-rc2-> ./easyrsa build-client-full client1


Note: using Easy-RSA configuration from: ./vars
Generating a 2048 bit RSA private key
...............+++
.................................................................................
..............................................+++
```

```
writing new private key to '/home/ecrist/EasyRSA-3.0.0-rc2/pki/private/
client1.key'
Enter PEM pass phrase:
Verifying - Enter PEM pass phrase:
-----
Using configuration from /home/ecrist/EasyRSA-3.0.0-rc2/openssl-1.0.cnf
Enter pass phrase for /home/ecrist/EasyRSA-3.0.0-rc2/pki/private/ca.key:
Check that the request matches the signature
Signature ok
The Subject's Distinguished Name is as follows
commonName                :PRINTABLE:'client1'
Certificate is to be certified until Oct 18 19:37:40 2024 GMT (3650 days)


Write out database with 1 new entries
Data Base Updated
```

We can use the `openssl` command to verify the key usage parameters:

```
ecrist@computer:~/EasyRSA-3.0.0-rc2-> openssl x509 -noout -text -in /usr/
local/etc/easy-rsa/pki/issued/client1.crt
Certificate:
    Data:
        Version: 3 (0x2)
        Serial Number: 2 (0x2)
    Signature Algorithm: sha256WithRSAEncryption
        Issuer: CN=Mastering OpenVPN
        Validity
            Not Before: Oct 21 19:37:40 2014 GMT
            Not After : Oct 18 19:37:40 2024 GMT
        Subject: CN=client1
        Subject Public Key Info:
            Public Key Algorithm: rsaEncryption
                Public-Key: (2048 bit)
                Modulus:
                    ...
                Exponent: 65537 (0x10001)
```

```
          X509v3 extensions:
              X509v3 Basic Constraints:
                  CA:FALSE
              X509v3 Subject Key Identifier:
                  47:80:59:8D:5F:63:4B:1C:21:C6:DE:C6:C0:7B:DE:6A:5D:53
  :F9:37
              X509v3 Authority Key Identifier:
                  keyid:F0:AF:20:ED:6F:A7:47:0F:C7:F2:B0:EC:CF:8B:30:09:02:
  E4:81:A0

                  DirName:/CN=Mastering OpenVPN
                  serial:84:9E:B9:14:2B:62:B4:50

              X509v3 Extended Key Usage:
                  TLS Web Client Authentication
              X509v3 Key Usage:
                  Digital Signature
      Signature Algorithm: sha256WithRSAEncryption
          . . .
```

As noted in the server section, we look to the x509v3 Extended Key Usage.
In the case of the client, we look for TLS Web Client Authentication.
Again, this is used when verifying remote client certificate type.

PKI using ssl-admin

The ssl-admin project was started during a time when Easy-RSA was considered
abandoned and broken. It is a menu-driven, interactive utility written in Perl.
Like Easy-RSA, ssl-admin is a wrapper for the OpenSSL command line utilities.

To install ssl-admin on FreeBSD, install the security/ssl-admin port. For all
other Unix-based systems, including OS X, an svn export is the simplest method.
The following examples are run on Mac OS X, but it will be similar for other
operating systems.

To obtain ssl-admin on an OS other than FreeBSD, use the SVN command-line
utility to export the current version:

```
ftp://ftp.secure-computing.net/pub/ssl-admin/
```

```
ecrist@computer:~-> curl -o ssa.tgz ftp://ftp.secure-computing.net//pub/
ssl-admin/ssl-admin-1.2.1.tar.gz
```

% Total	% Received	% Xferd	Average Dload	Speed Upload	Time Total	Time Spent	Time Left	Current Speed
100 11196	100 11196	0	0	17568	0	--:--:--	--:--:--	--:--:-- 17548

The server `ftp2.secure-computing.net` can be used as an alternative if the primary, `ftp.secure-computing.net`, is offline.

```
ecrist@computer:~-> tar -xzvf ssa.tgz
x ssl-admin-1.2.1/
x ssl-admin-1.2.1/man5/
x ssl-admin-1.2.1/man1/
x ssl-admin-1.2.1/ssl-admin
x ssl-admin-1.2.1/ssl-admin.conf
x ssl-admin-1.2.1/Makefile
x ssl-admin-1.2.1/configure
x ssl-admin-1.2.1/openssl.conf
x ssl-admin-1.2.1/ssl-admin-e
x ssl-admin-1.2.1/man1/ssl-admin.1
x ssl-admin-1.2.1/man1/ssl-admin.1-e
x ssl-admin-1.2.1/man5/ssl-admin.conf.5
x ssl-admin-1.2.1/man5/ssl-admin.conf.5-e
```

To install after the export, change dir to your exported tree and run `./configure`, followed by `make install`:

```
ecrist@computer:~/ssl-admin-1.2.1-> ./configure
```

The Bourne shell is the only requirement for configure. This is not a typical configure rule set, it just mimics the behavior of one.

```
ecrist@computer:~/ssl-admin-1.2.1-> sudo make install
```

Once installed, running the `ssl-admin` command will initially display an error:

```
ecrist@computer:~/ssl-admin-> ssl-admin
/Library/ssl-admin/ssl-admin.conf doesn't exist.  Did you copy the sample
from /Library/ssl-admin/ssl-admin.conf.sample? at /usr/local/bin/ssl-
admin line 40.
```

 Some versions of ssl-admin refer to the following file:
`ssl-admin.conf.default`.

To begin using the software, you must copy the default file to the location listed
in the error. This will vary across operating systems according to their standard
filesystem hierarchy. Here, we will copy `ssl-admin.conf.sample` to `ssl-admin.
conf` and fix the permissions on the new file.

 `ssl-admin` requires all operations to be done as root. This is a
known poor practice and will be fixed in an upcoming release.

The commands for it are as follows:

```
ecrist@computer:~/ssl-admin-> sudo csh
Password:
```

There is no specific reason to use `csh`, this was just a preference of the author (for
better or worse).

```
root@computer:~/ssl-admin-> cd /Library/ssl-admin/
root@computer:/Library/ssl-admin-> cp ssl-admin.conf.sample ssl-admin.
conf
root@computer:/Library/ssl-admin-> chmod ug+rw ssl-admin.conf
root@computer:/Library/ssl-admin-> ls -1
total 12
-r--r--r--  1 root  wheel  2511 Oct  1 12:02 openssl.conf.sample
-rw-rw-r--  1 root  wheel   531 Oct  1 12:11 ssl-admin.conf
-r--r--r--  1 root  wheel   531 Oct  1 12:02 ssl-admin.conf.sample
```

From here, we can edit the configuration file. Generally, only the bottom variables need to be changed:

- $ENV{'KEY_COUNTRY'}
- $ENV{'KEY_PROVINCE'}
- $ENV{'KEY_CITY'}
- $ENV{'KEY_ORG'}
- $ENV{'KEY_EMAIL'}
- $ENV{'KEY_COUNTRY'}

The variable KEY_COUNTRY must be two letters. This is a limitation/restriction of the standard, not ssl-admin. These values align with the similarly named variables in Easy-RSA. These should not be changed once a CA has been generated, as openssl will throw errors for mismatched values.

 $ENV{'KEY_CRL_LOC'} should be left alone if your organization does not have a valid URL for CRL distribution. A blank value will cause errors with openssl.

Once the configuration file has been edited, we can start the program. On first execution, ssl-admin will inspect its certificate store. If a valid CA and structure is not present there, the user has the ability to import an existing PKI or create a new PKI. As with Easy-RSA, we are generating a new CA. On some operating systems, the file /etc/openssl.cnf needs to be copied manually to your certificate store root. This error was not encountered on Mac OS X. On Linux systems, simply copy /etc/openssl.cnf to /etc/ssl-admin/openssl.cnf. This will be fixed in a later release of ssl-admin.

```
root@computer:/Library/ssl-admin-> ssl-admin
This program will walk you through requesting, signing,
organizing and revoking SSL certificates.

Looks like this is a new install, installing...
You will first need to edit the /Library/ssl-admin/ssl-admin.conf
default variables.  Have you done this? (y/n): y
I need the CA credentials.  Would you like to create a new CA key and
certificate now?  (y/n): y
Please enter certificate owner's name or ID.
```

Usual format is first initial-last name (jdoe) or
hostname of server which will use this certificate.
All lower case, numbers OK.
Owner []: Mastering OpenVPN

File names will use Mastering_OpenVPN.

===> Creating private key with 2048 bits and generating request.
Do you want to password protect your CA private key? (y/n): y
Generating RSA private key, 2048 bit long modulus
.....................................+++
............+++
e is 65537 (0x10001)
Enter pass phrase for Mastering_OpenVPN.key:
Verifying - Enter pass phrase for Mastering_OpenVPN.key:
===> Self-Signing request.
Enter pass phrase for /Library/ssl-admin/Mastering_OpenVPN.key:
===> Moving certficate and key to appropriate directory.
===> Creating initial CRL.Using configuration from /Library/ssl-admin/
openssl.conf
Enter pass phrase for /Library/ssl-admin/active/ca.key:
ssl-admin installed Wed Oct 1 12:28:23 CDT 2014
OPTIONAL: I can't find your OpenVPN client config. Please copy your
config to
/Library/ssl-admin/packages/client.ovpn


```
========================================================
#              SSL-ADMIN v1.2.1                     #
========================================================
```
Please enter the menu option from the following list:
1) Update run-time options:
      Key Duration (days): 3650
      Current Serial #: 01

```
     Key Size (bits): 2048
     Intermediate CA Signing: NO
2) Create new Certificate Request
3) Sign a Certificate Request
4) Perform a one-step request/sign
5) Revoke a Certificate
6) Renew/Re-sign a past Certificate Request
7) View current Certificate Revokation List
8) View index information for certificate.
i) Generate a user config with in-line certifcates and keys.
z) Zip files for end user.
dh) Generate Diffie Hellman parameters.
CA) Create new Self-Signed CA certificate.
S) Create new Signed Server certificate.
q) Quit ssl-admin
```

```
Menu Item:
```

As you can see, ssl-admin is considerably more verbose and interactive than Easy-RSA. Also, ssl-admin automatically generates the initial CRL for you.

Before the menu was displayed, there was an OPTIONAL warning about OpenVPN configuration. If you provide your client.ovpn configuration, ssl-admin can automatically package configuration files with embedded certificates or multifile ZIP files. The certificate lines of the configuration file should be generic:

```
ca ca.crt
cert client.crt
key client.key
```

These values will be automatically replaced with inline keys, or files will be renamed according to how the OpenVPN certificates, keys, and configurations are distributed. Now that we initialized the PKI by creating a root certificate authority key pair, we can start creating our server and client certificates.

OpenVPN server certificates

First, we will create the certificate for use on the OpenVPN server. Menu option s will generate a CSR, a key, and will prompt to sign the certificate by the CA:

```
Menu Item: S
Please enter certificate owner's name or ID.
Usual format is first initial-last name (jdoe) or
hostname of server which will use this certificate.
All lower case, numbers OK.
Owner []: Mastering OpenVPN Server



File names will use Mastering_OpenVPN_Server.
Please enter certificate owner's name or ID.
Usual format is first initial-last name (jdoe) or
hostname of server which will use this certificate.
All lower case, numbers OK.
Owner [Mastering_OpenVPN_Server]:
Would you like to password protect the private key (y/n): y
Generating a 2048 bit RSA private key
.................+++
.........+++
writing new private key to 'Mastering_OpenVPN_Server.key'
Enter PEM pass phrase:
Verifying - Enter PEM pass phrase:
-----
===> Serial Number = 01
Using configuration from /Library/ssl-admin/openssl.conf
Enter pass phrase for /Library/ssl-admin/active/ca.key:
Check that the request matches the signature
Signature ok
The Subject's Distinguished Name is as follows
countryName           :PRINTABLE:'ZA'
stateOrProvinceName   :PRINTABLE:'Enlightenment'
localityName          :PRINTABLE:'Overall'
```

```
organizationName        :PRINTABLE:'Mastering OpenVPN'
commonName              :PRINTABLE:'Mastering OpenVPN Server'
emailAddress            :IA5STRING:'root@example.org'
```

Certificate is to be certified until Sep 28 17:48:20 2024 GMT (3650 days)

```
Write out database with 1 new entries

Data Base Updated

=========> Moving certificates and keys to /Library/ssl-admin/active for
production.
```

Can I move signing request (Mastering_OpenVPN_Server.csr) to the csr directory for archiving? (y/n): y

```
===> Mastering_OpenVPN_Server.csr moved.
```

MENU

 To save space, the menu printed by `ssl-admin` will be omitted, instead it is replaced with the word MENU.

In the preceding code, we used a certificate CN with spaces to demonstrate `ssl-admin` behavior. Here, it warned that the spaces would be replaced with the underscore character, and gave the user the opportunity to change the CN, if needed. Further along, we opted to secure the private key with a passphrase. Finally, the user was asked if the CSR could be archived.

To show the added server tokens, we again run the `openssl` command to output certificate details. The following output omits some key details for brevity:

```
root@computer:/Library/ssl-admin-> openssl x509 -noout -text -in active/
Mastering_OpenVPN_Server.crt
Certificate:
    Data:
        Version: 3 (0x2)
        Serial Number: 1 (0x1)
        Signature Algorithm: sha1WithRSAEncryption
        Issuer: C=ZA, ST=Enlightenment, L=Overall, O=Mastering OpenVPN,
CN=Mastering OpenVPN/emailAddress=root@example.org
        Validity
            Not Before: Oct  1 17:48:20 2014 GMT
            Not After : Sep 28 17:48:20 2024 GMT
```

```
        Subject: C=ZA, ST=Enlightenment, O=Mastering OpenVPN,
CN=Mastering OpenVPN Server/emailAddress=root@example.org
        Subject Public Key Info:
            Public Key Algorithm: rsaEncryption
            RSA Public Key: (2048 bit)
                Modulus (2048 bit):

                    ...

                Exponent: 65537 (0x10001)
        X509v3 extensions:
            X509v3 Basic Constraints:
                CA:FALSE
            Netscape Cert Type:
                SSL Server
            Netscape Comment:
                ssl-admin (OpenSSL) Generated Server Certificate
            X509v3 Subject Key Identifier:
                FB:A8:91:01:E3:51:5D:A7:29:8C:54:63:9F:22:7F:F8:DE:AB:
5A:39
            X509v3 Authority Key Identifier:
                keyid:1F:85:DF:90:5C:3F:73:A9:03:B9:F4:E6:C2:2C:A3:27:CF:
5B:44:95
                DirName:/C=ZA/ST=Enlightenment/L=Overall/O=Mastering
OpenVPN/CN=Mastering OpenVPN/emailAddress=root@example.org
                serial:D2:93:32:F0:8E:BC:58:EE

            X509v3 Extended Key Usage:
                TLS Web Server Authentication
            X509v3 Key Usage:
                Digital Signature, Key Encipherment
    Signature Algorithm: sha1WithRSAEncryption
```

Note that x509v3 Extended Key Usage includes TLS Web Server Authentication. An older standard, nsCertType as Netscape Cert Type, is also included for backwards-compatibility. Not only is this pertinent for OpenVPN, but ssl-admin was written as a general x509 CA management utility.

OpenVPN client certificates

Client certificates are generated in much the same way as the server certificate. Option 4 on the menu will create a Certificate Signing Request (CSR) and subsequently sign the CSR:

```
Menu Item: 4
Please enter certificate owner's name or ID.
Usual format is first initial-last name (jdoe) or
hostname of server which will use this certificate.
All lower case, numbers OK.
Owner []: client1



File names will use client1.
Please enter certificate owner's name or ID.
Usual format is first initial-last name (jdoe) or
hostname of server which will use this certificate.
All lower case, numbers OK.
Owner [client1]:
Would you like to password protect the private key (y/n): n
Generating a 2048 bit RSA private key
.........................................................................
.........................................................+++
.........+++
writing new private key to 'client1.key'
-----
===> Serial Number = 02
=========> Signing request for client1
Using configuration from /Library/ssl-admin/openssl.conf
Enter pass phrase for /Library/ssl-admin/active/ca.key:
Check that the request matches the signature
Signature ok
The Subject's Distinguished Name is as follows
countryName           :PRINTABLE:'ZA'
stateOrProvinceName   :PRINTABLE:'Enlightenment'
```

```
localityName            :PRINTABLE:'Overall'
organizationName        :PRINTABLE:'Mastering OpenVPN'
commonName              :PRINTABLE:'client1'
emailAddress            :IA5STRING:'root@example.org'
Certificate is to be certified until Sep 28 18:05:14 2024 GMT (3650 days)


Write out database with 1 new entries

Data Base Updated

=========> Moving certificates and keys to /Library/ssl-admin/active for
production.

Can I move signing request (client1.csr) to the csr directory for
archiving? (y/n): ===> client1.csr moved.

MENU
```

 Later exercises will use up to three client certificates, so it's recommended that you repeat the preceding steps for `client2` and `client3`.

Using the `openssl` binary to inspect the certificate, we can see that the `client1` certificate is missing the server key usage extensions that existed in the server certificate we created earlier.

```
root@computer:/Library/ssl-admin-> openssl x509 -noout -text -in active/
client1.crt
Certificate:
    Data:
        Version: 1 (0x0)
        Serial Number: 2 (0x2)
        Signature Algorithm: sha1WithRSAEncryption
        Issuer: C=ZA, ST=Enlightenment, L=Overall, O=Mastering OpenVPN,
CN=Mastering OpenVPN/emailAddress=root@example.org
        Validity
            Not Before: Oct  1 18:05:14 2014 GMT
            Not After : Sep 28 18:05:14 2024 GMT
        Subject: C=ZA, ST=Enlightenment, O=Mastering OpenVPN, CN=client1/
emailAddress=root@example.org
        Subject Public Key Info:
```

```
          Public Key Algorithm: rsaEncryption
          RSA Public Key: (2048 bit)
              Modulus (2048 bit):

      ...

              Exponent: 65537 (0x10001)
      Signature Algorithm: sha1WithRSAEncryption

        ...
```

This certificate obviously has a simpler structure than the server certificate, and the server key usage parameters are missing.

After creating our CA, server and three client certificates, we're left with the following directory structure:

```
root@computer:/Library/ssl-admin-> ls -lrth
total 16
-rw-rw-r--  1 root   wheel    541B Oct  1 12:22 ssl-admin.conf
drwxr-x---  2 root   wheel     68B Oct  1 12:24 revoked
-rw-rw----  1 root   wheel    2.5K Oct  1 12:27 openssl.conf
drwxr-x---  2 root   wheel    102B Oct  1 12:28 packages
-r--r--r--  1 root   wheel    531B Oct  1 12:43 ssl-admin.conf.sample
-r--r--r--  1 root   wheel    2.5K Oct  1 12:43 openssl.conf.sample
drwxr-x---  2 root   wheel    340B Oct  1 13:05 prog
drwxr-x---  2 root   wheel    340B Oct  1 13:05 csr
drwxr-x---  2 root   wheel    544B Oct  1 13:05 active
```

The active directory contains all the certificates and keys that have not been revoked, including the CA certificate and key. As certificates are revoked, they are moved from active to revoked. In order to utilize the OpenSSL utilities to revoke a certificate, the certificate must be present. Without the certificate, potentially problematic editing needs to be done manually to the index.txt file. As its name would suggest, the csr directory contains all of the CSRs. These are generally safe to delete, and are only kept for troubleshooting, or if a certificate needs to be regenerated.

It is suggested that the administrator leave the contents of the certificate store to the management of the utility. This applies to both ssl-admin and Easy-RSA.

The prog directory contains the operational files of openssl and the latest CRL. It is not recommended these files be disturbed, as there is potential to render your PKI unusable if mistakes are made.

Finally, the `packages` directory will contain all the files you can distribute to your end users: not just the OpenVPN clients, but web server administrators and so on. Packaging the certificates and keys ensures the end user receives all the necessary files and that they are in the proper format.

Other features

The ssl-admin utility has some other features that someone managing a PKI may find interesting. The index is searchable (option 8), which shows a given certificate's status. Display of the current CRL is also possible (option 7). ssl-admin is capable of packaging OpenVPN configuration files with certificates for users both in an inline format (option i), as well as separate files—all contained in a zip file (option z). These last two options will be discussed further into this book, as we generate server and client configurations.

Multiple CAs and CRLs

Easy-RSA 3.0 fairly easily supports multiple root CAs. By creating a separate CA directory under EASYRSA root, and having different vars files for each, each individual CA can be managed with Easy-RSA.

Currently, ssl-admin does not support multiple root CAs, but creation of intermediate CAs is supported.

With OpenVPN, a single server instance can support multiple root CAs, with client connections that have been signed by either CA being accepted. To enable such support, the CA certificate for each authorized CA needs to be concatenated together into a single file that can be called with the `--ca` OpenVPN option. The same can be done with the certificate revocation list.

Generally, it is not recommended to use multiple CA certificates for a single OpenVPN instance; exceptions could be server, or certificate authority migration, company or organization acquisitions, and so on.

Under no circumstances would it be ideal to use a web browser root certificate authority for an OpenVPN certificate chain. There is no way to ascertain who has a certificate, and anyone that falls within that CAs hierarchy would be able to possibly connect to your VPN instance.

Moving forward, there are plans to merge the `ssl-admin` and Easy-RSA projects into a single, fully capable PKI administrative suite. The desire is for Easy-RSA 4.0 to realize these migrations using the best features of both utilities.

Extra security – hardware tokens, smart cards, and PKCS#11

In this section, we will provide some background information on cryptographic hardware devices. You will learn how to generate a private key on a hardware token, and how to copy the associated X.509 certificate to the token as well. After that, we will discuss how OpenVPN can find and use this certificate/private key pair to establish a VPN connection.

Background information

Starting with Version 2.1, OpenVPN supports two-factor authentication by providing **PKCS#11** support. Two-factor authentication is based on the idea that in order to use a system (like a VPN) you need to provide two things:

- Something you **know**, for example, a password
- Something you **possess**, for example, a smart card or hardware token

PKCS#11 is an industry standard for communicating with smart cards or hardware tokens, and there are both open source and commercial drivers available. The PKCS#11 standard was originally published by RSA Laboratories and is sometimes also referred to as the **cryptoki** standard, which stands for **CRYPtographic TOKen Interface**.

Apart from the terms hardware token and smart card, the term **Hardware Security Module (HSM)** is also often used for two-factor authentication. In this section, we will mostly use the term hardware token. The main difference between hardware tokens and smart cards is the form factor: a hardware token usually comes as a USB device, whereas a smart card looks like an ATM card or credit card. In order to use a smart card, a special card reader is required, which is sometimes integrated into laptops and even some desktop computers. Some countries issue national e-ID cards, which typically classify as smart cards.

An HSM is more often an appliance that can securely store and manage cryptographic keys, often providing hardware acceleration as well for speeding up encryption and decryption.

A hardware token, smart card or HSM, is typically a small device with an embedded chip on it. This embedded chip runs a miniature operating system (often referred to as Card OS), which is responsible for securely generating, storing, and managing SSL private keys. Most hardware tokens are also capable of storing other information, such as SSL certificates, so that a valid certificate/private key pair can be stored securely on a single device.

Supported platforms

The major difficulty when using two-factor authentication is the software support on different platforms. While most hardware token and smart card vendors provide operating system drivers for Microsoft Windows, there are far fewer cards and tokens supported on Linux or even Mac OS X. Note that this is not related to OpenVPN itself: if a particular hardware token is supported by the operating system you are using, and a PKCS#11 driver is provided then, in general, OpenVPN can make use of that hardware token or smart card.

For this book, we used an Aladdin eToken Pro 72K USB hardware token. (Aladdin Systems was bought by SafeNet (`http://www.safenet.com`). However, just recently SafeNet merged with Gemalto.) This hardware token is supported only using the closed-source SafeNet Authentication Client, which is available for Microsoft Windows, Mac OS X, and Linux.

Older versions of these tokens had the advantage that they could use either the paid, closed-source driver from SafeNet or the free, open source driver from the OpenSC project (found nowadays at `https://github.com/OpenSC/OpenSC/wiki`). Unfortunately, these older tokens can no longer be purchased, and the current hardware tokens from SafeNet use a different card OS, that is not supported by OpenSC.

The general process and concept apply to most hardware tokens you may use. These older devices were used simply for testing and demonstration purposes. Many vendors utilize a mobile application, usually on a user's smart phone, as the hardware token. SafeNet also has such a product: MobilePASS.

Also, the drivers and tools from the OpenSC project are not as mature as the software from commercial software vendors.

Other vendors of smart cards and hardware tokens are Aktiv Co and Feitian (with open source support).

Please note that OpenVPN depends purely on a working PKCS#11 driver. When selecting a hardware token, it will be important to verify whether the device is supported on the platforms needed, not if it will work with OpenVPN itself. Also, note that it is not required (or even recommended!) to use a hardware token on an OpenVPN server.

Initializing a hardware token

It is assumed that either the Aladdin `pkiclient` or SafeNet `AuthenticationClient` is installed and that the hardware token is recognized by the driver software. If the eToken has already been initialized, then skip this step.

First, bring up the eToken client properties window, and click on **Initialize eToken**. This will bring up the following dialog box:

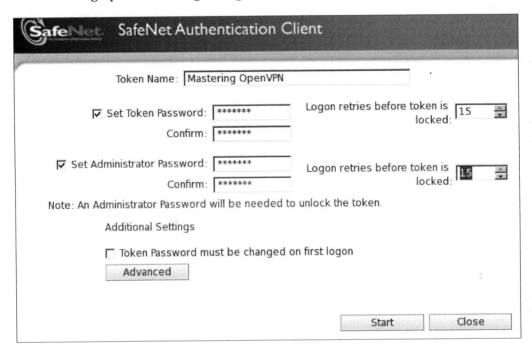

Fill in the token password and administrator password, uncheck the **Token Password must be changed on first logon** checkmark, and click on **Start**.

All contents on the token will now be destroyed and the eToken will be initialized with the new token and administrator passwords.

Generating a certificate/private key pair

When using a hardware token, the process of generating a certificate and private key pair is a little different compared to using the ssl-admin or Easy-RSA tools. With the ssl-admin or Easy-tools, the private key, certificate request, and X.509 certificate are generated in a single step. With a hardware token, we first need to generate a private key on the token.

Using this private key, we then need to create the CSR. This CSR is then signed by the CA, which results in an X.509 certificate. This certificate is then written back to the token. The ssl-admin and Easy-RSA tools actually follow the same process, but they hide the CSR file from the user.

Generating a private key on a token

In order to generate a private key on an eToken, we need the `pkcs11-tool` command, which is part of the OpenSC package. The OpenSC package is available for Microsoft Windows, Mac OS X, and Linux. The `pkcs11-tool` command provides an interface to hardware tokens using a PKCS#11 driver. The PKCS#11 driver included with the Aladdin/SafeNet driver software is `libeTPkcs11.so` (Linux and Mac OS X) or `eTPkcs11.dll` (Windows). The following command was issued on a 64-bit Linux machine and it generates a 2048-bit RSA key identified using the label `movpn` and the ID `20141001`. As we are generating a private key, it is mandatory to log in to the token:

```
# pkcs11-tool --module libeTPkcs11.so \
  --keypairgen --key-type rsa:2048 \
  --label "movpn" --id 20141001 --login
Using slot 0 with a present token (0x0)
Logging in to "Mastering OpenVPN".
Please enter User PIN: [enter Token password]
Key pair generated:
Private Key Object; RSA
  label:      movpn
  ID:         20141001
  Usage:      decrypt, sign, unwrap
Public Key Object; RSA 2048 bits
  label:      movpn
  ID:         20141001
  Usage:      encrypt, verify, wrap
```

It will take some time to generate a 2048-bit key on the hardware token, during which the red light on the hardware token is off. Afterwards the light will come back on again.

The output of the command above tells us that an RSA private key was generated, along with a public 2048-bit RSA public key. This is *not* the same as an SSL certificate. In order to generate an SSL or X.509 certificate, we first need to generate a certificate request.

Generating a certificate request

We need to use the OpenSSL engine `engine_pkcs11` to generate a certificate request using a private key from the hardware token. The `engine_pkcs11` engine is best used with a custom `openssl.cnf` file. We first create this file:

```
openssl_conf = openssl_def

[ openssl_def ]
engines = engine_section

[ engine_section ]
pkcs11 = pkcs11_section

[ pkcs11_section ]
engine_id = pkcs11
dynamic_path = /usr/lib64/openssl/engines/engine_pkcs11.so
MODULE_PATH = /usr/lib64/libeTPkcs11.so
init = 0

[ req ]
distinguished_name = req_distinguished_name

[ req_distinguished_name ]
```

This file was generated for a 64-bit CentOS Linux system. On other systems, the paths and names of the drivers will be different. Note that the statements in the `openssl.cnf` file are case sensitive!

We now generate a certificate request with the subject /CN=movpn, using the following `openssl` command:

```
$ openssl req -engine pkcs11 -keyform engine -key 20141001 \
  -new -text -out movpn.csr -config openssl.cnf \
  -subj "/CN=movpn"
engine "pkcs11" set.
PKCS#11 token PIN: [enter Token password]
```

The command produces no further output when successful. There should now be a `movpn.csr` file, which needs to be signed by the CA set up earlier in this chapter. It is assumed that the signed certificate will be named `movpn.crt`.

Writing an X.509 certificate to the token

OpenVPN expects the X.509 certificate to be present on the hardware token. Therefore, we must first write the X.509 certificate from the previous step to the eToken.

First, convert the signed certificate to the DER format:

```
$ openssl x509 -in movpn.crt -outform der -out movpn.der
```

Next we write the DER file to the token:

```
$ pkcs11-tool --module libeTPkcs11.so \
    --write-object movpn.der --type cert \
    --label movpn --id 20141001 --login
Using slot 0 with a present token (0x0)
Logging in to "Mastering OpenVPN".
Please enter User PIN: [enter Token password]
Created certificate:
Certificate Object, type = X.509 cert
    label:      movpn
    ID:         20141001
```

We need to verify that the IDs of the private key and certificate match:

```
$ pkcs11-tool --module libeTPkcs11.so --login -O
Using slot 0 with a present token (0x0)
Logging in to "Mastering OpenVPN".
Please enter User PIN: [enter Token password]
Private Key Object; RSA
    label:      movpn
    ID:         20141001
    Usage:      decrypt, sign, unwrap
Public Key Object; RSA 2048 bits
    label:      movpn
    ID:         20141001
    Usage:      encrypt, verify, wrap
Certificate Object, type = X.509 cert
    label:      movpn
    ID:         20141001
```

The token is now ready to be used with OpenVPN.

Getting a hardware token ID

In order to use a certificate and private key from a hardware token, you must first find out the hardware token ID that OpenVPN expects. This is done using the `--show-pkcs11-id` option:

```
$ openvpn --show-pkcs11-ids  /usr/lib64/libeTPkcs11.so
The following objects are available for use.
Each object shown below may be used as parameter to
--pkcs11-id option please remember to use single quote mark.


Certificate
        DN:                CN=movpn
        Serial:            01
        Serialized id:     SafeNet\x20Inc\x2E/eToken/00a3659e/Mastering\
x20OpenVPN/20141001
```

The serialized ID consists of the following:

- The name of the PKCS#11 driver (`SafeNet Inc`)
- The name of the product (`eToken`)
- The serial number of the token (`00a3659e`)
- The name of the token (`Mastering OpenVPN`)
- The ID of the certificate and private key on the token (`20141001`)

The label of the certificate or private key is not used, but it is a good practice to keep them in sync with each other as well.

Using a hardware token with OpenVPN

We are now finally ready to use the hardware token in OpenVPN. In order to use it, we replace the lines in the OpenVPN configuration file:

```
cert myclient.crt
key  myclient.key
```

With the options `pkcs11-providers` and `pkcs11-id`:

```
pkcs11-providers /usr/lib64/libeTPkcs11.so
pkcs11-id 'SafeNet\x20Inc\x2E/eToken/00a3659e/Mastering\
x20OpenVPN/20141001'
```

Summary

In this chapter, we discussed the tools and methods to create a root certificate authority, and the underlying server and client certificates. Additionally, the concept of PKCS#11 was covered, though the underlying technology is ever evolving. Now, you should have a full PKI and the tools to extend it.

The next chapter will introduce a routed VPN setup. Use of the tun network device and the layer 3 requirements for a working connection will be also be discussed.

Client/Server Mode with tun Devices

4

The most commonly used deployment model for OpenVPN is a single server with multiple remote clients capable of routing IP traffic. We refer to this deployment model as the *client/server mode with tun devices*.

In this chapter, we start off with a basic client/server setup. We will add more features as we go along, and some advanced examples on how to set up OpenVPN in client/server tun mode are given at the end of this chapter. In the next chapter, we will explain how to integrate a client/server tun-based setup in an existing network setup, including topics such as Windows file sharing and policy based routing.

The following topics will be covered in this chapter:

- Setting up the Public Key Infrastructure
- Initial setup of the client/server mode
- Adding extra security with production-level configuration files
- Routing and server-side routing
- Client-specific configuration using CCD files
- Client-side routing
- Redirecting the default gateway
- The OpenVPN status file
- The OpenVPN management interface
- Session key renegotiation
- Using IPv6
- Proxy ARP
- Handing out public IP addresses

Understanding the client/server mode

The client/server mode was first introduced with OpenVPN 2.0. In this mode, the server is a single OpenVPN process to which multiple clients can connect. Each authenticated and authorized client is assigned an IP address from a pool of IP addresses that the OpenVPN server manages. Clients cannot communicate directly with one another. All traffic flows via the server, which has both advantages and disadvantages.

The advantages are as follows:

- Control: The VPN server administrator can control which traffic is allowed to flow between clients. By default, no traffic is allowed to flow between clients. However, using either the OpenVPN option `client-to-client` or by using clever firewall and routing rules, it is possible to allow clients to communicate with each other.

- Ease of deployment: It is much easier to set up a single server that can be reached by many different clients than it is to ensure connectivity between a multitude of clients, each with their own network and firewall configurations.

The disadvantages are as follows:

- Scalability: As all traffic is flowing from client to server (and vice versa), the server can quickly become the bottleneck in large scale VPN setups.

- Performance: As all traffic between two clients (clients A and B) needs to flow from client A to the server and then from the server to client B, the performance of this type of VPN will always be lower when compared to a direct client-to-client connection.

The most common deployment scenario for this mode is an OpenVPN server at a corporate site that the various VPN clients connect to. Clients may include satellite offices, road warriors, people working at home, as well as smart phone and tablet users.

This deployment model covers 95 percent of the typical requirements for VPNs, and is preferable over more complicated setups using advanced features such as bridging. Only if there are specific requirements to route non-IP traffic (for example, legacy IPX traffic) or if there is a need to form a single network broadcast domain, then this deployment model will not suffice.

Setting up the Public Key Infrastructure

In the client/server mode, OpenVPN is configured using a **Public Key Infrastructure (PKI)** with X.509 certificates and private keys. Before we can set up a client/server VPN, we need to set up this PKI first. The PKI comprises of the CA, the private keys, and the certificates (public keys) for both the client and server. In *Chapter 3, PKIs and Certificates*, we will discuss in detail how to set up such a PKI. This chapter builds upon the certificates and keys generated in that chapter.

First, we copy the certificate and keys to a separate location. In general, it is a good security practice to keep the PKI files in a separate location, if possible even on a separate computer. Special care should be taken to protect the ca.key file, as the entire security of your PKI is dependent on this file. If the ca.key file is compromised in any way, the entire PKI is rendered insecure, and should be abandoned. In the following commands, it is assumed that the PKI files are generated using ssladmin and are stored in a directory <PKI_DIR>, where <PKI_DIR> represents a real directory on the system. Execute the following commands to copy over the necessary PKI files for the server:

```
[root@server] # mkdir -p /etc/openvpn/movpn

[root@server] # chmod 700 /etc/openvpn/movpn

[root@server] # cd /etc/openvpn/movpn

[root@server] # PKI=<PKI_DIR>/ssladmin/active

[root@server] # cp -a $PKI/ca.crt movpn-ca.crt

[root@server] # cp -a $PKI/Mastering_OpenVPN_Server.crt server.crt

[root@server] # cp -a $PKI/Mastering_OpenVPN_Server.key server.key
```

We also need to generate a **Diffie-Hellman (DH)** parameter file that is required for VPN session keys. The session keys are ephemeral or temporary keys and are generated when the connection between client and server is first set up. To ensure optimal security, the ephemeral keys are regenerated during the session at fixed intervals. The default key interval for OpenVPN is one hour, but this can be tuned using various OpenVPN options. This will be explained later in this chapter in the section *Session key renegotiation*.

To generate a DH parameter file, execute the following commands:

```
[root@server] # cd /etc/openvpn/movpn

[root@server] # openssl dhparam -out dh2048.pem 2048

Generating DH parameters, 2048 bit long safe prime, generator 2
```

```
This is going to take a long time
........+........................................................
..................................................................+......
```

In this example, we choose a DH key size of 2048 bits, which is the recommended size. You may also use larger DH key sizes, but it will make the initial connection process for each OpenVPN client slower. We are now ready to set up and start the OpenVPN server.

Initial setup of the client/server mode

In order to set up a basic OpenVPN server, we first create a server configuration file using the following steps:

1. Create the following file

    ```
    proto udp
    port 1194
    dev tun
    server 10.200.0.0 255.255.255.0
    topology subnet
    persist-key
    persist-tun
    keepalive 10 60

    dh       /etc/openvpn/movpn/dh2048.pem
    ca       /etc/openvpn/movpn/movpn-ca.crt
    cert     /etc/openvpn/movpn/server.crt
    key      /etc/openvpn/movpn/server.key

    user   nobody
    group nobody   # use 'group nogroup' on Debian/Ubuntu

    verb 3
    daemon
    log-append /var/log/openvpn.log
    ```

2. Then, save it as `movpn-04-01-server.conf`. A detailed explanation of each of the configuration lines will be given later.

3. Start the OpenVPN server:

    ```
    [root@server] # openvpn --config movpn-04-01-server.conf
    ```

4. The command will not produce any output on the command line, as all output is redirected to the log file `/var/log/openvpn.log`. Check this file for OpenVPN's startup message details:

```
OpenVPN 2.3.2 x86_64-redhat-linux-gnu [SSL (OpenSSL)] [LZO]
[EPOLL] [PKCS11] [eurephia] [MH] [IPv6] built on Sep 12 2013

Enter Private Key Password:

WARNING: this configuration may cache passwords in memory -- use
the auth-nocache option to prevent this

TUN/TAP device tun0 opened

do_ifconfig, tt->ipv6=0, tt->did_ifconfig_ipv6_setup=0

/sbin/ip link set dev tun0 up mtu 1500

/sbin/ip addr add dev tun0 10.200.0.1/24 broadcast 10.200.0.255

GID set to nobody

UID set to nobody

UDPv4 link local (bound): [undef]

UDPv4 link remote: [undef]

Initialization Sequence Completed
```

5. Please note that normally each log file entry starts with a timestamp. For the sake of clarity, this timestamp has been removed.

6. Next, create the client configuration file:

```
client
proto udp
remote openvpnserver.example.com
port 1194
dev tun
nobind
ca   /etc/openvpn/movpn/movpn-ca.crt
cert /etc/openvpn/movpn/client1.crt
key  /etc/openvpn/movpn/client1.key
```

Save it as `movpn-04-01-client.conf`.

7. Transfer the PKI files to the client using a secure channel, for example, using the `scp` command:

```
[root@client]# mkdir -p /etc/openvpn/movpn

[root@client]# chmod 700 /etc/openvpn/movpn

[root@client]# cd /etc/openvpn/movpn

[root@client]# PKI_HOST=openvpnserver.example.com

[root@client]# PKI=<PKI_DIR>/ssladmin/active
```

```
[root@client]# scp root@$PKI_HOST:$PKI/ca.crt movpn-ca.crt
[root@client]# scp root@$PKI_HOST:$PKI/client1.crt client1.crt
[root@client]# scp root@$PKI_HOST:$PKI/client1.key client1.key
```

8. Start the OpenVPN client:

```
[root@client]# openvpn --config movpn-04-01-client.conf
--suppress-timestamps
OpenVPN 2.3.2 x86_64-redhat-linux-gnu [SSL (OpenSSL)] [LZO]
[EPOLL] [PKCS11] [eurephia] [MH] [IPv6] built on Sep 12 2013
WARNING: No server certificate verification method has been
enabled.  See http://openvpn.net/howto.html#mitm for more info.
UDPv4 link local: [undef]
UDPv4 link remote: [AF_INET]openvpnserver:1194
[Mastering OpenVPN Server] Peer Connection Initiated with [AF_
INET]openvpnserver:1194
TUN/TAP device tun0 opened
do_ifconfig, tt->ipv6=0, tt->did_ifconfig_ipv6_setup=0
/sbin/ip link set dev tun0 up mtu 1500
/sbin/ip addr add dev tun0 10.200.0.2/24 broadcast 10.200.0.255
Initialization Sequence Completed
```

9. The timestamps are again missing, but this time they are suppressed using the OpenVPN option `suppress-timestamps`, as specified on the command line.

10. After the connection has come up, check for the following message:

```
Initialization Sequence Completed
```

11. You can verify that the connection is functioning correctly by pinging the VPN address of the server:

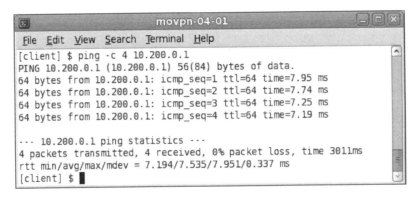

Detailed explanation of the configuration files

As this is the first client/server example, a detailed explanation of the server and client configuration files is in order. The server configuration file contains the following lines:

- `proto udp`: While this is the default protocol, it is wise to explicitly list it in the configuration file to avoid any confusion.

- `port 1194`: This is the local port that OpenVPN will listen on. The default value is 1194, but any valid and available port number can be used.

- `dev tun`: This specifies the name of the tun device that will be used for the server. By not adding a number behind the tun, we instruct OpenVPN to open a new tun device. This new device will be assigned the first available number in the system kernel, starting at 0 (tun0, tun1, tun2 and so on). For Windows servers, it is advisable to keep this line as is. If a specific Windows device needs to be used, then the option `dev-node` is required.

- `server 10.200.0.0 255.255.255.0`: The `server` statement puts OpenVPN in server mode. The IP subnet and subnet mask specify the subnet and mask to use for the VPN server and clients. The VPN server is assigned the first address, which in this case is `10.200.0.1`. The first client is assigned the address `10.200.0.2` (because we are using `topology subnet`). The `server` statement for this configuration is internally expanded as follows:

```
mode server
tls-server
push "topology subnet"

ifconfig 10.200.0.1 255.255.255.0
ifconfig-pool 10.200.0.2 10.200.0.254 255.255.255.0
push "route-gateway 10.200.0.1"
```

This is taken from the OpenVPN manual page at `https://community.openvpn.net/openvpn/wiki/Openvpn23ManPage`. If these configuration lines are used instead of the macro server, the same configuration is used.

 The expansion includes `push "topology subnet"` because we have also specified `topology subnet` in the configuration file. Without this line, the expansion would not have occurred.

- `topology subnet`: This specifies the topology for the VPN. The current default topology is `net30`, in which the server and each client are assigned a separate miniature `/30` subnet space. More details on the use of *topology subnet versus topology net30* are given in the following section.

- `persist-tun` and `persist-key`: Instruct OpenVPN to neither reopen the tun device, nor generate new keying material whenever the tunnel is restarted. These options are particularly useful in combination with `user nobody`, as the `user nobody` normally does not have the access rights to open a new tun interface.

- `keepalive 10 60`: This is used to make sure that the VPN connection remains up, even if there is no traffic flowing over the tunnel. The `keepalive` statement is a macro for the `ping` and `ping-restart` commands. The statement `keepalive 10 60` in a server-side configuration expands to:

```
ping 10
ping-restart 120
push "ping 10"
push "ping-restart 60"
```

  The preceding code means:

  - Send a ping message to each client every 10 seconds
  - Restart the connection if a client does not respond within 120 seconds *(2 * 60 = 120)*
  - Push the statements `ping 10` and `ping-restart 60` to each client

- `dh <path to Diffie Hellman file>`: This specifies the path to the DH file that is required for the OpenVPN server. Without this file, the server cannot establish a secure TLS connection with the clients. It is advisable to use an absolute path for this file (as well as the other certificate and private key paths).

- `ca <path to CA file>`: This specifies the path to the CA file. The CA file needs to contain the CA certificate (or even set of certificates) that was used to sign the **client certificates**. It does not necessarily have to be the same CA as the one that was used to sign the server certificate, although in our PKI setup we used the same CA. It is advisable to use an absolute path for this file (as well as the other certificate and private key paths).

- `cert <path to X.509 certificate file>`: This specifies the path to the server X.509 public certificate file. This certificate is needed by the OpenVPN server, even if the clients are connection without using certificates. It is advisable to use an absolute path for this file (as well as the other certificate and private key paths).

- `key <path to private key file>`: This specifies the path to the server private key file. This private key file is needed by the OpenVPN server, even if the clients are connecting without using certificates or private keys. This file needs to be readable by the root (or administrator) user only, as anyone with read access to private keys can decrypt OpenVPN traffic. Note that OpenVPN will read this file before dropping user privileges. It is advisable to use an absolute path for this file (as well as the other certificate and private key paths).

- `user nobody` and `group nobody`: This instructs OpenVPN to drop to Unix `user nobody` and `group nobody` after the connection has come up. This further enhances security, as an attack on the tunnel will less likely result in a root exploit. Note that on Debian/Ubuntu the group `nogroup` is used.

- `verb 3`: This sets the verbosity level to the default value of 3. Increase this number to view more detailed output of the OpenVPN process. If the verbosity is set to 0, then hardly any logging output is produced. However, this is not recommended.

- `daemon`: This tells OpenVPN to *daemonize* itself, which means that the OpenVPN process will keep running even after the terminal window in which OpenVPN was started is closed.

- `log-append <path to log file>`: This specifies the path to the server log file. By using `log-append` instead of `log <path to file>`, we prevent OpenVPN from truncating the log file each time it starts. For this file, it is also advisable to use an absolute path.

The client configuration file contains:

- `client`: This puts OpenVPN into client mode. It instructs OpenVPN to connect to the remote server and to `pull` and process configuration parameters from the server after a successful connection has been made. The client statement is internally expanded as follows:

```
tls-client
pull
```

- `proto udp`: This specifies the protocol to use. While this is the default protocol, it is wise to explicitly list it in the configuration file to avoid any confusion.

- `remote openvpnserver.example.com`: This specifies the name of the VPN server to connect to. The name can be either a **Fully qualified domain name (FQDN)** or an IPv4 address. Later in this chapter, we will see how to connect to an IPv6-based VPN server.

- `port 1194`: This is the port that the OpenVPN client will use to connect to the server. The default value is 1194, but any valid and available port number can be used.

> There are multiple ways to specify a remote address and port for the VPN server. For example, it is also possible to use `remote openvpnserver.example.com:1194`.

- `dev tun`: This specifies the name of the tun device that will be used for the server. By not adding a number behind the tun, we instruct OpenVPN to open a new tun device. This new device will be assigned the first available number in the system kernel, starting at 0 (tun0, tun1, tun2 and so on). For Windows servers, it is advisable to keep this line as is. If a specific Windows device needs to be used, then the option `dev-node` is required.

- `nobind`: This instructs the OpenVPN client not to bind to (and not listen on) the port specified using `port`. Instead, the OpenVPN client will use a port in the anonymous port range, which is typically 1024-65335.

- `ca <path to CA file>`: This specifies the path to the CA file. This CA file needs to contain the CA certificate (or even set of certificates) that was used to sign the server certificate. It does not necessarily have to be the same CA as the one that was used to sign the client certificate, although we used the same CA in our PKI setup. On Linux/Unix it is advisable to use an absolute path for this file (as well as the other certificate and private key paths).

- `cert <path to X.509 certificate file>`: This specifies the path to this client's X.509 public certificate file. It is possible to configure OpenVPN to use username/password authentication instead of certificates, but this is considered less secure. On Linux/Unix, it is advisable to use an absolute path for this file (as well as the other certificate and private key paths).

- `key <path to private key file>`: This specifies the path to the client private key file. This file needs to be readable by the root (or administrator) user only, as OpenVPN will read this file before dropping user privileges. On Linux, it is advisable to use an absolute path for this file (as well as the other certificate and private key paths).

Note that we did not specify `daemon` or `log-append` for the client configuration, as in most cases a wrapper application will launch the `openvpn` process. This wrapper application will then control the logging of OpenVPN. The most commonly used wrapper applications are:

Operating system	Wrapper applications
Windows	OpenVPN-GUI.exe (part of OpenVPN installer package)
Mac OS X	Tunnelblick or Viscosity
Linux	NetworkManager (with OpenVPN plugin)

Topology subnet versus topology net30

OpenVPN supports several topologies in tun mode:

- net30 (default, may change with v2.4)
- subnet
- p2p

To start off with the last one, topology p2p is hardly ever used anymore and was the first method to assign a single IP address to a VPN client. However, it only works on Linux and Unix derivatives, and hence was never very widely used.

Topology net30 is the current default. In this mode, OpenVPN sets up a Point-to-Point network interface for each client (and for the server) and it assigns a /30 subnet to each. This means that the server and each client are assigned a block of four IP addresses. In the server configuration file, the `server 10.200.0.0 255.255.255.0` was specified. With `topology net30`, this causes OpenVPN to assign the following IP blocks:

- The OpenVPN server is assigned from 10.200.0.0 to 10.200.0.3.
- The first client is assigned from 10.200.0.4 to 10.200.0.7.
- The second client is assigned from 10.200.0.8 to 10.200.0.11 and so on. Each /30 subnet consist of four addresses; for the first client, these addresses are as follows:
  - 10.200.0.4: This is the /30 subnet network address. Each subnet is normally required to have such an address associated with it.
  - 10.200.0.5: This is the virtual endpoint address. This address is required for OpenVPN to function, but it cannot actually be used, and is not even pingable.

- ° 10.200.0.6: This is the client VPN IP address.
- ° 10.200.0.7: This is the /30 subnet broadcast address. Each subnet is required to have such a broadcast address associated with it.

As you can see, this is not a very efficient method of assigning IP addresses—for each VPN client, four IP addresses are assigned. For small VPN setups, this method works fine, but this method does not scale for a server with more than 100 clients connected.

To overcome this problem, the topology subnet mode was introduced. It allows OpenVPN to assign a single IP address to all clients, which makes it much easier to manage a large-scale VPN. There are some issues with server-side routing (for more details, see the *Routing and server-side routing* section later in this chapter) that have prevented this topology mode from becoming the default, but it is expected that as of Version 2.4 this will be the default topology mode.

Adding extra security

The initial set of configuration files is a good starting point for a client/server deployment. However, for a production-level system, we want to add more security. Security can be enhanced in two ways:

- By adding tls-auth keys
- By checking the extended key usage attributes of the certificates used

Using tls-auth keys

In the client/server mode, OpenVPN will attempt to establish a TLS control channel for each client that tries to connect. Setting up a TLS control channel is resource consuming, which makes OpenVPN susceptible to denial-of-service attacks: an attacker could launch a multitude of misconfigured clients that all try to connect to the OpenVPN server. For each of these, the OpenVPN server would attempt to set up a TLS connection, which will effectively lead to a denial of service for well-configured clients. This is especially true when OpenVPN is running using proto udp (the recommended default). UDP traffic is connectionless, which means that for each new UDP packet that the server receives, it must verify if it is a valid OpenVPN packet.

To address this possible vulnerability, OpenVPN introduced an extra authentication layer to the TLS control channel using the tls-auth option. This TLS authentication must be done using a pre-shared key, as the server does not yet know if a valid client is attempting to connect. The pre-shared keys used for this are the exact same keys as the keys used in point-to-point mode, as described in *Chapter 2, Point-to-point Mode*.

Generating a tls-auth key

To generate a `tls-auth` key, we use the same command as described in *Chapter 2, Point-to-point Mode*:

```
[root@server]# openvpn --genkey --secret /etc/openvpn/movpn/ta.key
```

Just like the client's private key file, this file needs to be copied to each client using a secure channel, or it needs to be included in a secure client configuration package:

```
[root@client]# cd /etc/openvpn/movpn
[root@client]# scp root@openvpnserver:/etc/openvpn/movpn/ta.key .
```

Checking certificate key usage attributes

When X.509 certificates are generated, special **Extended Key Usage (EKU)** attributes can be added to the certificate. This allows us to specify a purpose for the certificate, for example as a *server-only* certificate or a *client-only* certificate. Certificates used by secure websites make use of the same EKU attributes.

The `easy-rsa` scripts and the `ssladmin` tool set the EKU attributes by default when generating a server certificate or a non-server (client) certificate. To check the EKU attributes of a certificate, use the following commands:

```
$ openssl x509 -text -noout -in server.crt | \
    grep -C 1 "Key Usage"


        X509v3 Extended Key Usage:
            TLS Web Server Authentication
        X509v3 Key Usage:
            Digital Signature, Key Encipherment
```

This tells us that the `server.crt` certificate can be used only for server authentication.

Older certificates may not have these EKU attributes set, but instead use the (deprecated) `Netscape Cert Type` attribute. The `easy-rsa` scripts and the `ssladmin` tool set this attribute as well:

```
$ openssl x509 -text -noout -in server.crt | \
    grep -C 1 "Netscape Cert"


        Netscape Cert Type:
            SSL Server
```

However, this certificate can only be set for server-side certificates.

OpenVPN security can be increased by checking these attributes. For this, we use the option `remote-cert-tls`.

The option `remote-cert-tls client` instructs the OpenVPN server to only allow connections from VPN clients that have a certificate with the X.509 EKU attribute set to `TLS Web Client Authentication`.

This prevents a hacker from setting up a rogue OpenVPN server using a client certificate.

Similarly, for the client, the option `remote-cert-tls server` instructs the OpenVPN client to only allow connections to a VPN server that has a certificate with the X.509 EKU attribute set to `TLS Web Server Authentication`.

This prevents a malicious client from setting up a rogue OpenVPN server to attract connections from other VPN users.

It is also possible to check for the `Netscape Cert Type` attribute. As this is an attribute of the server certificate, the OpenVPN client needs to check this attribute when connecting. For this, the option `ns-cert-type server` can be used. Preferably, the option `remote-cert-tls` should be used.

Basic production-level configuration files

We extend the previous client and server configuration files to use the newly created `tls-auth` key. We do this by adding a line to the configuration file `movpn-04-01-server.conf`, as well as the second security-enhancing option:

```
proto udp
port 1194
dev tun
server 10.200.0.0 255.255.255.0
topology subnet
persist-key
persist-tun
keepalive 10 60

remote-cert-tls client
tls-auth /etc/openvpn/movpn/ta.key 0
dh       /etc/openvpn/movpn/dh2048.pem
ca       /etc/openvpn/movpn/movpn-ca.crt
cert     /etc/openvpn/movpn/server.crt
```

```
key        /etc/openvpn/movpn/server.key

user   nobody
group  nobody

verb 3
daemon
log-append /var/log/openvpn.log
```

 Note that the order of the statements in this configuration file is random. The remote-cert-tls and tls-auth lines could have been added at any point in the file.

This server configuration file is a basic server configuration file that we will reuse throughout this chapter and others. Save it as basic-udp-server.conf so that we can reuse it later.

We add two similar lines to the client configuration file movpn-04-01-client.conf:

```
client
proto udp
remote openvpnserver.example.com
port 1194
dev tun
nobind

remote-cert-tls server
tls-auth /etc/openvpn/movpn/ta.key 1
ca   /etc/openvpn/movpn/movpn-ca.crt
cert /etc/openvpn/movpn/client1.crt
key  /etc/openvpn/movpn/client1.key
```

Save it as basic-udp-client.conf.

The second parameter to the tls-auth option is the so-called direction of the key. OpenVPN supports the use of *directional* keys, that is, different keys are used for incoming versus outgoing data. This further enhances security. The direction flag needs to be set to 0 on one end and to 1 on the other end. In the client/server mode, this means that the server has the parameter 0 for the direction, and all clients have the direction parameter set to 1.

When we start the OpenVPN server, we can see that the TLS control channel is now protected using a static key:

```
[root@server]# openvpn --config basic-udp-server.conf --suppress-
timestamps

OpenVPN 2.3.2 x86_64-redhat-linux-gnu [SSL (OpenSSL)] [LZO] [EPOLL]
[PKCS11] [eurephia] [MH] [IPv6] built on Sep 12 2013

Enter Private Key Password:

WARNING: this configuration may cache passwords in memory -- use the
auth-nocache option to prevent this

Control Channel Authentication: using '/etc/openvpn/movpn/ta.key' as a
OpenVPN static key file

TUN/TAP device tun0 opened

do_ifconfig, tt->ipv6=0, tt->did_ifconfig_ipv6_setup=0

/sbin/ip link set dev tun0 up mtu 1500

/sbin/ip addr add dev tun0 10.200.0.1/24 broadcast 10.200.0.255

GID set to nobody

UID set to nobody

UDPv4 link local (bound): [undef]

UDPv4 link remote: [undef]

Initialization Sequence Completed
```

Similarly, when we start the OpenVPN client we see:

```
[root@client]# openvpn --config basic-udp-client.conf --suppress-
timestamps

OpenVPN 2.3.2 x86_64-redhat-linux-gnu [SSL (OpenSSL)] [LZO] [EPOLL]
[PKCS11] [eurephia] [MH] [IPv6] built on Sep 12 2013

Control Channel Authentication: using '/etc/openvpn/movpn/ta.key' as a
OpenVPN static key file

UDPv4 link local: [undef]

UDPv4 link remote: [AF_INET]openvpnserver:1194

[Mastering OpenVPN Server] Peer Connection Initiated with [AF_INET]
openvpnserver:1194

TUN/TAP device tun0 opened

do_ifconfig, tt->ipv6=0, tt->did_ifconfig_ipv6_setup=0

/sbin/ip link set dev tun0 up mtu 1500

/sbin/ip addr add dev tun0 10.200.0.2/24 broadcast 10.200.0.255

Initialization Sequence Completed
```

TCP-based configuration

The default protocol that OpenVPN uses is the UDP protocol. It is very simple to create TCP-based versions based on the configuration files created previously. In both client and server configuration files, change the line `proto udp` to `proto tcp`. The entire TCP-based server configuration file is listed here:

```
proto tcp
port 1194
dev tun
server 10.200.0.0 255.255.255.0
topology subnet
persist-key
persist-tun
keepalive 10 60

remote-cert-tls client
tls-auth /etc/openvpn/movpn/ta.key 0
dh       /etc/openvpn/movpn/dh2048.pem
ca       /etc/openvpn/movpn/movpn-ca.crt
cert     /etc/openvpn/movpn/server.crt
key      /etc/openvpn/movpn/server.key

user   nobody
group  nobody

verb 3
daemon
log-append /var/log/openvpn.log
```

Save this configuration file as `basic-tcp-server.conf`.

Similarly, for the client configuration file:

```
client
proto tcp
remote openvpnserver.example.com
port 1194
dev tun
nobind

remote-cert-tls server
tls-auth /etc/openvpn/movpn/ta.key 1
ca   /etc/openvpn/movpn/movpn-ca.crt
cert /etc/openvpn/movpn/client1.crt
key  /etc/openvpn/movpn/client1.key
```

Save it as `basic-tcp-client.conf`.

Configuration files for Windows

The basic configuration files for the Windows platform are slightly different from the ones for the Linux/Unix or Mac OS platforms. On the Windows platform, the Openvpn-GUI.exe wrapper is used, which expects that all configuration files are stored in the directory C:\Program Files\OpenVPN\config or a subdirectory thereof. The name of the directory Program Files may be different for other languages. In all languages, the Windows environment variable %PROGRAMFILES% will point to the proper location.

Thus, the basic UDP and TCP configuration files are actually slightly shorter. Create the UDP client configuration file:

```
client
proto udp
remote openvpnserver.example.com
port 1194
dev tun
nobind

remote-cert-tls server
tls-auth ta.key 1
ca        movpn-ca.crt
cert      client1.crt
key       client1.key
```

Save it as basic-udp-client.ovpn so that we can re-use it later in this book.

Similarly, create the client configuration:

```
client
proto tcp
remote openvpnserver.example.com
port 1194
dev tun
nobind

remote-cert-tls server
tls-auth ta.key 1
ca        movpn-ca.crt
cert      client1.crt
key       client1.key
```

Save it as basic-tcp-client.ovpn.

Routing and server-side routing

A VPN is only truly useful when the VPN clients have access to server-side resources. In order to access these resources, routing is needed in most cases. OpenVPN has many options to automatically set up and tear down extra routes whenever a client connects or disconnects.

It should be stated that most OpenVPN troubleshooting issues are related to routing. Setting up a VPN connection is one thing, getting network traffic to flow properly is another. This often has little to do with OpenVPN itself, but more with the routing tables and firewall rules on both client and server side.

The most common layout for accessing resources on the server-side network is depicted here:

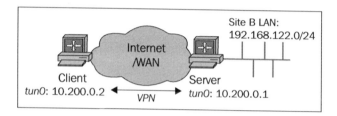

The server-side LAN is **192.168.122.0/24**. The resources that the VPN clients need to access are located on this subnet. Thus, the server needs to instruct the VPN clients that an extra route needs to be set. This is done using a push option, where the route configuration is pushed to the client. It could also be achieved by adding the route to the client configuration file itself, but this does not scale well. This is because for each new server-side network route, all client configuration files would need to be updated.

We start out with the `basic-udp-server.conf` file, and add one line:

```
proto udp
port 1194
dev tun
server 10.200.0.0 255.255.255.0
topology subnet
persist-key
persist-tun
keepalive 10 60

remote-cert-tls client
```

```
tls-auth /etc/openvpn/movpn/ta.key 0
dh       /etc/openvpn/movpn/dh2048.pem
ca       /etc/openvpn/movpn/movpn-ca.crt
cert     /etc/openvpn/movpn/server.crt
key      /etc/openvpn/movpn/server.key

user  nobody
group nobody

verb 3
daemon
log-append /var/log/openvpn.log

push "route 192.168.122.0 255.255.255.0"
```

We save it as `movpn-04-03-server.conf` and we start the OpenVPN server using this configuration file. This time, we use a Windows 7 64-bit Professional machine as the OpenVPN client, on which the X86_64 Version of OpenVPN 2.3.4-I004 is installed. Copy over the following files to the Windows machine:

- `basic-udp-client.ovpn`
- `movpn-ca.crt`
- `client1.crt`
- `client1.key`

Take and place them in `C:\Program Files\OpenVPN\config` (or `%PROGRAMFILES%\config`).

Launch the OpenVPN GUI application, select the configuration `basic-udp-client` and click on **Connect**:

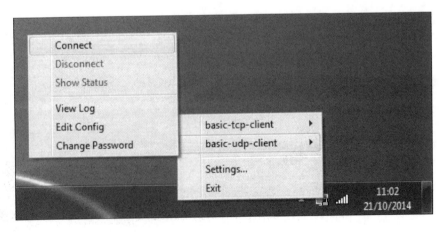

Once the connection is successfully established, the OpenVPN GUI icon turns green and connection information is shown when hovering over the icon:

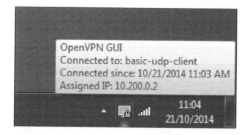

We can now verify that the VPN connection to the server is working by opening a command shell and pinging the server:

```
c:\Users\janjust\movpn>ping 10.200.0.1

Pinging 10.200.0.1 with 32 bytes of data:
Reply from 10.200.0.1: bytes=32 time=3ms TTL=64
Reply from 10.200.0.1: bytes=32 time=3ms TTL=64
Reply from 10.200.0.1: bytes=32 time=6ms TTL=64
Reply from 10.200.0.1: bytes=32 time=4ms TTL=64

Ping statistics for 10.200.0.1:
    Packets: Sent = 4, Received = 4, Lost = 0 (0% loss),
Approximate round trip times in milli-seconds:
    Minimum = 3ms, Maximum = 6ms, Average = 4ms

c:\Users\janjust\movpn>
```

After we verify that we can reach the OpenVPN server, we need to ensure that the OpenVPN server is forwarding IP traffic and we need to add an extra route on the server side gateway to ensure that the VPN traffic is routed correctly back via the VPN server. Without this route, the machines on the server-side network will now know where the VPN traffic with IP addresses `10.200.0.0/24` is coming from, and will most likely wrongly route or drop the packets:

```
[root@server]# sysctl -w net.ipv4.ip_forward=1
[router]# ip route add 10.200.0.0/24 via 192.168.122.1
```

Now, we check the routing table on the client side, and we verify that we can reach a machine on the server-side LAN:

```
c:\Users\janjust\movpn>route print | find "10.200.0"
      10.200.0.0    255.255.255.0        On-link      10.200.0.2      286
      10.200.0.2    255.255.255.255      On-link      10.200.0.2      286
    10.200.0.255    255.255.255.255      On-link      10.200.0.2      286
   192.168.122.0    255.255.255.0      10.200.0.1     10.200.0.2       30
       224.0.0.0        240.0.0.0        On-link      10.200.0.2      286
 255.255.255.255    255.255.255.255      On-link      10.200.0.2      286

c:\Users\janjust\movpn>ping 192.168.122.184

Pinging 192.168.122.184 with 32 bytes of data:
Reply from 192.168.122.184: bytes=32 time=4ms TTL=63
Reply from 192.168.122.184: bytes=32 time=7ms TTL=63
Reply from 192.168.122.184: bytes=32 time=3ms TTL=63
Reply from 192.168.122.184: bytes=32 time=4ms TTL=63

Ping statistics for 192.168.122.184:
    Packets: Sent = 4, Received = 4, Lost = 0 (0% loss),
Approximate round trip times in milli-seconds:
    Minimum = 3ms, Maximum = 7ms, Average = 4ms
```

The first part of the output shows that multiple routes for the VPN subnet `10.200.0.0/24` were added to the routing tables, including a route for the pushed network `192.168.122.0/24`. Note the last column in the output, which shows the route metric. Windows calculates a metric (286 in this case), but this can be overruled using the right `route` statements. The route added using `push route 192.168.122.0 255.255.255.0` has a lower metric as the OpenVPN default metric of 30 was specified.

Special parameters for the route option

Analogous to what is explained in *Chapter 2, Point-to-point Mode* the configuration statement `push route <network> <netmask> [vpn_gateway] [metric]` is vital in this setup. The `route` option accepts up to four parameters, two mandatory and two optional. It is the third parameter which plays an important role in this setup. The word `vpn_gateway` is a special OpenVPN keyword, and it specifies the VPN remote endpoint address. Normally, this keyword does not have to be specified, *unless* it is also necessary to specify the metric for this route.

The full syntax for the `route` statement is `route <network> <netmask> [gateway] [metric]`, where `gateway` can either be explicitly set as an IPv4 address or either of the special keywords `vpn_gateway` or `net_gateway` can be used. If no gateway and no metric are specified, then `vpn_gateway` is used.

The keyword `net_gateway` is useful to specify a subnet that should explicitly *not* be routed via the VPN. For `net_gateway`, the default gateway before the VPN connection was established is substituted.

The metric has a default metric that can be set using `route-metric m`, which then applies to all routes. If you wish to overrule the metric for a particular route (as we have done in this example), then it is required to specify the gateway (`vpn_gateway` in our case) followed by the metric for that particular route.

Masquerading

Sometimes, it is not possible to add a server-side route to redirect all VPN traffic back to the OpenVPN server. In this case, a quick and dirty approach is to use masquerading. On Linux, you can use the `iptables` command to set up masquerading on the server:

```
[root@server]# iptables -t nat -I POSTROUTING -o eth0 \
                -s 10.200.0.0/24 -j MASQUERADE
```

This `iptables` statement instructs the Linux kernel to rewrite all traffic that is coming from the VPN subnet `10.200.0.0/24` and that is leaving the Ethernet interface `eth0`. The traffic leaving the `eth0` interface has its source address rewritten so that it appears as if it is coming from the OpenVPN server itself and not from the OpenVPN client. This is an easy shortcut to get routing to work, but the disadvantage is that it is no longer possible to distinguish whether such traffic is coming from the OpenVPN server itself, or from one of the connected clients.

Redirecting the default gateway

A very common use of a VPN is to route all the traffic over a secure tunnel. This allows one to safely access a network, or even the Internet itself, from within a *hostile* environment (for example, a poorly protected Internet cafe).

Redirecting the default gateway is achieved by adding the line `push "redirect-gateway [def1 local bypass-dhcp bypass-dns]"` to the server configuration file.

The parameters to `redirect-gateway` listed previously are optional, but they can play a very important role:

- No parameters added: In this case, OpenVPN will replace the existing default gateway (0.0.0.0/0) with the address of the OpenVPN server itself. An extra route to the OpenVPN server itself is also added so that the OpenVPN traffic itself is sent directly to the server, instead of via the tunnel. The disadvantage is that if the OpenVPN connection is stopped or breaks down, the original default gateway is lost. This usually causes a full loss of network connectivity.

- Parameter `def1`: Instead of replacing the existing default gateway, OpenVPN will add two new routes, 0.0.0.0/1 and 128.0.0.0/1. These routes together also cover all IPv4 space, and are more specific (`/1`) than the regular gateway (`/0`). Routing always takes place over the more specific routes, and thus all traffic is sent over the VPN. The advantage of this trick is that the default gateway is left intact. If the VPN connection is stopped, the original gateway can be restored. Note that in this case, OpenVPN will add an explicit route to the OpenVPN server itself, so the encrypted traffic itself will not be sent over the tunnel.

- Parameter `bypass-dhcp`: Sometimes, it is useful to add an explicit route to the local DHCP server on the client-side LAN. This avoids DHCP renewals to also be tunneled over the VPN, although in most network setups this does not happen, as there usually is a more specific route to the network segment on which the local DHCP server resides.

- Parameter `bypass-dns`: Sometimes, it can be necessary to add an explicit route to the local DNS server, as DNS resolution breaks down otherwise. This happens only if you want to use the client-side DNS server, yet you want to route all traffic over the tunnel.

Apart from the option `redirect-gateway`, we could also specify the option `push "redirect-private [def1 local bypass-dhcp bypass-dns]"` to the server configuration file. This option takes the same parameters as `redirect-gateway`, but it does not change the existing default gateway at all. This can be useful for pushing private subnets.

For now, we add `push "redirect-gateway def1"` to the `basic-udp-server.conf` configuration file. Save it as `movpn-04-06-server.conf`, start the OpenVPN server, and reconnect the client using the default configuration file.

After the connection is established, we verify that all traffic is now flowing via the VPN using the `traceroute` command (use `tracert -d` in a command shell on Windows):

```
┌─────────────────────────────────────────────────────────────────────┐
│ ▣                          Mastering OpenVPN                   ─ □ ✕  │
├─────────────────────────────────────────────────────────────────────┤
│ File  Edit  View  Search  Terminal  Help                              │
│ [client]$ traceroute -n openvpn.net                                   │
│ traceroute to openvpn.net (198.41.191.212), 30 hops max, 60 byte packets│
│  1   10.200.0.1      3.117 ms  3.140 ms  3.155 ms                     │
│  2   .....           3.164 ms  6.403 ms  6.439 ms                     │
│  3   .....           8.796 ms  8.807 ms  8.827 ms                     │
│  4   198.41.191.212 11.728 ms  8.792 ms  8.875 ms                     │
│                                                                       │
│ [client]$ ▌                                                           │
└─────────────────────────────────────────────────────────────────────┘
```

The first `hop` in the `traceroute` output is `10.200.0.1`, which is the IP address of the OpenVPN server. This proves that traffic is flowing via the VPN by default.

The configuration option `redirect-gateway def1` tells the OpenVPN client to add three routes to the client operating system:

`10.198.1.1 via 192.168.4.254 dev eth0`

`0.0.0.0/1 via 10.200.0.1 dev tun0`

`128.0.0.0/1 via 10.200.0.1 dev tun0`

The first route is an explicit route from the client to the OpenVPN server via the LAN interface. This route is needed as all the traffic for the OpenVPN server itself would go through the tunnel otherwise.

The other two routes are a clever trick to overrule the default route so that all the traffic is sent through the tunnel instead of to the default LAN gateway.

The advantage of this method is that the original default gateway is left intact. When the VPN is disconnected, the original gateway address automatically takes over again. If we would simply use `redirect-gateway`, there is a chance that the default gateway is lost when the VPN is disconnected, resulting in a complete loss of network connectivity.

The downside of this method is with Windows 7 and above clients: Windows sometimes refuses to trust the TAP-Win adapter without a default route, and therefore marks it as a *public* adapter. It is not possible to use a public adapter in Windows 7 for file or printer sharing. We will see in the next chapter how to work around this peculiarity.

Client-specific configuration – CCD files

In a setup where a single server can handle many clients, it is sometimes necessary to set per-client options that overrule the global options, or to add extra options to a particular client. The option `client-config-dir` is very useful for this. It allows the VPN administrator to assign a specific IP address to a client, in order to push specific options such as a DNS server to a particular client or to temporarily disable a client altogether. This option is also vital if you want to route a subnet from the client side to the server side, as we will see later on.

A `client-config-dir` or CCD file can contain the following options:

- `push`: This is useful for pushing DNS and WINS servers, routes, and so on
- `push-reset`: This is useful to overrule global push options
- `iroute`: This is useful for routing IPv4 client subnets to the server
- `iroute-ipv6`: This is useful for routing IPv6 client subnets to the server
- `ifconfig-push`: This is useful for assigning a specific IPv4 address to a client
- `ifconfig-ipv6-push`: This is useful for assigning a specific IPv6 address to a client
- `disable`: This is useful for temporarily disabling a client altogether
- `config`: This is useful for including another CCD configuration file

In order to use CCD files, we add a line to the `basic-udp-server.conf` configuration file:

```
client-config-dir /etc/openvpn/movpn/clients
```

Save it as `movpn-04-04-server.conf`. Next, create the CCD directory and create a CCD file in it for the client with certificate `client1.crt`:

```
[root@server]# mkdir -p /etc/openvpn/movpn/clients
[root@server]# echo "ifconfig-push 10.200.0.99 255.255.255.0" \
                > /etc/openvpn/movpn/clients/client1
[root@server]# chmod 755 /etc/openvpn/movpn/clients
[root@server]# chmod 644 /etc/openvpn/movpn/clients/client1
```

The name of the CCD file is based on the certificate subject's common name (the "/CN=" part), as found in the `client1.crt` file:

```
$ openssl x509 -subject -noout -in client1.crt
```

```
subject= /C=ZA/ST=Enlightenment/O=Mastering OpenVPN/CN=client1/
emailAddress=root@example.org
```

The filename needs to be just `client1` with no extension in this case, not even on Windows! If there are spaces present in the common name, then they need to be converted to underscores (_). If the Windows Explorer is configured to hide extensions for common file types, then it is easiest to open a command shell (`cmd.exe`) window, and remove the extension using the following commands:

```
C:\> cd %PROGRAMFILES%\openvpn\config\clients

C:\> rename client1.txt client1,145.102.134.201:35519
```

Next, we start the OpenVPN server using this configuration file and we connect the VPN client. The connection log shows that the client is assigned the address 10.200.0.99:

```
[root@client]# openvpn --config basic-udp-client.conf

OpenVPN 2.3.2 x86_64-redhat-linux-gnu [SSL (OpenSSL)] [LZO] [EPOLL]
[PKCS11] [eurephia] [MH] [IPv6] built on Sep 12 2013

Control Channel Authentication: using '/etc/openvpn/movpn/ta.key' as a
OpenVPN static key file

UDPv4 link local: [undef]

UDPv4 link remote: [AF_INET]openvpnserver:1194

[Mastering OpenVPN Server] Peer Connection Initiated with [AF_INET]
openvpnserver:1194

TUN/TAP device tun0 opened

do_ifconfig, tt->ipv6=0, tt->did_ifconfig_ipv6_setup=0

/sbin/ip link set dev tun0 up mtu 1500

/sbin/ip addr add dev tun0 10.200.0.99/24 broadcast 10.200.0.255

Initialization Sequence Completed
```

The server-side log does not show any messages about picking up the CCD file when using the default verbosity setting. Increase the verbosity setting to 5 or higher to view whether the CCD file is processed:

```
<client-ip>:49299 [client1] Peer Connection Initiated with [AF_
INET]<client-ip>:49299

client1/<client-ip>:49299 OPTIONS IMPORT: reading client specific options
from: /etc/openvpn/movpn/clients/client1client1/<client-ip>:49299 MULTI:
Learn: 10.200.0.99 -> client1/<client-ip>:49299
```

How to determine whether a CCD file is properly processed

Troubleshooting whether a CCD file is correctly processed can be a bit tricky. The following guidelines will aid in debugging CCD file issues:

- Always specify the full path for the `client-config-dir` option.
- Make sure the directory is accessible and the CCD file is readable to the user which is used to run OpenVPN (`nobody` or `openvpn` in most cases; in the configurations listed in this book, the `user nobody` is used).
- Make sure that the right filename is used for the CCD file, without any extensions.
- If possible, add the option `ccd-exclusive` to the server configuration file. This instructs OpenVPN to only allow client connections if there is a particular CCD file for that client. If there was a problem reading the CCD-file for a particular client, then the client will also be denied access. This way, you will know that your `client-config-dir` settings are misconfigured.

CCD files and topology net30

If you are using the (default) topology setting (`topology net30`), then the `ifconfig-push` statement is slightly different. As each client is now assigned a /30 subnet, the `ifconfig-push` statement needs to specify a valid VPN /30 subnet. The following rules apply:

- Each /30 subnet needs to start at an address divisible by 4 (4, 8, 12, and so on)
- The VPN local IP is the third address in this subnet
- The virtual remote endpoint IP is the second address

For example, a valid IP address for a VPN client is 10.200.0.50:

- The subnet is 10.200.0.48/32, where 48 is a multiple of 4
- The VPN IP address is 50 (*48+2 = 50*)
- The virtual remote endpoint is 49 (*48 + 1 = 49*)

The CCD file should now contain the following:

```
ifconfig-push 10.200.0.50 10.200.0.49
```

Client-side routing

Sometimes, it is useful to allow the VPN server (or other VPN clients) to access resources connected to a particular client. This is known as client-side routing. Client-side routing in OpenVPN requires a CCD file for that client containing an `iroute` statement. It also requires a corresponding `route` statement in the OpenVPN server configuration file.

Consider the following network layout:

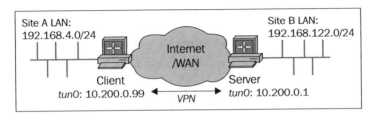

The subnet **192.168.4.0/24** needs to be accessible from the server-side LAN and the server-side subnet **192.168.122.0/24** needs to be accessible from the client-side LAN. This can be achieved as follows:

1. Add two lines to the `basic-udp-server.conf` configuration file:

   ```
   client-config-dir /etc/openvpn/movpn/clients
   route 192.168.4.0 255.255.255.0 10.200.0.1
   ```

   Save it as `movpn-04-05-server.conf`.

2. Create a CCD file `client1` in the directory `/etc/openvpn/movpn/clients` with contents:

   ```
   ifconfig-push 10.200.0.99 255.255.255.0
   iroute 192.168.4.0 255.255.255.0
   push "route 192.168.122.0 255.255.255.0"
   ```

3. Ensure that IP traffic forwarding is enabled and allowed on both client and server:

   ```
   [root@client]# sysctl -w net.ipv4.ip_forward=1

   [root@server]# sysctl -w net.ipv4.ip_forward=1
   ```

4. Start the OpenVPN server using the configuration file `movpn-04-05-server.conf`.

5. Connect the client using the default configuration file `basic-udp-client.conf`.

6. After the connection has been established, we verify that both subnets can reach each other using `ping`:

```
[root@client]# ping -c 3 192.168.122.184
PING 192.168.122.184 (192.168.122.184) 56(84) bytes of data.
64 bytes from 192.168.122.184: icmp_seq=1 ttl=63 time=3.29 ms
64 bytes from 192.168.122.184: icmp_seq=2 ttl=63 time=3.27 ms
64 bytes from 192.168.122.184: icmp_seq=3 ttl=63 time=3.31 ms

--- 192.168.122.184 ping statistics ---
3 packets transmitted, 3 received, 0% packet loss, time 2006ms
rtt min/avg/max/mdev = 3.277/3.296/3.317/0.016 ms
```

```
[root@server]# ping -c 3 192.168.4.10
PING 192.168.4.10 (192.168.4.10) 56(84) bytes of data.
64 bytes from 192.168.4.10: icmp_seq=1 ttl=63 time=6.31 ms
64 bytes from 192.168.4.10: icmp_seq=2 ttl=63 time=5.07 ms
64 bytes from 192.168.4.10: icmp_seq=3 ttl=63 time=5.14 ms

--- 192.168.4.10 ping statistics ---
3 packets transmitted, 3 received, 0% packet loss, time 2007ms
rtt min/avg/max/mdev = 5.073/5.512/6.317/0.575 ms
```

In-depth explanation of the client-config-dir configuration

In the first step, we add two new lines to the server configuration file. These lines set up `client-config-dir`, and they instruct OpenVPN to add a system network route for the subnet 192.168.4.0/24. We need to explicitly specify the gateway address `10.200.0.1` here, due to a minor bug in OpenVPN. This shortcoming is expected to be resolved in Version 2.4, after which you can specify `route 192.168.4.0 255.255.255.0` again.

The contents of the CCD file instruct OpenVPN that when the client with Common Name `client1` connects the IP address for this client is to be set to `10.200.0.99`. Furthermore, OpenVPN needs to set an internal route (`iroute`) for this client so that OpenVPN itself is aware that the subnet 192.168.4.0/24 is located behind this particular client.

Finally, the `push route` statement instructs OpenVPN to push a route for this particular subnet to client `client1`. This way, an OpenVPN server can push different routes to different clients in a transparent manner.

 Selectively pushing a route to a particular client can be handy, but it is not tamper-proof. A rogue VPN client that adds a route to this subnet by itself will also have access to it. If you need to control access to a particular subnet, use a firewalling solution such as `iptables` or `ipfw`.

This example shows the flexibility of the OpenVPN configuration options. Without having to change a single line in the client configuration file, it is possible to assign a different IP address, route a particular subnet to a client, or route a particular subnet from the client-side network to the server-side LAN.

Client-to-client traffic

OpenVPN also allows you to set up client-to-client traffic. By default, the VPN clients are not allowed to communicate directly with each other. This is a good security measure, but sometimes it is necessary to allow inter-client traffic. Be aware that all VPN client-to-client traffic will flow via the OpenVPN server: from `client1` to the VPN server and then again from the VPN server to `client 2`, and vice versa. This can easily lead to performance issues.

In tun mode, client-to-client connectivity can be achieved using either `iptables` or by using the OpenVPN option `client-to-client`. The option `client-to-client` has the advantage that it is faster: traffic from one client arriving at the server is automatically forwarded to the second client, without passing through the system routing tables or firewalling rules. The downside is that it is hard to monitor the traffic, and it is impossible to apply access control.

Without the `client-to-client` option, the traffic from one client is received by the OpenVPN server, forwarded out to the system routing and firewalling tables, and (if configured correctly) bounced back to the OpenVPN server again. The server then forwards it out to the second client.

If other VPN clients need to access the subnet 192.168.4.0/24 as specified in the preceding example, then the server configuration needs to be extended with a line:

```
push "192.168.4.0 255.255.255.0"
```

This instructs the OpenVPN server to push a route to all clients that subnet 192.168.4.0/24 is reachable through the VPN tunnel, except for client `client1`. The client `client1` itself is excluded due to the matching `iroute` entry.

The OpenVPN status file

OpenVPN offers several options to monitor the clients connected to a server. The most commonly used method is using a status file. The OpenVPN status file is continually updated by the OpenVPN process and contains the following information:

- Which clients are connected
- From which IP address the clients are connecting
- The number of bytes each client has received and transferred
- The time at which the client connected
- In addition, the routing table also shows which networks are routed to each client

We modify the `client-side routing` server configuration file `movpn-04-05-server.conf` by adding a line to the server configuration:

```
proto udp
port 1194
dev tun
server 10.200.0.0 255.255.255.0
topology subnet
persist-key
persist-tun
keepalive 10 60

remote-cert-tls client
tls-auth /etc/openvpn/movpn/ta.key 0
dh      /etc/openvpn/movpn/dh2048.pem
ca      /etc/openvpn/movpn/movpn-ca.crt
cert    /etc/openvpn/movpn/server.crt
key     /etc/openvpn/movpn/server.key
```

```
user    nobody
group nobody

verb 3
daemon
log-append /var/log/openvpn.log

client-config-dir /etc/openvpn/movpn/clients
route 192.168.4.0 255.255.255.0 10.200.0.1

status /var/run/openvpn.status 3
```

Save it as `movpn-04-07-server.conf`. After re-establishing the VPN connection, we then see the following contents in the status file, after the VPN client `client1` has connected and has transferred some data:

```
OpenVPN CLIENT LIST
Updated,Tue Oct 21 15:45:27 2014
Common Name,Real Address,Bytes Received,Bytes Sent,Connected Since
client1,<client-IP>:35519,7730,9342,Tue Oct 21 15:44:35 2014
ROUTING TABLE
Virtual Address,Common Name,Real Address,Last Ref
192.168.4.0/24,client1,145.102.134.201:35519,Tue Oct 21 15:44:35 2014
10.200.0.99,client1,145.102.134.201:35519,Tue Oct 21 15:44:35 2014
GLOBAL STATS
Max bcast/mcast queue length,0
END
```

The `CLIENT LIST` shows the list of connected clients, including information about the number of bytes received and bytes sent.

The `ROUTING TABLE` shows the list of OpenVPN internal routes:

- The subnet 192.168.4.0/24 is routed to `client1` due to the `iroute` statement in the server configuration
- The IP address 10.200.0.99 is the IP address of `client1` which we set explicitly in the CCD file named `client1`

When the client disconnects, the status file is updated after 3 seconds, and the connected client is no longer listed.

When a client disconnects, all information is removed from the status file and all statistics are reset. If the client connects again later, the number of received and sent bytes starts again from zero. The client-disconnect script is given all the status info when a client has been disconnected.

The second parameter to the `status` option is the interval after which the status file is updated (rewritten). The default value is 60 seconds.

Reliable connection tracking for UDP mode

The OpenVPN server cannot immediately detect when using the UDP protocol that a client is disconnected, either on purpose or due to a bad internet connection. This allows a client to reconnect to the VPN server without losing all tunneled connections in case of a bad connection. The downside is that it takes some time for the OpenVPN server to realize that a client is *gone*.

An OpenVPN client can explicitly notify the server that it is disconnecting using the option `explicit-exit-notify`. This option takes one parameter that specifies the number of explicit messages that the client attempts to send to the server. The default value is `1`, which does not work well if the underlying network connection itself is unstable. In that case it is recommended to increase this value to `3`.

When `explicit-exit-notify` is used, the OpenVPN server immediately receives a `remote-exit` message when the client disconnects, as can be seen in the server log file:

```
SIGTERM[soft,remote-exit] received, client-instance exiting
```

Note that this problem does not occur when `proto tcp` is used, as the termination of a TCP connection is immediately noticed by the server.

The OpenVPN management interface

One of the most powerful but less well-known options of OpenVPN is the management interface. The management interface is available on both the server side and the client side. On the server side, it can be used to collect statistics, monitor and control the connected clients, and perform other management related tasks. On the client side, it can be used to query for passwords, enter proxy information for establishing a connection with the VPN server, interact with a PKCS #11 device, and collect client-side statistics.

The OpenVPN plugin for the Linux NetworkManager makes extensive use of the management interface to control the startup and shutdown of the VPN connection.

To use the management interface, add a line `management 127.0.0.1 23000 stdin` to either the client or the server configuration file. This option instructs OpenVPN to set up the management interface on IP address 127.0.0.1, port 23000, and to use `stdin` to specify the management password.

If we add this to the `basic-udp-server.conf` configuration file and launch the OpenVPN server, then OpenVPN will first query us for the management password to use:

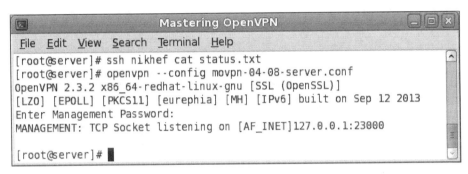

We can then use `telnet` to log in on the management interface (user input is listed in boldface):

```
[root#server]# telnet 127.0.01 23000
Trying 127.0.0.1...
Connected to 127.0.01.
Escape character is '^]'.
ENTER PASSWORD:[password]
SUCCESS: password is correct
>INFO:OpenVPN Management Interface Version 1 -- type 'help' for more
info
help
Management Interface for OpenVPN 2.3.2 x86_64-redhat-linux-gnu [SSL
(OpenSSL)]
[LZO] [EPOLL] [PKCS11] [eurephia] [MH] [IPv6] built on Sep 12 2013
Commands:
auth-retry t            : Auth failure retry mode
                          (none,interact,nointeract).
bytecount n             : Show bytes in/out, update every n secs
                          (0=off).
```

```
echo [on|off] [N|all]     : Like log, but only show messages in echo
                            buffer.
exit|quit                 : Close management session.
forget-passwords          : Forget passwords entered so far.
help                      : Print this message.
[...]
END
```

This raw telnet interface can be used to view the status of the server, providing the same output as the option `status` from the previous example. It can also be used to terminate a client connection immediately, using the following command:

```
kill client1
```

This will cause client `client1` one to be disconnected. Note that in most cases the client will automatically attempt to reconnect. Now, type `exit` to end the telnet session.

The management interface can be used to control OpenVPN in many different ways (adapted from the OpenVPN manual page `https://community.openvpn.net/ openvpn/wiki/Openvpn23ManPage`):

- `management IP port [pw-file]`: Enable a TCP server on IP:port to handle daemon management functions. `pw-file`, if specified, is a password file (password on first line) or `stdin` to prompt from standard input. The password provided will set the password which TCP clients will need to provide in order to access management functions.

  The management interface can also listen on a Unix domain socket, if supported. To use a domain socket, specify the Unix socket pathname in place of IP and set port to `unix`.

  The management interface provides a special mode where the TCP management link can operate over the tunnel itself. To enable this mode, set `IP = "tunnel"`. Tunnel mode will cause the management interface to listen for a TCP connection on the local VPN address of the TUN/TAP interface.

- `management-client`: The management interface will connect as a TCP/ Unix domain client to IP:port specified by `--management` rather than listen as a TCP server or on a Unix domain socket. If the client connection fails to connect or is disconnected, a SIGTERM signal will be generated, and cause OpenVPN to quit.

- `management-query-passwords`: This is the query management channel for private key password and `--auth-user-pass` username/password.

- `management-hold`: Start OpenVPN in a hibernating state, until a client of the management interface explicitly starts it with the hold release command.

- `management-signal`: Send SIGUSR1 signal to OpenVPN if management session disconnects. This is useful when you wish to disconnect an OpenVPN session on user logoff.

- `management-client-auth`: This gives management interface client the responsibility to authenticate clients after their client certificate has been verified.

Session key renegotiation

To ensure the security of each OpenVPN connection, the server periodically renegotiates the secret key for the data channel with each client. This is controlled using three options:

- `reneg-sec N`: Renegotiate data channel key after N seconds (default is 3600)

- `reneg-bytes N`: Renegotiate data channel key after N bytes (default=0=off)

- `reneg-pkts N`: Renegotiate data channel key after N packets (default=0=off)

If a VPN client is experiencing periodic timeouts when connected to the server, it is often useful to vary these parameters. If you set the `reneg-sec` parameter at a very short interval, however, the performance of the VPN will be severely degraded.

The `reneg` options can be specified on either the client or the server side, or both. The `reneg` option that runs the most frequently on either side will reset the counters on both ends. If the server specifies `reneg-sec 500` but the client specifies `reneg-sec 60`, then the data channel renegotiation will occur approximately every 60 seconds.

We create an example by adding three lines to the `basic-udp-server.conf` configuration file:

```
reneg-sec   10
reneg-pkts  1000
reneg-bytes 1000000
```

We save the configuration as `movpn-04-09-server.conf` and re-establish the VPN connection. The server log will now contain many lines stating `TLS: soft reset`:

```
Tue Oct 21 16:53:29 2014 <IP>:41679 [client1] Peer Connection Initiated
with [AF_INET]<IP>:41679

[...]
```

```
Tue Oct 21 16:53:39 2014 client1/<IP>:41679 TLS: soft reset sec=0
bytes=0/100000 pkts=0/100

[...]

Tue Oct 21 16:53:49 2014 client1/<IP>:41679 TLS: soft reset sec=0
bytes=53/100000 pkts=1/100

[...]

Tue Oct 21 16:53:59 2014 client1/<IP>:41679 TLS: soft reset sec=0
bytes=105/100000 pkts=2/100
```

With the option `reneg-sec 10` set we see from the server log timestamps that the data channel key is renegotiated every 10 seconds.

On the client side, we can also see the impact this key renegotiation has on the performance of the VPN connection. By letting a simple `ping` command run after the connection has come up, we can see when the key renegotiation is happening based on the spikes in the ping response times:

```
[client]$ ping 10.200.0.1
PING 10.200.0.1 (10.200.0.1) 56(84) bytes of data.
64 bytes from 10.200.0.1: icmp_seq=1 ttl=64 time=3.29 ms
64 bytes from 10.200.0.1: icmp_seq=2 ttl=64 time=3.55 ms
64 bytes from 10.200.0.1: icmp_seq=3 ttl=64 time=61.6 ms
64 bytes from 10.200.0.1: icmp_seq=4 ttl=64 time=16.6 ms
64 bytes from 10.200.0.1: icmp_seq=5 ttl=64 time=3.23 ms
64 bytes from 10.200.0.1: icmp_seq=6 ttl=64 time=3.22 ms
64 bytes from 10.200.0.1: icmp_seq=7 ttl=64 time=3.74 ms
64 bytes from 10.200.0.1: icmp_seq=8 ttl=64 time=3.25 ms
64 bytes from 10.200.0.1: icmp_seq=9 ttl=64 time=3.21 ms
64 bytes from 10.200.0.1: icmp_seq=10 ttl=64 time=3.26 ms
64 bytes from 10.200.0.1: icmp_seq=11 ttl=64 time=3.26 ms
64 bytes from 10.200.0.1: icmp_seq=12 ttl=64 time=3.55 ms
64 bytes from 10.200.0.1: icmp_seq=13 ttl=64 time=3.27 ms
64 bytes from 10.200.0.1: icmp_seq=14 ttl=64 time=3.26 ms
64 bytes from 10.200.0.1: icmp_seq=15 ttl=64 time=3.31 ms
64 bytes from 10.200.0.1: icmp_seq=16 ttl=64 time=3.28 ms
64 bytes from 10.200.0.1: icmp_seq=17 ttl=64 time=77.1 ms
...
```

The same thing will happen when the packet or byte *boundary* is crossed, at which moment the data channel keys will also be renegotiated.

A note on PKCS#11 devices

Especially when using PKCS#11 devices, the key renegotiation can be cumbersome. Some PKCS#11 devices put a heavy penalty on key renegotiation, causing the renegotiation process to take several seconds. During this time the VPN is unresponsive.

Setting the `reneg-sec` value to `0` will effectively disable key renegotiation, but this makes the VPN itself susceptible to man-in-the-middle and timing attacks, rendering the extra security of using a hardware security device useless.

Using IPv6

With OpenVPN 2.3 came solid support for IPv6, both within the OpenVPN tunnel as well as for transit of the tunnel itself. OpenVPN all the way back to 1.x had rudimentary support for IPv6, which was largely rewritten. Overall, inside an OpenVPN tunnel an administrator can choose to support Ethernet (layer 2), IPv4 (layer 3), and IPv6 (layer 3).

The diagram illustrates the logical relationship of the transit network path and the protected network path. Only a single transit method needs to be used, and a single OpenVPN configuration can contain both IPv4 and IPv6 `--remote` entries. All traffic, regardless of type, will be protected within the tunnel. It is perfectly acceptable to have an all-IPv6 tunnel, using IPv6 for both transit and protected traffic. With additional routing and proxying, it's even possible to use OpenVPN to aid in IPv6 to IPv4 translation.

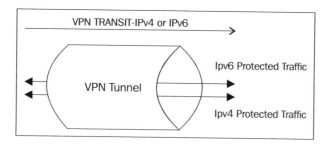

Protected IPv6 traffic

Building on the examples from the previous section, we can provide IPv6 addresses to clients and protect that traffic within the tunnel. To do this, we add a `--server-ipv6` option to our server configuration. This operates similarly to the `--server` directive, only for IPv6 instead of IPv4 and takes an IPv6 network address and netmask as arguments. Like `--server`, `--server-ipv6` is a macro for other options that can be passed individually: `--ifconfig-ipv6`, `--ifconfig-ipv6-pool`, `--tun-ipv6`, and `–push tun-ipv6`.

Just like with IPv4, IPv6 routes can be pushed from the main server configuration or from per-client configuration files in your `client-config` directory. In this example, however, we will simply push a default route for all IPv6 traffic.

There is not currently a `redirect-gateway` option in OpenVPN for IPv6. Routes are added similar to IPv6, with the keyword `route-ipv6` instead of `route`.

Now, modify the `movpn-04-01-server.conf` file, and add the `--server-ipv6` directive:

```
proto udp
port 1194
dev tun
server 10.200.0.0 255.255.255.0
server-ipv6 2001:DB8:100::/64
push "route-ipv6 ::/0"
topology subnet
persist-key
persist-tun
keepalive 10 60

dh        /etc/openvpn/movpn/dh2048.pem
ca        /etc/openvpn/movpn/movpn-ca.crt
cert      /etc/openvpn/movpn/server.crt
key       /etc/openvpn/movpn/server.key

user nobody
group nobody

verb 3
daemon
log-append /var/log/openvpn.log
```

Once the file has been saved, a restart of the OpenVPN server process is required. If the process started correctly with the new option, you should see something like this in your log file:

```
IFCONFIG POOL IPv6: (IPv4) size=252, size_ipv6=65536, netbits=64,
base_ipv6=2001:db8:100::1000
```

At this point, clients are able to pass traffic using IPv6 inside the tunnel, and the server is pushing a default route to clients for IPv6. Adding the server configuration options requires no additional corresponding options within the client configurations.

A connected client will show both an IPv4 and IPv6 address on the tunX interface.

Here's a FreeBSD example:

```
utun1: flags=8051<UP,POINTOPOINT,RUNNING,MULTICAST> mtu 1331
    inet 10.200.0.2 --> 10.200.0.2 netmask 0xffffff00
    inet6 fe80::5ab0:35ff:fef5:811f%utun1 prefixlen 64 scopeid 0x9
    inet6 2001:db8:100::1001 prefixlen 64
    nd6 options=1<PERFORMNUD>
```

Here's a Windows 7 example:

Note that the popup from hovering over the task bar icon doesn't display the IPv6 address, but the `ipconfig` command from a terminal does show both addresses.

```
OpenVPN GUI
Connected to: client1
Connected since: 10/18/2014 6:31 PM
Assigned IP: 10.200.0.2
```

Using IPv6 as transit

OpenVPN doesn't currently have the ability to listen on both IPv4 and IPv6 addresses at the same time, but most modern kernels can handle this for you with IPv6-mapped addresses. What this does is takes a Version 4 IP, such as 192.168.200.4 and maps it as the IPv6 address of ::ffff:192:168.:200:.:4. Also, instead of `proto udp`, the protocol will be `udp6` on both the client and the server.

After changing the `proto` statement from our sample config, `client2` is initialized and we can see the address are assigned. Both the OpenVPN server v4 and v6 addresses can be pinged and we can confirm that the transit over the tunnel is via IPv6 with `tcpdump`.

Here's the client tun interface:

```
ecrist@phillip:~-> ifconfig tun4
tun4: flags=8051<UP,POINTOPOINT,RUNNING,MULTICAST> metric 0 mtu 1500
  options=80000<LINKSTATE>
  inet6 fe80::216:3eff:fe09:5d4e%tun4 prefixlen 64 scopeid 0x9
  inet 10.200.0.2 --> 10.200.0.2 netmask 0xffffff00
  inet6 2001:db8:100::1000 prefixlen 64
  nd6 options=21<PERFORMNUD,AUTO_LINKLOCAL>
  Opened by PID 45391
```

Here's the IPv4 inside tunnel ping:

```
ecrist@phillip:~-> ping -c 1 10.200.0.1
PING 10.200.0.1 (10.200.0.1): 56 data bytes
64 bytes from 10.200.0.1: icmp_seq=0 ttl=64 time=0.490 ms

--- 10.200.0.1 ping statistics ---
1 packets transmitted, 1 packets received, 0.0% packet loss
round-trip min/avg/max/stddev = 0.490/0.490/0.490/0.000 ms
```

Here's the IPv6 inside tunnel ping:

```
ecrist@phillip:~-> ping6 -c 1 2001:db8:100::1
PING6(56=40+8+8 bytes) 2001:db8:100::1000 --> 2001:db8:100::1
16 bytes from 2001:db8:100::1, icmp_seq=0 hlim=64 time=0.591 ms


--- 2001:db8:100::1 ping6 statistics ---
1 packets transmitted, 1 packets received, 0.0% packet loss
round-trip min/avg/max/std-dev = 0.591/0.591/0.591/0.000 ms
```

Here's the `tcpdump` output (note the IPv6 keyword in the output):

```
root@terrance:/usr/local/etc/openvpn-> tcpdump -i xn0 host
2001:db8:5555:5555::1
tcpdump: verbose output suppressed, use -v or -vv for full protocol
decode
listening on xn0, link-type EN10MB (Ethernet), capture size 65535 bytes
19:14:05.449553 IP6 phillip.1194 > terrance.1194: UDP, length 53
19:14:05.449692 IP6 terrance.1194 > phillip.1194: UDP, length 53
19:14:08.389222 IP6 phillip.1194 > terrance.1194: UDP, length 93
19:14:08.389394 IP6 terrance.1194 > phillip.1194: UDP, length 93
19:14:09.389858 IP6 phillip.1194 > terrance.1194: UDP, length 93
```

Advanced configuration options

The next few sections illustrate some advanced configuration options. It is suggested you fully understands the impact to their network before deploying these in a production environment. These options are rarely used, but can be extremely beneficial in the right circumstances.

Proxy ARP

It is often desirable to make VPN clients appear as if they are part of the server-side network. This makes it easier to browse folders and share files and printers. To achieve this purpose, many setups resort to Ethernet bridging (see *Chapter 6, Client/ Server Mode with tap Devices*), which has its own drawbacks. The performance of a bridged configuration can be much lower compared to a nonbridged setup.

When the OpenVPN server runs on Linux or Unix, there is an alternative solution: most Unix kernels have Proxy ARP capabilities, which can be used to assign an OpenVPN client with an IP address on the server-side LAN, and make it appear as if it is part of that LAN. Note that this works only for IPv4 networks, as IPv6 networking does not use ARP.

Consider the following network layout:

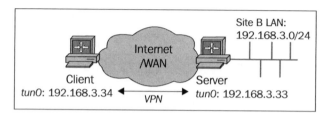

In this layout, the *standard* VPN subnet 10.200.0.0/24 cannot be used, as we have to integrate the VPN clients into the existing subnet, which for this example is **192.168.3.0/24**. Current machines in this subnet are in the range 192.168.3.10 - 192.168.3.24, thus we place the VPN addresses a little outside of this range. Make sure that the VPN addresses should not be advertised by a DHCP server on the server-side LAN, as we want OpenVPN to assign the addresses for the VPN clients.

For this example, we will make use of the OpenVPN capability to run scripts when a client connects or disconnects. The scripting abilities of OpenVPN are explained in more detail in *Chapter 7, Scripting and Plugins*.

1. We start out with the following server configuration file:

```
proto udp
port 1194
dev tun
server 192.168.3.32 255.255.255.224
push "route 192.168.3.0 255.255.255.0"
topology subnet
persist-key
persist-tun
keepalive 10 60

tls-auth /etc/openvpn/movpn/ta.key 0
```

```
dh         /etc/openvpn/movpn/dh2048.pem
ca         /etc/openvpn/movpn/movpn-ca.crt
cert       /etc/openvpn/movpn/server.crt
key        /etc/openvpn/movpn/server.key

verb 3
daemon
log-append /var/log/openvpn.log

script-security 2
client-connect     /etc/openvpn/movpn/proxyarp-connect.sh
client-disconnect /etc/openvpn/movpn/proxyarp-disconnect.sh
```

Note that we have added three statements to set the security level for the scripts, and to run a custom script whenever a client connects or disconnects.

2. Save this configuration file as `movpn-04-10-server.conf`.

3. Next, create the `proxyarp-connect.sh` script that is executed each time a VPN client connects:

    ```
    #!/bin/bash
    /sbin/arp -i eth0  -Ds ${ifconfig_pool_remote_ip} eth0 pub
    /sbin/ip route add ${ifconfig_pool_remote_ip}/32 dev tun0
    ```

4. Save the script as `/etc/openvpn/movpn/proxyarp-connect.sh`. The script location must match the absolute path specified in the `movpn-04-10-server.conf` file.

5. Then, create the `proxyarp-disconnect.sh` script that is executed when the client disconnects:

    ```
    #!/bin/bash
    /sbin/arp -i eth0  -d ${ifconfig_pool_remote_ip}
    /sbin/ip route del ${ifconfig_pool_remote_ip}/32 dev tun0
    ```

6. Save the script as `/etc/openvpn/movpn/proxyarp-disconnect.sh`.

> The device names `eth0` and `tun0` are hardcoded into the scripts. This is necessary as the device on which the extra ARP address needs to be published is unknown to OpenVPN. It is also possible to publish the extra ARP address on multiple interfaces (`eth0`, `eth1`, `wlan0`, and so on) by duplicating the `/sbin/arp` line in both scripts.

Make both scripts executable, and launch the OpenVPN server using the following commands:

```
[root@server]# chmod a+x /etc/openvpn/movpn/proxyarp-connect.sh
[root@server]# openvpn --config movpn-04-10-server.conf
```

7. As always, use the `basic-udp-client.conf` (or `basic-udp-client.ovpn`) configuration file to connect to the server. After the VPN client has successfully connected, we verify that the client is *seen* by other devices on the LAN. For this, we used an Android smart phone with the app Fing installed:

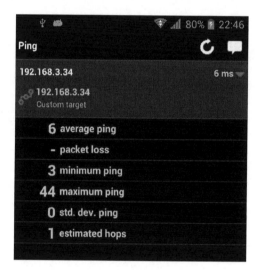

 No extra network routes were added on the Android device. The VPN client is truly integrated into the existing subnet.

8. We can also verify that the OpenVPN server machine is now publishing an extra IP address in its ARP tables:

```
[server]$ /sbin/arp -an | grep PERM
? (192.168.3.34) at * PERM PUP on eth0
```

How does Proxy ARP work?

Proxy ARP is a feature supported by most Unix and Linux kernels. It is used most often for connecting dial-in clients to a LAN, and nowadays also by ADSL and cable Internet providers.

The OpenVPN server borrows an IP address from its local LAN range when a client connects. This IP address is then assigned to this OpenVPN client. The server also creates a special entry in the system's ARP tables to tell the rest of site B's LAN that the OpenVPN server acts as a proxy for IP 192.168.3.34. This means that when another machine on the server-side LAN wants to know where to find the host with IP 192.168.3.34 then the OpenVPN server will respond with its own MAC address of the interface on which the Proxy ARP address was published.

The server configuration file contains a few statements that need some explanation:

```
server 192.168.3.32 255.255.255.224
push "route 192.168.3.0 255.255.255.0"
```

The preceding lines cause the OpenVPN server to assign the address 192.168.3.33 to the server VPN IP address, with a netmask of 255.255.255.224 (or /27). The first VPN client is assigned the address 192.168.3.34/27. However, this means that the VPN client itself cannot reach any IP addresses outside of this range. The push route statement is needed to tell the OpenVPN client that the entire subnet 192.168.3.0/24 is reachable via the VPN.

So far, the server configuration file normally included the following lines:

```
user nobody
group nobody
```

In this configuration file, they are absent because the client-connect and client-disconnect scripts need to run as user root. An alternative approach is to set up sudo rights so that the user nobody is allowed to execute the /sbin/arp command with root privileges.

Finally, the lines:

```
script-security 2
client-connect /etc/openvpn/movpn/proxyarp-connect.sh
client-disconnect /etc/openvpn/movpn/proxyarp-disconnect.
```

Set up OpenVPN's scripting features. The first line sets the security level of the scripts to 2, which means that certain environment variables are available to the script.

The client-connect and client-disconnect lines both specify an absolute path to the scripts to be executed.

Assigning public IP addresses to clients

As a follow up to the Proxy ARP example, we will now look at how we can hand out public IPv4 addresses to OpenVPN clients. Let's assume that the following set of (example only) public IPv4 addresses is available to us:

Our public IPv4 network is 192.0.2.160/28, which gives us 16 addresses. These addresses are used as follows:

IP address	Use
192.0.2.160	This is the subnet's network address
192.0.2.161	This is used for the server's VPN IP address
192.0.2.162	Not available
192.0.2.163	Not available
192.0.2.164 - 192.0.2.170	This is available for VPN clients
192.0.2.171	This is the LAN address of the OpenVPN server itself
192.0.2.172	Not available
192.0.2.173	Not available
192.0.2.174	This is the router on the remote LAN
192.0.2.175	This is the network broadcast address

We now want to set up an OpenVPN server that is capable of handing out the addresses 192.0.2.164 through 192.0.2.170, with the OpenVPN server itself at the address 192.0.2.161:

1. First we create the server configuration file:

    ```
    proto udp
    port 1194
    dev tun

    mode server
    tls-server
    ifconfig 192.0.2.161 255.255.255.240
    ifconfig-pool 192.0.2.164 192.0.2.170
    push "route 192.0.2.171 255.255.255.255 net_gateway"
    push "route-gateway 192.0.2.174"
    push "redirect-gateway def1"
    push "topology subnet"
    ```

```
topology subnet
persist-key
persist-tun
keepalive 10 60

tls-auth /etc/openvpn/movpn/ta.key 0
dh          /etc/openvpn/movpn/dh2048.pem
ca          /etc/openvpn/movpn/movpn-ca.crt
cert        /etc/openvpn/movpn/server.crt
key         /etc/openvpn/movpn/server.key

verb 3
daemon
log-append /var/log/openvpn.log

script-security 2
client-connect    /etc/openvpn/movpn/proxyarp-connect.sh
client-disconnect /etc/openvpn/movpn/proxyarp-disconnect.sh
```

2. Save this file as `movpn-04-11-server.conf`. We will reuse the `proxyarp-connect.sh` and `proxyarp-disconnect.sh` scripts from the previous example. Create `proxyarp-connect.sh` that is executed each time a VPN client connects:

```
#!/bin/bash
/sbin/arp -i eth0  -Ds ${ifconfig_pool_remote_ip} eth0 pub
/sbin/ip route add ${ifconfig_pool_remote_ip}/32 dev tun0
```

3. Save it as `/etc/openvpn/movpn/proxyarp-connect.sh`.

4. Then, create the `proxyarp-disconnect.sh` script that is executed when the client disconnects:

```
#!/bin/bash
/sbin/arp -i eth0  -d ${ifconfig_pool_remote_ip}
/sbin/ip route del ${ifconfig_pool_remote_ip}/32 dev tun0
```

5. Save it as `/etc/openvpn/movpn/proxyarp-disconnect.sh`. Make both scripts executable and launch the OpenVPN server:

```
[root@server]# chmod a+x /etc/openvpn/movpn/proxyarp-connect.sh[
[root@server]# openvpn --config movpn-04-11-server.conf
```

6. Use the basic configuration file to connect the OpenVPN client to the server. The first client will be assigned the address 192.0.2.164.

Check the IP address of the first client by browsing to `https://www.whatismyip.com`.

The server configuration file is similar to the file `movpn-04-10-server.conf` with the exception of this block:

```
mode server
tls-server
ifconfig 192.0.2.161 255.255.255.240
ifconfig-pool 192.0.2.164 192.0.2.170
push "route 192.0.2.171 255.255.255.255 net_gateway"
push "route-gateway 192.0.2.174"
push "redirect-gateway def1"
push "topology subnet"
```

Earlier in this chapter, it was explained that the macro `server 10.200.0.0 255.255.255.0` expands as follows:

```
mode server
tls-server
push "topology subnet"

ifconfig 10.200.0.1 255.255.255.0
ifconfig-pool 10.200.0.2 10.200.0.254 255.255.255.0
push "route-gateway 10.200.0.1"
```

When handing out public IP addresses, we usually do not have the luxury of wasting IPv4 addresses. The option `topology subnet`, which was introduced in OpenVPN 2.1, is really useful here.

After examining our public IPv4 space, we forsake the `server` statement and include our own version of the `ifconfig` and `ifconfig-pool` options:

- `ifconfig 192.0.2.161 255.255.255.240`: This specifies that the server VPN IP address is 192.0.2.161/28.

- `ifconfig-pool 192.0.2.164 192.0.2.170`: This specifies that the pool of available IP addresses for VPN clients ranges from 192.0.2.164 to 192.0.2.170 for a total of seven addresses. Note that an `ifconfig-pool` range needs to be contiguous.

 If there are 'holes' in a range then it is often easier to assign IP addresses using a script, as we will learn in *Chapter 7, Scripting and Plugins*.

- push "route 192.0.2.171 255.255.255.255 net_gateway": This route to the LAN address of the VPN server needs to be explicitly pushed to the clients. Normally, this route is added automatically by the OpenVPN client to ensure that traffic that is intended for the OpenVPN server itself is not injected into the tunnel again, which would cause a packet loop. With our special ifconfig and ifconfig-pool setup, it is advisable to add an explicit route to the LAN address of the OpenVPN server.

- push "route-gateway 192.0.2.174": route-gateway specifies the gateway address that is used to direct all tunnel traffic to. Normally route-gateway is equal to the VPN server IP address. In this case, it would only cause a route hop, as the VPN server would immediately forward it to the real gateway, 192.0.2.174, which is on the same subnet. Hence, we specify the IP address of the LAN gateway.

- push "redirect-gateway def1": For an OpenVPN client to use the public address for all its traffic, it must route all traffic over the VPN tunnel.

- push "topology subnet": Normally, the server macro takes care of this push for us, but as we are not using the server macro here we must explicitly push this option. If this option is omitted, then the server would be assigning linear addresses (because it has a line topology subnet in its configuration), yet the VPN clients would assume that they are assigned topology net30 addresses, which is the current default. The explicit push circumvents this potential misconfiguration.

Summary

In this chapter, a wide variety of features and options of client/server mode with tun devices were covered. We established a basic set of configuration files for both the OpenVPN server and the client, for both the UDP and TCP protocol as means of transport, and for both Windows and Linux/Unix clients. This set of basic configuration files will be used throughout the rest of the book.

We discussed how to set up an OpenVPN server serving both IPv4 addresses and IPv6 addresses. We covered server-side and client-side routing, including redirecting all traffic over the VPN tunnel. We also saw how to hand out public IPv4 addresses using OpenVPN.

In the next chapter, we will explore the advanced features that OpenVPN offers. Also, in *Chapter 6, Client/Server Mode with tap Devices*, several options and examples will be explained that are useful for tun mode as well.

5
Advanced Deployment Scenarios in tun Mode

The basic configuration of a VPN is relatively simple but integrating that VPN with the rest of the network is a much more difficult task. In this chapter, we will explore some advanced deployment scenarios for OpenVPN, which goes beyond the basic installation and configuration of a VPN. Some of these scenarios are based on actual questions from users on the OpenVPN mailing lists, forum, and IRC channel. We will cover the following topics:

- Enabling (Windows) file sharing over the VPN
- Integration with backend authentication mechanisms such as PAM and LDAP
- Filtering VPN traffic (firewall)
- Policy-based routing for enhanced security
- Dealing with public versus private network adapters in Windows 7
- Using OpenVPN with HTTP or SOCKS proxies

The examples presented throughout this chapter rely on the examples from the previous chapter, *Chapter 4, Client/Server Mode with tun Devices*. Most notably, the *Basic production-level configuration files* and *Adding extra security* sections will be used.

Enabling file sharing over VPN

As stated in the *Routing and server-side routing* section in the previous chapter, a VPN is only truly useful when the VPN clients have access to server-side resources. In order to access these server-side resources, routing is needed. This ensures the proper flow of network traffic between the server-side LAN and the VPN.

One of the most common use cases for setting up a VPN is to allow remote workers to access resources on a corporate network. Files on a corporate network are often stored on a Windows-based file server. In order to browse Windows file shares using network names, a WINS server will be required.

Again, a very common layout for accessing resources on the server-side network is depicted here:

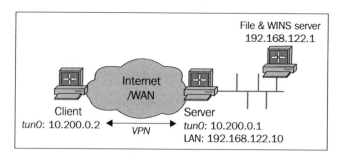

The server-side LAN is **192.168.122.0/24,** and on this subnet, the resources are located that the VPN clients need to access.

We start out with the `basic-udp-server.conf` file and add three lines:

```
proto udp
port 1194
dev tun
server 10.200.0.0 255.255.255.0
topology subnet
persist-key
persist-tun
keepalive 10 60

remote-cert-tls client
tls-auth /etc/openvpn/movpn/ta.key 0
dh       /etc/openvpn/movpn/dh2048.pem
ca       /etc/openvpn/movpn/movpn-ca.crt
cert     /etc/openvpn/movpn/server.crt
key      /etc/openvpn/movpn/server.key
```

```
user    nobody
group nobody # use 'group nogroup' on Debian/Ubuntu

verb 3
daemon
log-append /var/log/openvpn.log

push "route 192.168.122.0 255.255.255.0"
push "redirect-gateway"
push "dhcp-option WINS 192.168.122.1"
```

Save this file as movpn-05-01-server.conf.

The first extra line adds the server-side LAN to the set of networks that need to be routed via the VPN. The second line redirects all network traffic via the VPN tunnel. This line is needed to ensure that OpenVPN's TAP-Win adapter is considered *private*. File sharing is possible only using network adapters that are *private* (as opposed to *public* network adapters). The last extra line instructs the OpenVPN server to push an extra DHCP option to the OpenVPN client, containing the IP address of the WINS server.

We start the OpenVPN server using this configuration file. We again use a 64 bit Windows 7 Professional machine as the OpenVPN client, on which the X86_64 Version of OpenVPN 2.3.5-I001 is installed.

Launch the OpenVPN GUI application, select the configuration **basic-udp-client**, and click on **Connect**.

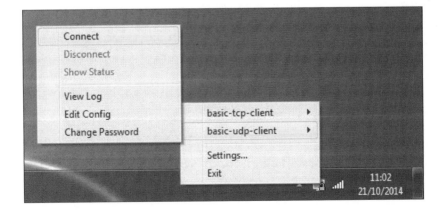

Like we did in the *Routing and server-side routing* section example in the previous chapter, we ensure that the OpenVPN server is forwarding IP traffic and that an extra route is added on the server-side gateway to allow the VPN traffic to be routed correctly back via the VPN server.

After the VPN connection has been established, we go to **Network and Sharing Center** to verify that the TAP adapter (named vpn0 in the following screenshot) is marked as **non-public** and that it is part of either the **Home** or **Work** networks/ groups/locations/. If the TAP adapter is marked **public**, this means that Windows does not trust traffic coming in from this adapter and it will refuse file sharing via the VPN. In the *Windows network locations – public versus private* section of this chapter, we will go into the details of this topic.

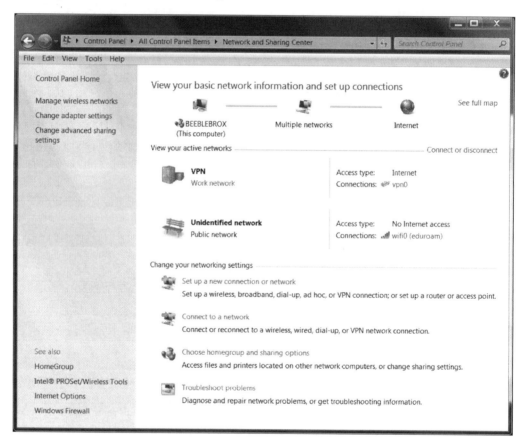

As we can see, the OpenVPN connection vpn0 is part of the **Work** network, which means that file sharing is allowed.

The first method to test that file sharing is working is to browse to the file server using its IP address. You can do this by opening a command prompt window and typing the following lines:

```
C:> start \\192.168.122.1
```

At this point, an authentication dialog will pop up.

Enter your credentials for the file server. Now, a Windows explorer window with the contents of the remote shares will open.

Using NetBIOS names

Instead of browsing file shares by their IP addresses, it is much more convenient to use the Windows Network name of the file server. For this, a WINS server address is needed by the Windows client. The line push "dhcp-option WINS 192.168.122.1" pushes out this WINS address to all connecting OpenVPN clients. After the VPN connection has been established, we can verify that the proper WINS server is used by issuing an ipconfig /all command in a command shell.

```
Console

        Connection-specific DNS Suffix  . :
        Description . . . . . . . . . . . : TAP-Win32 Adapter V9 #2
        Physical Address. . . . . . . . . : 00-FF-63-96-4A-DF
        Dhcp Enabled. . . . . . . . . . . : Yes
        Autoconfiguration Enabled . . . . : Yes
        IP Address. . . . . . . . . . . . : 10.200.0.2
        Subnet Mask . . . . . . . . . . . : 255.255.255.0
        Default Gateway . . . . . . . . . : 10.200.0.1
        DHCP Server . . . . . . . . . . . : 10.200.0.254
        Primary WINS Server . . . . . . . : 192.168.122.1
        Lease Obtained. . . . . . . . . . : Tuesday, November 11, 2014 23:07:55
        Lease Expires . . . . . . . . . . : Wednesday, November 11, 2015 23:07:55

C:\users\janjust>
```

The IP address of the WINS server is listed on the line **Primary WINS Server**, which indicates that Windows will use this server for resolving WINS names.

Now, when the **Network and Sharing Center** is opened, the file server will show up with its NetBIOS name (FILESERVER):

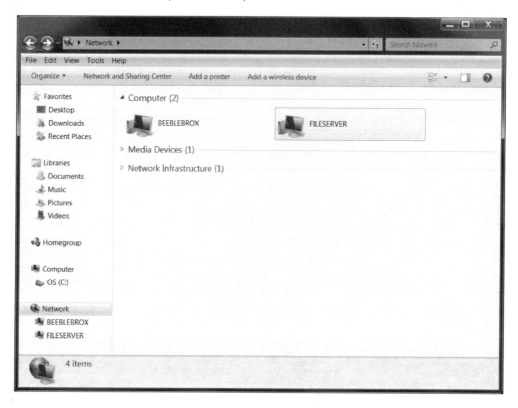

When we click on this icon, we will see the available shares on the file server:

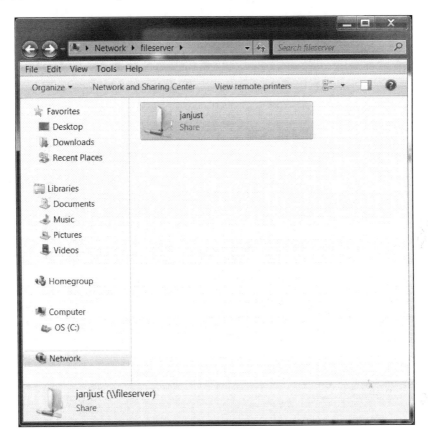

When we click on the share again, an authentication dialog pops up. Enter your credentials for the file server. A Windows explorer window with the contents of the remote share opens up, just like when using an IP address.

Using nbtstat to troubleshoot connection problems

The Windows command-line tool **nbtstat** is very valuable when troubleshooting Windows file sharing problems. You can look up a Windows NetBIOS name and view the available shares, or you can find the NetBIOS name that corresponds to a particular IP address. In both cases, the output will be something like this:

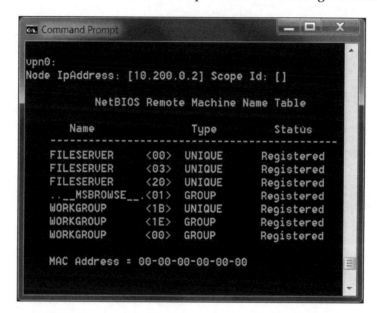

Using LDAP as a backend authentication mechanism

Normally, the security of a VPN is based on a X.509 certificate / private key pair, which all users of the VPN must possess in order to gain access. The security of your VPN can be further increased by requiring users to also supply a username and password when they connect to the OpenVPN server.

On the server side, the verification of the username and password can be done using several mechanisms:

- Using a server-side password file that contains the username and their hashed passwords.
- Using **PAM** (short for **Pluggable Authentication Module**), which is normally included in all Linux/UNIX operating systems.
- Using a central directory server based on **Lightweight Directory Access Protocol (LDAP)**. Note that both LDAP and Active Directory can be used with various PAM modules as well.

It is also possible to authenticate against a Windows Active Directory domain, as this is very similar to using a standalone LDAP server. In this example, we will show you how to authenticate users against an LDAP server.

The easiest way to support LDAP backend authentication is to use the `openvpn-plugin-ldap` module. On most Linux distributions, this module needs be installed separately. For example, on RPM-based systems, you would use the following command:

```
sudo yum install openvpn-auth-ldap
```

We start out with the `basic-udp-server.conf` file and add one line:

```
proto udp
port 1194
dev tun
server 10.200.0.0 255.255.255.0
topology subnet
persist-key
persist-tun
keepalive 10 60

remote-cert-tls client
tls-auth /etc/openvpn/movpn/ta.key 0
dh       /etc/openvpn/movpn/dh2048.pem
ca       /etc/openvpn/movpn/movpn-ca.crt
cert     /etc/openvpn/movpn/server.crt
key      /etc/openvpn/movpn/server.key

user  nobody
```

```
group nobody # use 'group nogroup' on Debian/Ubuntu

verb 3
daemon
log-append /var/log/openvpn.log
```

```
plugin /usr/lib64/openvpn/plugin/lib/openvpn-authldap.so \
        "/etc/openvpn/movpn/movpn_ldap.conf"
```

Save this file as `movpn-05-02-server.conf` and create the `movpn_ldap.conf` file:

```
<LDAP>
  URL               ldaps://ldap.example.org
  Timeout           15
  TLSEnable       no
  FollowReferrals  yes
  TLSCACertFile    /etc/pki/tls/certs/ca-bundle.crt
  TLSCACertDir      /etc/pki/tls/certs
</LDAP>

<Authorization>
  BaseDN          "ou=LocalUsers,dc=example,dc=org"
  SearchFilter      "(&(uid=%u)(authorizedService=login))"
  RequireGroup    false
</Authorization>
```

This is a very basic `authldap` configuration file using the secure LDAP server found at the URI `ldaps://ldap.example.org`, port `636`, and an LDAP search filter based on the User ID (`uid=%u`) and the LDAP attribute `authorizedService=login`. The URI indicates an SSL connection to the server with the `ldaps://` service. These settings are highly dependent on the LDAP server used, but the `openvpn-ldap-auth` plugin can be adapted to almost any configuration. For example, in this setup, no binding is used to connect to the LDAP server. However, this as well as other connection options can be added.

Next we add a line to client config `basic-udp-client.ovpn`:

auth-user-pass

Save it as `movpn-05-02-client.ovpn` and launch the client. The client first initiates the connection with the server using its X.509 certificate and private key file, after which the user is prompted for a username and password.

If the proper credentials are entered, then the connection is established. Otherwise, the server refuses access.

Instead of using the `openvpn-ldap-auth` plugin, we could also use the PAM plugin. OpenVPN will then query the PAM subsystem for authentication. If the PAM subsystem is properly configured to authenticate users against an LDAP database, then the same functionality would be achieved. The OpenVPN server configuration file would then look like this:

```
proto udp
port 1194
dev tun
server 10.200.0.0 255.255.255.0
topology subnet
persist-key
persist-tun
keepalive 10 60

remote-cert-tls client
tls-auth /etc/openvpn/movpn/ta.key 0
dh       /etc/openvpn/movpn/dh2048.pem
ca       /etc/openvpn/movpn/movpn-ca.crt
cert     /etc/openvpn/movpn/server.crt
key      /etc/openvpn/movpn/server.key

user   nobody
group nobody # use 'group nogroup' on Debian/Ubuntu

verb 3
daemon
log-append /var/log/openvpn.log

plugin /usr/lib64/openvpn/plugin/lib/openvpn-auth-pam.so "login login
USERNAME password PASSWORD"
```

Troubleshooting the LDAP backend authentication

Troubleshooting the LDAP backend authentication plugin can be tricky. The most important thing to do first is to ensure that the VPN server is capable of connecting to the LDAP server and the user information can be retrieved. For this, the `ldapsearch` tool is very handy. This tool is included in the OpenLDAP client utilities package.

Using `BaseDN` and `SearchFilter` from the `movpn_ldap.conf` file, we can query the LDAP server:

```
$ ldapsearch -x -H ldaps://ldap.example.org \
    -b ou=LocalUsers,dc=example,dc=org \
     "(&(uid=janjust)(authorizedService=login))"
```

The `-x` option signifies an anonymous (unauthenticated) bind to the server, and the `-H` option indicates the server URI. Note that the URI is different from a host name, as it will include the protocol (SSL or plain text) as well as the hostname. The `ldapsearch` output should be something like this:

```
# extended LDIF
#
# LDAPv3
# base <ou=LocalUsers,dc=example,dc=org> with scope subtree
# filter: (&(uid=janjust)(authorizedService=login))
# requesting: ALL
#


# janjust, LocalUsers, example.org
dn: uid=janjust,ou=LocalUsers,dc=example,dc=org
loginShell: /bin/bash
uid: janjust
cn: Jan Just Keijser
...
authorizedService: login


# search result
search: 2
result: 0 Success


# numResponses: 2
# numEntries: 1
```

Make sure this is working before attempting to connect an OpenVPN client. If this works but the client cannot connect to the OpenVPN server, then increase the verbosity on the server and watch for LDAP messages. Add the following line to the bottom of the configuration file and restart the server:

```
verb 5
```

Reconnect the client and watch the server log for any LDAP authentication messages. For a failed connection attempt, the server logs will contain lines like this:

```
LDAP bind failed: Invalid credentials


Incorrect password supplied for LDAP DN "uid=janjust,ou=LocalUsers,dc=exa
mple,dc=org".


[...] PLUGIN_CALL: POST /usr/lib64/openvpn/plugin/lib/openvpn-auth-ldap.
so/PLUGIN_AUTH_USER_PASS_VERIFY status=1


[...] PLUGIN_CALL: plugin function PLUGIN_AUTH_USER_PASS_VERIFY failed
with status 1: /usr/lib64/openvpn/plugin/lib/openvpn-auth-ldap.so


[...] TLS Auth Error: Auth Username/Password verification failed for peer


Whereas a successful connection attempt will show
[...] PLUGIN_CALL: POST /usr/lib64/openvpn/plugin/lib/openvpn-auth-ldap.
so/PLUGIN_AUTH_USER_PASS_VERIFY status=0


[...] TLS: Username/Password authentication succeeded for username
'janjust'
```

In these log messages, the connection-specific details such as the client IP address and the UDP port number were replaced with [...].

Filtering OpenVPN

Just like any other interface on a system or server, the tun and tap adapter interfaces can be filtered using your operating system appropriate firewall software. In many cases, both for routing and filtering purposes, it's best to logically place the OpenVPN server in a network-central location, such as at or near the border router. For homes, this is likely a cable or DSL modem. On corporate networks, this will generally be an actual core router such as a Cisco or Juniper edge device.

Depending on the platform and your own or business preferences, the firewall can be a separate device between the OpenVPN server and the unprotected Internet, or it can be software running on the same system as your OpenVPN server. Larger installations may even have multiple firewalls.

The first image shows a network with a separate firewall inserted between the OpenVPN server and the border router and Internet:

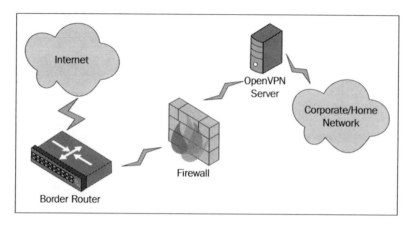

The next image shows how, logically, the firewall and the OpenVPN server can be on the same machine:

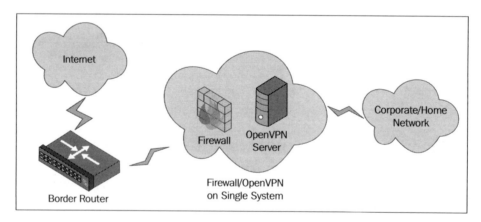

Projects such as pfSense (`https://www.pfsense.org`) and OpenWRT (`https://openwrt.org`) integrate Internet connections, LANs, and VPNs in a single system. These systems run software that provides a simple graphical interface to manage wireless networking, Internet connections, VPN instances, and a firewall rule set to protect them all.

For our examples, we are going to allow only ports `80` and `443` from VPN clients to the rest of the network.

FreeBSD example

On FreeBSD, we will use `pf` to filter traffic in and out of our VPN. On FreeBSD, the OpenVPN interface is `tun0`. First, `pf` needs to be enabled in `rc.conf`:

```
pf_enable="YES"
```

To start, we'll create an extremely simple ruleset in the default `/etc/pf.conf`:

```
pass all
```

Then, start `pf`:

```
root@server:~-> /etc/rc.d/pf start
Enabling pf
No ALTQ support in kernel
ALTQ related functions disabled
```

Using `pfctl`, we can list the rules and their counters:

```
root@server:~-> pfctl -vvv -s rules
No ALTQ support in kernel
ALTQ related functions disabled
@0 pass all flags S/SA keep state
  [ Evaluations: 209      Packets: 13       Bytes: 624         States:
2    ]
  [ Inserted: uid 0 pid 71163 State Creations: 7       ]
```

At this point, we have a simple ruleset that simply allows all packets on all interfaces. As this isn't a book on mastering `pf`, we won't go into the minute details of the entire configuration. Here's a sample filter that allows all traffic on all interfaces, except `tun0`. Traffic on `tun0` will be filtered inbound, so only connections on ports `80` and `443` to the LAN can be made from the VPN clients. Traffic outbound on `tun0` will be allowed.

```
# Mastering OpenVPN - FreeBSD Filtering Example
vpn_if="tun0"
out_if="xn0"
in_if="xn0"

lanv4="10.50.0.0/24"
lanv6="2001:db8:900::/64"
vpnv4="10.200.0.0/24"
vpnv6="2001:db8:100::/64"

pass on {$in_if, $out_if} all
pass out on $vpn_if all
block in on $vpn_if
pass in on $vpn_if inet proto tcp to $lanv4 port {http, https}
pass in on $vpn_if inet6 proto tcp to $lanv6 port {http, https}
```

Both OpenVPN and FreeBSD have a `pf` packet filter. In the above example, we are using the kernel supported `pf` and not the `pf` built into OpenVPN.

A Windows example

Assuming you already have an OpenVPN server running on a Windows 7 Professional system, you'll access the firewall configuration through **Control Panel**. Once **Control Panel** is open, type `firewall` in the search box and click on **Windows Firewall**. From the options available on the left-hand side panel of the window, click on **Advanced Settings**. This will present the firewall configuration utility.

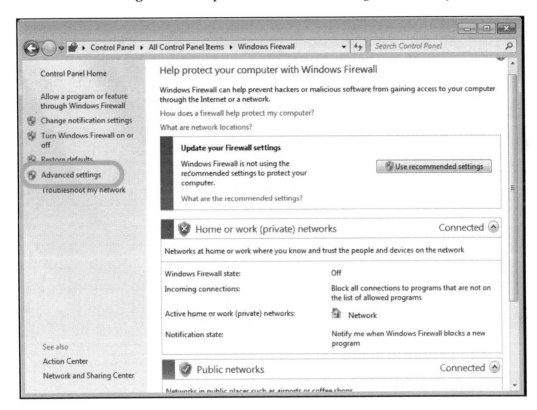

Click on **Advanced settings** to open the **Windows Firewall with Advanced Security** program, as shown in the following figure:

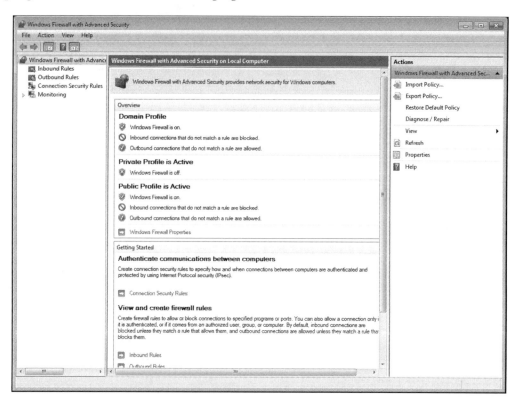

Once in the utility, we need to create two inbound rules. The first rule will block all traffic from the VPN, and the second one will allow traffic on ports 80 and 443 from the VPN.

Once the **New Inbound Rule Wizard** has opened, select the option to create a custom rule, as shown in the following screenshot. This allows us to identify all the specific inbound address ranges and ports needed to be effective.

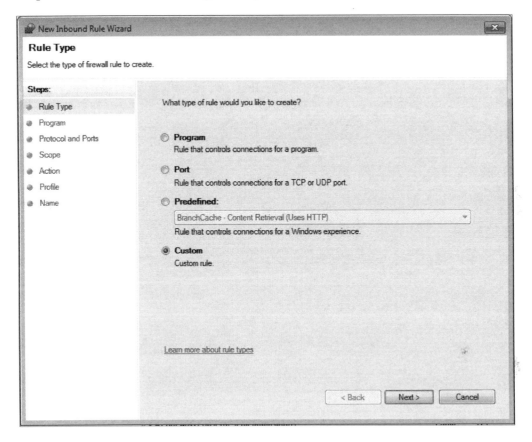

On the second page, select the radio button for **All programs** to apply this rule to all programs:

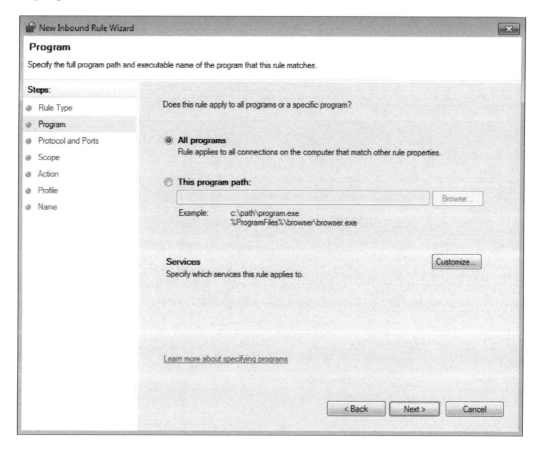

On the third inbound rule screen, specify TCP ports `80` and `443` on the inbound rule, and allow them from *all* remote ports. This is shown in the following screenshot:

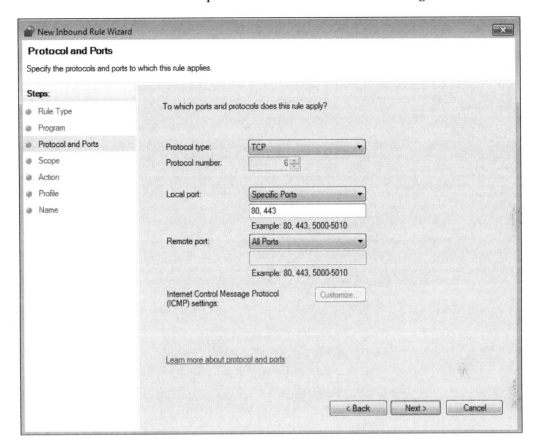

For the scope page, specify the local VPN IP ranges:

- `10.200.0.0/24` (IPv4)
- `2001:db8:100::/64` (IPv6)

Then, allow all remote IP addresses by selecting **Any IP address** (this is the default). Later, when creating the block rule, you will leave the defaults—both for **All Ports** on this page.

You could apply this to the VPN IP ranges as well to only allow the VPN host addresses to contact VPN resources. Omitting this restriction allows other remote subnets you may desire to route (using `--iroute`, for example).

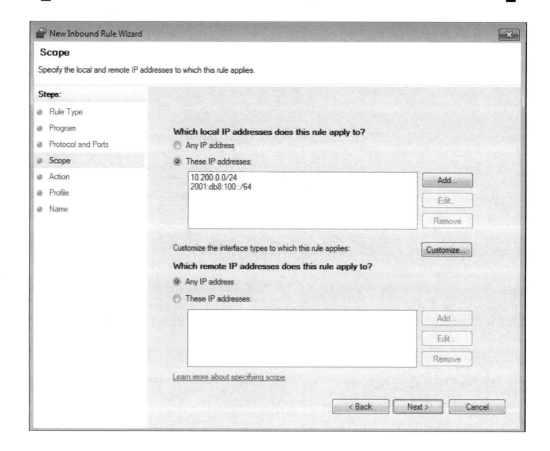

Next, select **Allow the connection** from the list of actions. Later, when creating the block rule, you will need to select **Block the connection** on this page.

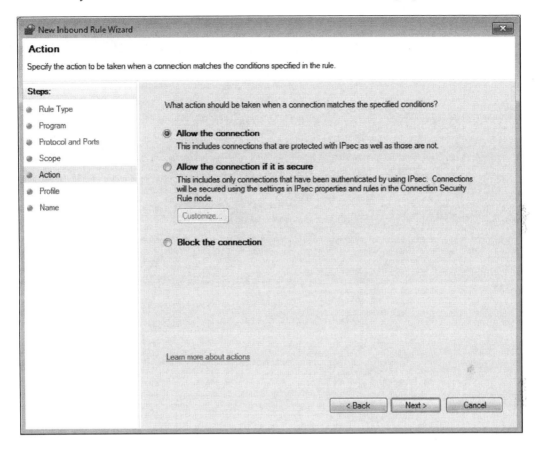

Check all three boxes on the **Profile** page of the wizard. This will allow the rule to function regardless of the interface profile assigned (**Public, Private,** or **Domain**). We will discuss this later.

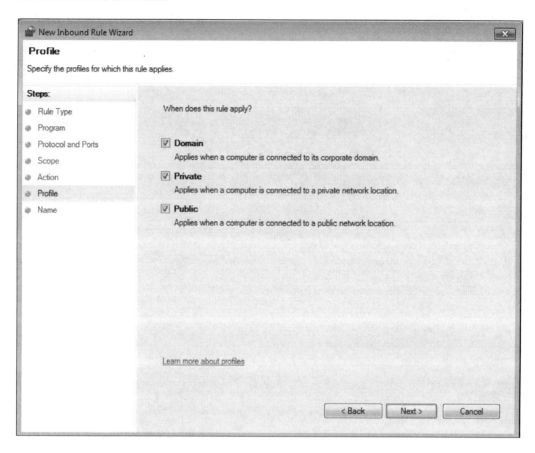

The last page of the inbound rule wizard allows you to set a name. Choose something descriptive that allows an administrator to quickly identify the rule and how it is applied. In our case, we set the name to VPN - Allow 80, 443 for the allow rule.

Now that the allow rule is created, go through these steps again and create your block rule. This rule will block all traffic from the VPN. When coupled with the allow rule we already created, it will only allow our VPN clients to connect through the VPN on ports 80 and 443.

Use the following settings for your block rule on each page of the wizard:

- **Rule Type** should be **Custom**
- For the **Program** option, select **All programs**
- Select **All Ports** for both local ports and remote ports
- **Scope** should be **Any IP address** (for local and remote)
- **Action** should be **Block the connection**
- Choose **Select all profiles** for **Profile**
- Set the **Name** as VPN - Block All

Once saved, you will have a pair of VPN rules at the top of the list.

Inbound Rules					
Name	Group	Profile	Enabled	Actior	
VPN - Allow 80, 443		All	Yes	Allow	
VPN - Block All		All	Yes	Block	

Windows Firewall with Advanced Security is a first-match firewall type. This means that as soon as a firewall rule matches a given network packet, processing of the ruleset stops and the given action in that rule is applied. The Linux iptables packet filter is another first-match filter. Other packet filters, such as OpenBSD's pf, are last-match, which means the rules continue to process through to the end.

OpenVPN has a built-in filtering capability, but the code has been untouched for a number of years and requires additional plugins to operate. The developers don't think the code is viable at this time, but the feature may be brought back in the future.

Doing many "server" type tasks on a desktop version of Windows generally requires the administrator to go a bit off the beaten path. Windows Server 2008, for example, has better firewall editing tools than Windows 7 Professional, which is used in the above example.

Policy-based routing

Policy-based routing utilizes a firewall or other packet filter to route traffic based on not only the source and destination IP addresses, but also the source or destination ports. One common use of policy-based routing is to send all of the unprotected port 80 traffic across the VPN, but allow other traffic, such as SSL traffic on port 443, to traverse the general Internet.

Policy-based routing is something that needs to be done at the source. In most cases, this means it will be applied at the OpenVPN client. In some instances, this can be augmented at the OpenVPN server, but the flexibility is greatly diminished.

Every firewall or packet filtering software handles policy routing differently. We were unable to configure the Windows 7 firewall to route based on source or destination ports, and even the OpenBSD pf packet filter has specific caveats.

The following figure demonstrates a simple port 80 or port 443 policy routing decision matching our example scenario from the preceding section:

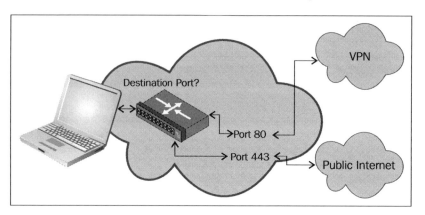

Windows network locations – public versus private

A recurring question on the OpenVPN mailing lists is how to change the network location of OpenVPN's TAP-Win virtual network adapter from public to private. This question started popping up with the introduction of Windows Vista. The answer to this question is unfortunately quite lengthy. In this section, we will explore different methods that allow us to change the network location of the TAP-Win adapter on Windows clients.

Background

Starting with Windows Vista, Microsoft introduced the concept of network locations. In Windows 7, there are three network locations: **Home**, **Work**, and **Public**. These network locations apply to all network adapters: wired network adapters, wireless adapters, and also OpenVPN's virtual TAP-Win network adapter.

The **Home** network location is intended for a home network and provides a high level of trust. It also includes the **Home group** feature, where a computer can easily connect to all other devices at home. Similarly, the **Work** network location provides a high level of trust at work, allowing the computer to share files, connect to printers, and so on. In Windows 8, the **Home** and **Work** network locations are merged together to become the **Private** network location.

The **Public** network location is not trusted and access to network resources, both inbound and outbound, is severely restricted by Windows—even when the Windows firewall is disabled.

When the Windows firewall is enabled, the **Private** firewall profile is applied to all network adapters in the **Home** and **Work** network locations, and the **Public** firewall profile is applied to all network adapters in the **Public** network location.

For a network adapter to be trusted, it must advertise a default gateway or the network adapter must be part of a Windows domain. There is some documentation about this online:

```
http://blogs.technet.com/b/networking/archive/2009/02/20/why-is-my-
network-detected-as-unknown-by-windows-vista-or-windows-server-2008.
aspx
```

When Windows cannot determine the *location* of a network, it automatically chooses the **Public** network location. Unfortunately, it is not possible to change the status when a network adapter is classified as **Public**.

Changing the TAP-Win adapter location using the redirect-gateway

OpenVPN can set a default gateway on the remote TAP-Win adapter using the configuration directive:

```
redirect-gateway
```

Normally, it is recommended that you add the parameter def1 to this option. The def1 option causes OpenVPN to not add a new default gateway (in network terms, a route 0.0.0.0/0.0.0.0), but rather to add two routes with netmask 128.0.0.0, as explained in the previous chapter. The disadvantage of the def1 option is that Windows does not recognize the TAP-Win adapter as having a default gateway. For more details on the different alternatives to the redirect-gateway option, see *Chapter 4, Client/Server Mode with tun Devices.*

In order to test this option, we add a line to the basic-udp-server.conf file:

```
proto udp
port 1194
dev tun
server 10.200.0.0 255.255.255.0
topology subnet
persist-key
persist-tun
keepalive 10 60

remote-cert-tls client
tls-auth /etc/openvpn/movpn/ta.key 0
dh       /etc/openvpn/movpn/dh2048.pem
ca       /etc/openvpn/movpn/movpn-ca.crt
cert     /etc/openvpn/movpn/server.crt
key      /etc/openvpn/movpn/server.key

user   nobody
group nobody # use 'group nogroup' on Debian/Ubuntu

verb 3
daemon
log-append /var/log/openvpn.log

push "redirect-gateway"
```

Now, save it as movpn-05-03-server.conf. Start the OpenVPN server using this configuration file and connect a Windows 7 client using the default basic-udp-client.ovpn configuration.

This time, after the client successfully connects, Windows will ask in which *location* to place the new network:

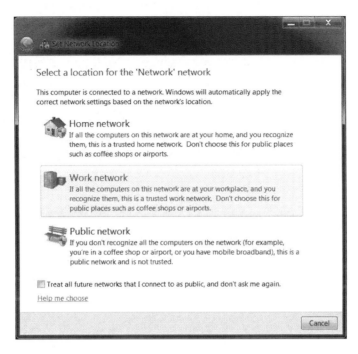

Select the **Work** network, after which Windows will let you choose your own name and icon for the VPN network:

We chose the name VPN, choose a different icon, and click on **OK**.

The TAP-Win adapter is now trusted and Windows file sharing is allowed over this network, as well as other trusted protocols.

One of the downsides of using *redirect-gateway* is that the VPN adapter is now the only adapter with a default gateway, and hence is trusted. The wireless network adapter, connected to the Wi-Fi network eduroam, now lacks a default route and all of a sudden is part of an *unidentified network* and is no longer trusted. This can be seen in the following screenshot of the Windows 7 **Network and Sharing Center**:

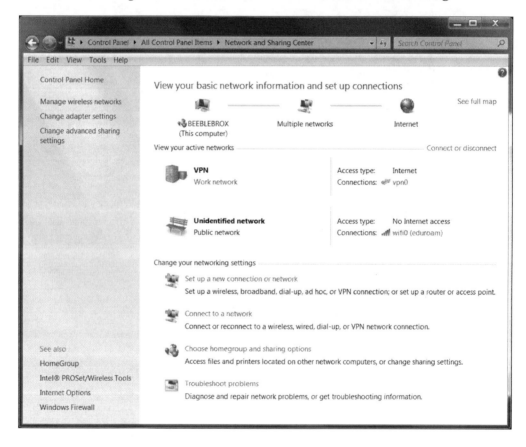

The biggest disadvantage of using *redirect-gateway* without `def1` becomes apparent when the VPN connection is stopped or dropped. As the default gateway on the Windows OpenVPN client has been replaced, it is no longer possible to reliably restore the default gateway that existed before the VPN was started and all Internet connectivity is lost. In most cases, the (wireless) local network connection needs to be restarted for the gateway to be restored.

Using the Group Policy editor to force an adapter to be private

A second approach to changing the location of the TAP-Win adapter is to use the Windows Group Policy editor. Using this tool, it is possible to force the TAP-Win adapter (or any unidentified adapter) to be either *private* or *public*:

1. Open the **Command prompt** and start the **Group Policy** editor:

   `gpoledit.msc`

2. Select **Network List Manager policies** and double-click on **Unidentified Networks** in the right-hand side pane, as shown in the following screenshot:

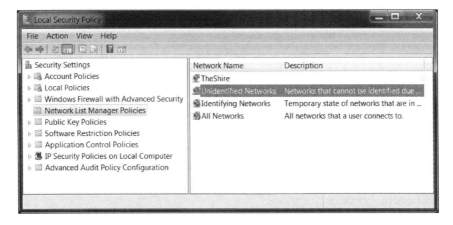

3. A new **Unidentified Networks Properties** window will pop up. Set the **Location Type** to **Private** and click **OK**, as shown in the following screenshot:

4. Restart the OpenVPN client without the *redirect-gateway* flag.

Windows will now automatically mark the adapter as **Private** and will again ask in which network the adapter should be placed: **Home** or **Work**. However, this time the icon and name of the network type chosen cannot be modified.

> The preceding instructions will set *all* unidentified networks to **Private** and could possibly preset other negative security side-effects. Make sure you understand the full implications of this change before setting this.

Changing the TAP-Win adapter location using extra gateways

A more elegant approach to change the adapter location is to add an extra gateway address to the server configuration:

```
push "route 0.0.0.0 0.0.0.0"
```

When the OpenVPN client connects, it will add an extra default route to the system routing tables. This route will always have a higher metric than the regular default gateway, but the adapter is now trusted.

In Windows 7, the metric of an adapter normally is calculated automatically as the sum of the gateway metric and the interface metric. The interface metrics are based on the type and speed of the adapter. As OpenVPN's TAP-Win adapter is registered as a 10 Mbps adapter, it will always have a higher metric (that is, it will be less preferable) than wired or wireless adapters, which have higher speeds.

These metrics can be shown using the `netsh int ip show config` command:

```
C:\>netsh int ip show config

Configuration for interface "vpn0"
    DHCP enabled:                          Yes
    IP Address:                            10.200.0.2
    Subnet Prefix:                         10.200.0.0/24 (...)
    Default Gateway:                       10.200.0.1
    Gateway Metric:                        70
    InterfaceMetric:                       30
    DNS servers configured through DHCP:   192.0.2.12
    Register with which suffix:            Primary only
    WINS servers configured through DHCP:  192.0.2.60

Configuration for interface "wifi0"
    DHCP enabled:                          Yes
    IP Address:                            192.0.2.233
    Subnet Prefix:                         192.0.2.0/24 (...)
    Default Gateway:                       192.0.2.254
    Gateway Metric:                        0
```

```
InterfaceMetric:                        20
DNS servers configured through DHCP:    192.0.2.17
                                        192.0.2.12
Register with which suffix:             None
WINS servers configured through DHCP:   192.0.2.121
                                        192.0.2.20
```

It is possible to turn off the automatic metric calculation and revert to the behavior of older versions of Windows. In order to do this, go the **Advanced TCP/IP Properties** dialog of the **TCP/IPv4 Properties** option of a network adapter:

In this case, the metric specified in the **TCP/IPv4 Properties** window will determine the default route in the system. If the metric of the TAP-Win adapter is higher than that of the non-VPN adapter, then effectively all traffic is routed over the VPN!

The advantage of this approach is that the *old* default gateway is left intact, thus avoiding the problem of the lost default gateway when the VPN connection is dropped or stopped.

Redirecting all traffic in combination with extra gateways

As a final example of how the network location can be influenced using OpenVPN configuration options, we will both add an extra gateway and redirect the default gateway using `def1`:

```
proto udp
port 1194
dev tun
server 10.200.0.0 255.255.255.0
topology subnet
persist-key
persist-tun
keepalive 10 60

remote-cert-tls client
tls-auth /etc/openvpn/movpn/ta.key 0
dh       /etc/openvpn/movpn/dh2048.pem
ca       /etc/openvpn/movpn/movpn-ca.crt
cert     /etc/openvpn/movpn/server.crt
key      /etc/openvpn/movpn/server.key

user   nobody
group nobody # use 'group nogroup' on Debian/Ubuntu

verb 3
daemon
log-append /var/log/openvpn.log

push "route 0.0.0.0 0.0.0.0"
push "redirect-gateway def1"
```

Save the file as `movpn-05-04-server.conf`. Start the OpenVPN server using this configuration file and connect a Windows 7 client using the default `basic-udp-client.ovpn` configuration.

After the OpenVPN client reconnects, the IPv4 routing table now has the following entries:

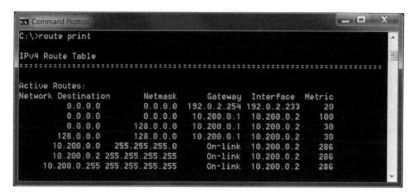

The first route is the original gateway. The second route is the extra `0.0.0.0/0` route for the TAP-Win adapter. This causes Windows to trust the adapter. The third and fourth routes are set by the `redirect-gateway def1` command by adding the routes `0.0.0.0/1` and `128.0.0.0`.

OpenVPN provides two new routes that are more specific than the default `0.0.0.0/0` route. TCP/IP routing specifies that the more specific route should always be chosen, regardless of the interface metric. Therefore, all traffic is redirected over the VPN tunnel.

The **Network & Sharing Center** window now shows both the LAN network and the VPN network as trusted:

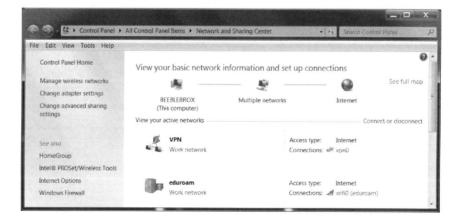

The advantages of this approach are as follows:

- Both the original network (Wi-Fi `eduroam` in the preceding example) and the VPN network are trusted. This means file and printer sharing is available on both networks.

- All network traffic is correctly redirected over the VPN, regardless of the interface metrics.

- When the VPN connection is dropped or stopped, the original default gateway is correctly restored.

A quick check of the link `https://www.whatismyip.com` will show that all traffic is now routed over the VPN. Another way to verify this is to use `tracert` in a Windows command shell:

```
c:\>tracert -4 -d www

Tracing route to www.nikhef.nl [192.16.199.160]
over a maximum of 30 hops:

  1     95 ms    119 ms     83 ms   10.200.0.1
  3    103 ms    119 ms     83 ms   192.0.2.133
  4    115 ms    101 ms    101 ms   192.16.199.160

Trace complete.
```

 On Mac OS X, the Tunnelblick client for OpenVPN has the ability to check if the external IP has changed once connected to the VPN, and then notify the user if that IP does not change.

The first hop in the `traceroute` output is the VPN server address, which proves that the default gateway of the system is now indeed the VPN adapter.

Using OpenVPN with HTTP or SOCKS proxies

OpenVPN supports operation through an HTTP or SOCKS proxy with no authentication, with basic authentication and with NTLM authentication. We will cover both HTTP and SOCKS proxy servers, both with and without authentication.

HTTP proxies

HTTP proxies require the use of TCP for the OpenVPN tunnel transport. If you are currently using UDP, the protocol argument in both the server as well as the client configurations will need to be updated:

```
proto tcp
```

Once configured, add proxy support to the client by adding the `--http-proxy` configuration directive. As an example, let's assume your local area network requires an anonymous proxy for outbound connections and that server is at `192.168.4.4` on the default port `1080`. Your configuration would be something like this:

```
http-proxy 192.168.4.4 1080 none
```

This will allow your OpenVPN client connection to connect to your remote OpenVPN server through the proxy server on your local network. An authenticated HTTP proxy isn't much different, simply replace `none` in the preceding command with the authentication information:

```
http-proxy 192.168.4.4 1080 stdin basic
```

The preceding command connects to the same proxy server and port as we did before, but queries on standard input for the username and password to use for HTTP basic authentication. Additionally, support authentication methods include an `auth` file, which is similar to the core OpenVPN password file—just a username and password in clear text on two separate lines:

```
someuser
somepass
```

The `auth` file path and filename are passed in place of the `stdin` keyword in the preceding example. Setting `auto` allows OpenVPN to determine where to query credentials from, including via the management console.

Some HTTP proxies may restrict access or authentication based on the HTTP user agent passed, or other HTTP options. These can be defined using the `http-proxy-option` configuration argument for almost any arbitrary HTTP option. Common examples are the user agent string and the HTTP version string:

```
http-proxy-option VERSION 1.1
http-proxy-option AGENT "Definitely NOT OpenVPN"
```

All of these options can be defined in the standard OpenVPN client configuration or on the command line at run time.

If you want to have OpenVPN retry connections to a flapping HTTP proxy, specify the `--http-proxy-retry` option. This will result in OpenVPN mimicking a `SIGUSR1` reset on the OpenVPN process, causing a reconnection of the tunnel.

SOCKS proxies

In addition to HTTP proxies, OpenVPN supports SOCKS proxies. If you want to understand more about the differences between HTTP and SOCKS proxies, Wikipedia has a good comparison at `http://en.wikipedia.org/wiki/SOCKS` or you can review the protocol-specific **Request For Comments (RFC)** at the following URLs:

- **SOCKS5**: `https://www.ietf.org/rfc/rfc1928.txt`
- **HTTP**: `https://www.ietf.org/rfc/rfc2616.txt`

For our examples, we'll again assume a proxy server `192.168.4.4` on the default port `1080`. But this time, it will be a SOCKS5 proxy. Unlike the HTTP proxy example, it is permissible to use either UDP or TCP for the tunnel transport with a standard SOCKS5 proxy server. However, there are caveats to this.

Add the following line to your OpenVPN client configuration to point it to our example proxy server:

```
socks-proxy-server 1080 socks_auth.txt
```

Like with the other authentication files, a plain text file with username and password on separate lines suffices:

```
socks5user
socks5pass
```

As earlier, `stdin` works in place of the path and filename for the `auth` file. Also, if reconnection/retry is desired when a connection is lost or falters to the proxy server, specify the option `--socks-proxy-retry` to allow OpenVPN to mimic a `SIGUSR1` to restart the VPN.

> You can use the SSH protocol to create a SOCKS5 local server and tunnel OpenVPN through that tunnel. One restriction to doing this is that the SSH SOCKS5 proxy requires TCP-only connections. Your traffic within OpenVPN can be TCP/UDP, but the OpenVPN tunnel itself must be `--proto tcp`.

Summary

In this chapter, you learned how to integrate OpenVPN into your existing network and computer infrastructure. This applies to the server side. We also saw how to use LDAP as a backend authentication system, and how to use policy-based routing to seamlessly integrate the VPN offered by OpenVPN into the regular network. On the client side, we addressed the integration of OpenVPN in to the Windows operating system, as well as a scenario where the OpenVPN server cannot be contacted directly.

These are, of course, only a few examples of advanced deployment scenarios, and we were restricted to tun mode only. This was done on purpose so that we could show that tun mode is suitable for most OpenVPN deployments. There are deployment scenarios that require tap mode or even bridging, and these are covered in the next chapter.

6
Client/Server Mode with tap Devices

The *other* deployment model for OpenVPN is a single server with multiple remote clients capable of routing Ethernet traffic. We refer to this deployment model as *client/server mode with tap devices*.

The main difference between tun and tap mode is the type of adapter used. A tap adapter provides a full virtual Ethernet (layer 2) interface, whereas a tun adapter is seen as a point-to-point (layer 3) adapter by most operating systems. Computers connected using (virtual) Ethernet adapters can form a single *broadcast domain*, which is needed for certain applications. With point-to-point adapters, this is not possible. Also, note that not all operating systems support tap adapters. For example, both iOS and Android support tun devices only.

In this chapter, we start with a basic client/server setup, which is very similar to the basic setup described in *Chapter 4, Client/Server Mode with tun Devices*. However, there are subtle differences that will be discussed using several examples. Also, tap mode enables a bridging setup, where a regular network adapter is bridged with the virtual tap adapter. This topic will be discussed in detail for both the Linux and Windows operating systems.

The following topics will be covered in this chapter:

- Basic setup
- Enabling client-to-client traffic using `pf`
- Bridging
- Bridging on Linux
- Bridging on Windows

- Using an external DHCP server
- Checking broadcast and non-IP traffic
- Comparing tun mode to tap mode

The basic setup

The basic setup for OpenVPN in tap mode is almost exactly the same as in the tun mode. In tap mode, we use the following line in the server configuration file:

```
dev tap
```

While in tun mode, we use the following lines:

```
dev tun
topology subnet
```

The option `topology subnet` is not required, but provides a network addressing scheme that is more sensible and will be the default in a future version of OpenVPN.

For the sake of completeness, we first create the server configuration file:

```
proto udp
port 1194
dev tap
server 10.222.0.0 255.255.255.0

persist-key
persist-tun
keepalive 10 60

remote-cert-tls client
tls-auth /etc/openvpn/movpn/ta.key 0
dh       /etc/openvpn/movpn/dh2048.pem
ca       /etc/openvpn/movpn/movpn-ca.crt
cert     /etc/openvpn/movpn/server.crt
key      /etc/openvpn/movpn/server.key

user    nobody
group nobody

verb 3
daemon
log-append /var/log/openvpn.log
```

We will reuse this basic tap-mode server configuration file in this chapter and others. Save it as `tap-udp-server.conf` so that we can reuse it later.

 The `topology subnet` option was removed as the `topology` option is a tun-specific configuration option. In tap-mode, the server will always hand out a single IP address to each client, with a corresponding netmask.

Similarly, we create the client configuration file, which is again nearly identical to the `basic-udp-client.conf` file from *Chapter 4, Client/Server Mode with tun Devices*:

```
proto udp
port 1194
dev tap

client
remote openvpnserver.example.com
nobind

remote-cert-tls server
tls-auth /etc/openvpn/movpn/ta.key 1
ca    /etc/openvpn/movpn/movpn-ca.crt
cert /etc/openvpn/movpn/client1.crt
key  /etc/openvpn/movpn/client1.key
```

Save this file as `tap-udp-client.conf`. Similarly, for Windows clients, create the configuration file `tap-udp-client.ovpn`.

Start the OpenVPN server and connect a client using these configuration files. The server-side connection log shows some subtle differences compared to the tun-based setup, which are highlighted in the following section:

```
OpenVPN 2.3.6 x86_64-redhat-linux-gnu [SSL (OpenSSL)] [LZO] [EPOLL]
[PKCS11] [MH] [IPv6] built on Dec  2 2014
library versions: OpenSSL 1.0.1e-fips 11 Feb 2013, LZO 2.03
[...]
TUN/TAP device tap0 opened
TUN/TAP TX queue length set to 100
do_ifconfig, tt->ipv6=0, tt->did_ifconfig_ipv6_setup=0
/sbin/ip link set dev tap0 up mtu 1500
/sbin/ip addr add dev tap0 10.222.0.1/24 broadcast 10.222.0.255
GID set to nobody
UID set to nobody
```

```
UDPv4 link local (bound): [undef]
UDPv4 link remote: [undef]
MULTI: multi_init called, r=256 v=256
IFCONFIG POOL: base=10.222.0.2 size=253, ipv6=0
Initialization Sequence Completed
CLIENT_IP:60728 TLS: Initial packet from [AF_INET]CLIENT_IP:60728,
sid=d4d7f1fd 988e4ff3
[...]
client1/CLIENT_IP:60728 PUSH: Received control message: 'PUSH_REQUEST'

client1/CLIENT_IP:60728 SENT CONTROL [client1]: 'PUSH_REPLY,route-
gateway 10.222.0.1,ping 10,ping-restart 60,ifconfig 10.222.0.2
255.255.255.0' (status=1)
client1/CLIENT_IP:60728 MULTI: Learn: 8e:66:e4:43:35:a1 -> client1/
CLIENT_IP:60728
```

The last line of the server connection log is actually the most interesting one: the
MULTI: Learn line shows that the server is now using the MAC address of the
remote client to distinguish it from other clients, whereas in tun-mode it could rely
solely on the IP address assigned to the client. This is necessary as a tap-based client
can also send non-IP traffic in which no IP address is used.

Enabling client-to-client traffic

When multiple **Virtual Private Network (VPN)** clients are connected to the server,
they are not permitted to exchange traffic. This is true for both tap mode and tun
mode. In order to enable client-to-client traffic, there are two options:

- Use the configuration option client-to-client. This allows OpenVPN to
  handle client-to-client traffic internally, bypassing the system routing tables
  as well as the system firewall/iptables rules.

- Use the system routing tables and firewall/iptables rules to send traffic from
  one client to another and back.

The first option is the fastest option, both in terms of configuration and in terms
of performance. If there are no restrictions on the traffic between VPN clients,
add the line client-to-client to the configuration file tap-udp-server.conf,
save it as movpn-06-01-server.conf, and restart the OpenVPN server using this
configuration file:

```
$ openvpn --config movpn-06-01-server.conf
```

Reconnect the VPN clients. The first client is assigned IP address 10.222.0.2 and the second client 10.222.0.3. The clients can now reach each other:

```
C:\ Console                                              _ □ ×

C:\Program Files\OpenVPN\config>ping 10.222.0.2          ▲

Pinging 10.222.0.2 with 32 bytes of data:

Reply from 10.222.0.2: bytes=32 time=652ms TTL=64
Reply from 10.222.0.2: bytes=32 time=321ms TTL=64
Reply from 10.222.0.2: bytes=32 time=325ms TTL=64
Reply from 10.222.0.2: bytes=32 time=327ms TTL=64

Ping statistics for 10.222.0.2:
    Packets: Sent = 4, Received = 4, Lost = 0 (0% loss),
Approximate round trip times in milli-seconds:
    Minimum = 321ms, Maximum = 652ms, Average = 406ms    ▼
```

The high latency (that is, a `ping` time of more than 300 ms) in the preceding screenshot, immediately shows one of the drawbacks of using client-to-client traffic over a VPN. All traffic flows via the OpenVPN server, thus a `ping` from `client1` to `client2` takes longer:

1. The ping request message is sent from `client1` to the OpenVPN server.
2. The OpenVPN server forwards the message to `client2`.
3. `client2` sends back a ping reply message, again to the server.
4. The OpenVPN server forwards the ping reply back to `client1`.

If the VPN clients are connected over a high-latency network, then the use of a client/server-model VPN will increase the latency when sending traffic between clients. OpenVPN is such a client/server-model VPN, as are most commercial VPN solutions available. Some peer-to-peer VPN solutions exist, but they are outside the scope of this book.

Filtering traffic between clients

A drawback of the `client-to-client` option is the lack of filtering. When this option is added, *all* traffic between *all* clients is allowed, bypassing the system firewall/iptables rules.

A second method of allowing traffic to flow between clients is to use the system's routing tables. In tun mode, this is quite easy to achieve, but it is a little trickier when using tap mode. When `client1` wishes to reach `client2`, it will first need to know the MAC (hardware) address of `client2`. An ARP request is sent out over the client's tap adapter and reaches the OpenVPN server. The OpenVPN server process forwards the ARP request out of its own tap adapter and waits for the response. However, the response needs to come from *another* VPN client, which is connected to the same tap adapter. Thus, the ARP request needs to be sent back out to all connected clients by the OpenVPN server. Normally, this reissuing of the ARP request is not done and client-to-client traffic fails.

On modern Linux kernels (2.6.34+ or kernels with back-ported options), a special `proxy_arp_pvlan` flag can be set per interface. This flag instructs the Linux kernel to resend the ARP request back out of the same interface from where it came. It is exactly this flag that is needed for client-to-client traffic to work. Thus, we enable client-to-client traffic in tap mode without using the `client-to-client` option by setting this flag:

```
# echo 1 >  /proc/sys/net/ipv4/conf/tap0/proxy_arp_pvlan
```

This system flag can only be set after the `tap0` adapter has been set up. The tap adapter can be created prior to starting OpenVPN (see the *Bridging on Linux* section) or the flag can be set after OpenVPN has started. In that case, it can be set automatically using an `up` script, as explained in *Chapter 7, Scripting and Plugins*.

When `client1` wishes to reach `client2`, the flow of network traffic with this flag set is as follows:

1. `client1` sends an ARP request out its tap adapter.

2. The OpenVPN server receives the ARP request and forwards it out of its own `tap0` adapter.

3. The ARP request passes through the system routing and iptables forward table.

4. If the request is allowed through, the request is sent out to all network interfaces on the OpenVPN server, including the `tap0` adapter where it originated. The latter is caused by the `proxy_arp_pvlan` flag.

5. OpenVPN receives the ARP request and forwards it out to all connected OpenVPN clients.

6. `client2` receives the request and responds. An ARP reply is now sent back to the OpenVPN server.

7. The OpenVPN server forwards the ARP reply to `client1`.

8. `client1` now knows where to find `client2` and can send network traffic to `client2`.

The second step allows us to filter out traffic between different clients. Filtering rules (for example, using `iptables`) can be added to allow only certain types of traffic, or only traffic between special clients. For example, the following `iptables` rule will block traffic between the first and second OpenVPN client:

```
# iptables -I FORWARD -i tap0 -o tap0 \
    -s 10.222.0.2 -d 10.222.0.3 -j DROP
```

Note that by blocking traffic in one direction, both clients cannot reach each other. For unidirectional blocking, more advanced iptables rules are required.

 There does not seem to be an equivalent for the `proxy_arp_pvlan` flag on the Windows or Mac OS operating systems.

Disadvantage of the proxy_arp_pvlan method

A major disadvantage of using this special kernel flag is that it does not turn the VPN into a single Ethernet broadcast domain. With the `proxy_arp_pvlan` flag, the VPN clients can reach each other using ARP messages. However, they will not receive broadcast traffic coming from other clients. When the `client-to-client` option is used, all connected VPN clients automatically receive each other's broadcast messages, but filtering traffic is harder (as we will see in the next section).

Filtering traffic using the pf filter of OpenVPN

A second method to filter traffic from OpenVPN clients is to use OpenVPN's built-in `pf` filter. This filter is also fully supported in OpenVPN Access Server, the commercial offering from OpenVPN Technologies, Inc. The `pf` filter support is rudimentary compared to most firewalls, but is fully functional and supported on all platforms. We will now go through the steps to use this filter in the open source version of OpenVPN. This example is given only as a proof of concept; it will become clear that for a production-level service a different approach and/or tool is needed.

In order to use the `pf` filter, the management interface of OpenVPN must be used. This is achieved with the following configuration file:

```
proto udp
port 1194
dev tap
server 10.222.0.0 255.255.255.0

persist-key
persist-tun
keepalive 10 60

remote-cert-tls client
tls-auth /etc/openvpn/movpn/ta.key 0
dh       /etc/openvpn/movpn/dh2048.pem
ca       /etc/openvpn/movpn/movpn-ca.crt
cert     /etc/openvpn/movpn/server.crt
key      /etc/openvpn/movpn/server.key

user   nobody
group nobody

verb 3
daemon
log-append /var/log/openvpn.log

client-to-client
management 127.0.0.1 12000 stdin
management-client-auth
management-client-pf
```

Save this file as `movpn-06-02-server.conf` and start the OpenVPN server. The OpenVPN server will ask for a (new) management password. This password will be used to authenticate all connections to the management interface; VPN clients are authenticated separately. The `management-client-pf` option requires that the `management-client-auth` option is also set. The downside of this is that each client must now supply a (bogus) username and password, and that each client must be granted access on the server side, using the management interface.

The client configuration file now becomes:

```
proto udp
port 1194
dev tap

client
remote openvpnserver.example.com
nobind

remote-cert-tls server
tls-auth /etc/openvpn/movpn/ta.key 1
ca    /etc/openvpn/movpn/movpn-ca.crt
cert /etc/openvpn/movpn/client1.crt
key  /etc/openvpn/movpn/client1.key

auth-user-pass
```

Save it as `movpn-06-02-client.conf` (or `movpn-06-02-client.ovpn` for Windows).

On the server side, first start the management interface using `telnet`:

```
# telnet 127.0.0.1 12000
Trying 127.0.0.1...
Connected to 127.0.0.1.
Escape character is '^]'.
ENTER PASSWORD:
SUCCESS: password is correct
>INFO:OpenVPN Management Interface Version 1 -- type 'help' for more info
```

Next, start the OpenVPN client. The connection to the server will not be completed until the client is granted access via the management interface. In the management interface, you will now see this:

```
>CLIENT:CONNECT,0,0
>CLIENT:ENV,n_clients=0
>CLIENT:ENV,IV_VER=2.3.6
>CLIENT:ENV,IV_PLAT=linux
>CLIENT:ENV,IV_PROTO=2
[...]
```

After getting all the >CLIENT lines, authorize the client to connect. For this, the **Client Identifier (CID)** and **Key Identifier (KID)** are required. They are the parameters on the very first >CLIENT lines when the OpenVPN client connects. In this example, both CID and KID are 0. To grant this client access, the command client-auth-nt CID KID must be entered in the management interface:

```
client-auth-nt 0 0
SUCCESS: client-auth command succeeded
>CLIENT:ESTABLISHED,0CLIENT:CONNECT,0,0
```

The first OpenVPN client is now granted access. We can now apply access control rules to this client using the command client-pf CID. This is a multiline command. After the first line, we first specify the subnets that this client is allowed to access:

```
[SUBNETS ACCEPT]
-10.0.0.0/8
```

We grant the client access to all subnets *except* 10.0.0.0/8.

Next, we specify which clients this client is allowed to reach:

```
[CLIENTS ACCEPT]
-client3
```

We allow the client to contact all other VPN clients *except* the client with the certificate name /CN=client3. With the two END statements, one with brackets and one without, we close the client-pf command:

```
client-pf 0
[SUBNETS ACCEPT]
-10.0.0.0/8
[CLIENTS ACCEPT]
-client3
[END]
END
SUCCESS: client-pf command succeeded
```

This OpenVPN client will now be able to reach all subnets on the server side, except 10.0.0.0/8, and it is allowed to contact all other OpenVPN clients except client3.

There are many disadvantages to using this approach, but it does work on all platforms. The main disadvantages are as follows:

- Each client must supply a bogus username/password
- Each client must be authenticated using the management interface
- For each client, a `pf` filter must be set up
- The management interface currently does not have any commands to view the current filters

There is currently no tool for the open source version of OpenVPN to send these commands to the management interface. The commercial OpenVPN Access Server software, however, provides the needed mechanism to apply the filter rules.

Using the tap device (bridging)

A special use case for a tap-based configuration is bridging. The term bridging applies to a feature of the operating system to bridge two network adapters together. When two (or more) adapters are bridged, all Ethernet traffic that is received on one of the adapters is forwarded out to all other adapters that are part of that bridge. This makes it possible to join (bridge) two network segments together and make it appear as if it is a single Ethernet broadcast domain. Common use cases for bridges are as follows:

- The VPN clients need to be fully and transparently integrated into the server-side LAN. Note that the same effect can often be achieved using a `proxy-arp` setup.
- Some older computer games only allow multiuser games when all computers are part of the same broadcast domain.
- Some legacy network protocols, notably the original Microsoft NetBIOS (non-TCP/IP-based) protocol, do not work well across network routers, or even assume a fully "flat" network space with all clients connected directly.

Bridging has drawbacks too, most notably the loss of performance. *All* network traffic entering one of the bridge interfaces is replicated out through all other interfaces. Because of this, it is quite easy to overload a bridge with multicast or broadcast traffic. Especially in a VPN setup with clients using high-latency or low-bandwidth connections (for example, road warriors in a hotel), this performance loss can quickly make an OpenVPN setup unusable.

It should also be observed that a bridged setup is often not necessary. With modern operating systems and file sharing protocols, a tun-based setup can achieve the same results using less effort and with greater performance.

It is unfortunately still a common misconception that bridging is needed in order to use Windows file sharing over an OpenVPN setup. In the section *Enabling file sharing over VPN* of *Chapter 5, Advanced Deployment Scenarios in tun Mode*, a detailed explanation is given on how to achieve file sharing using a tun-based setup and a WINS server.

In some cases, a bridged setup remains desirable or necessary. We will now show how to set up a bridged OpenVPN configuration on both the Linux and Windows platforms.

Bridging on Linux

Consider the following network layout:

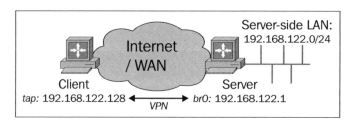

On the server side, a network bridge is used between the LAN adapter `eth0` and the OpenVPN virtual tap adapter. On Linux, this is achieved by creating the tap adapter prior to starting OpenVPN. For this, the system package `bridge-utils` needs to be installed. The steps are as follows:

1. First, we create a script to start the network bridge:

    ```
    #!/bin/bash

    br="br0"
    tap="tap0"
    eth="eth0"
    br_ip="192.168.122.1"
    br_netmask="255.255.255.0"
    ```

```
br_broadcast="192.168.122.255"
# Create the tap adapter
openvpn --mktun --dev $tap
# Create the bridge and add interfaces
brctl addbr $br
brctl addif $br $eth
brctl addif $br $tap
# Configure the bridge
ifconfig $tap 0.0.0.0 promisc up
ifconfig $eth 0.0.0.0 promisc up
ifconfig $br $br_ip netmask $br_netmask broadcast $br_broadcast
```

2. Save it as `movpn-bridge-start` and make sure it is executable using the following command:

   `# chmod 755 movpn-bridge-start`

3. Next, start the bridge using the following command:

   `# ./movpn-bridge-start`

   `Mon Jan 5 18:40:02 2015 TUN/TAP device tap0 opened`

   `Mon Jan 5 18:40:02 2015 Persist state set to: ON`

4. Now we create a configuration file for bridged setups using the following commands:

   ```
   tls-server
   proto udp
   port 1194

   dev tap0 ## the '0' is extremely important

   server-bridge 192.168.122.1 255.255.255.0 192.168.122.128
   192.168.122.200

   remote-cert-tls client
   tls-auth /etc/openvpn/movpn/ta.key 0
   dh       /etc/openvpn/movpn/dh2048.pem
   ca       /etc/openvpn/movpn/movpn-ca.crt
   cert     /etc/openvpn/movpn/server.crt
   key      /etc/openvpn/movpn/server.key

   persist-key
   persist-tun
   keepalive 10 60
   ```

```
user    nobody
group nobody

verb 3
daemon
log-append /var/log/openvpn.log
```

5. Save it as `movpn-06-03-server.conf`. The arguments to the `server-bridge` option are network gateway, subnet mask, pool start, and pool end. The pool addresses are those that can be assigned to clients.

> The line `dev tap0` in the preceding example is crucial for a bridged setup to work. We have created the tap adapter for the bridge prior to starting OpenVPN. In order to use this adapter, we must explicitly specify the name of the adapter. Otherwise, OpenVPN will create a new, non-bridged adapter at startup.

6. Start the OpenVPN server and connect the client using the `tap-udp-client. conf` configuration file created earlier in this chapter. On a Linux client, the connection log will show the following:

```
TUN/TAP device tap0 opened
do_ifconfig, tt->ipv6=0, tt->did_ifconfig_ipv6_setup=0
/sbin/ip link set dev tap0 up mtu 1500
/sbin/ip addr add dev tap0 192.168.122.128/24 broadcast
192.168.122.255
Initialization Sequence Completed
```

The client is assigned the first address, `192.168.122.128`, from the pool of available addresses.

7. Finally, we verify that we can reach a host on the server-side LAN:

```
[client]$ ping -c 4 192.168.122.246
PING 192.168.122.246 (192.168.122.246) 56(84) bytes of data.
64 bytes from 192.168.122.246: icmp_req=1 ttl=64 time=287 ms
64 bytes from 192.168.122.246: icmp_req=2 ttl=64 time=289 ms
64 bytes from 192.168.122.246: icmp_req=3 ttl=64 time=285 ms
64 bytes from 192.168.122.246: icmp_req=4 ttl=64 time=287 ms

--- 192.168.122.246 ping statistics ---
4 packets transmitted, 4 received, 0% packet loss, time 3003ms
rtt min/avg/max/mdev = 285.397/287.496/289.568/1.570 ms
```

Tearing down the bridge

When the OpenVPN server process is stopped, the network bridge is not automatically shut down as well. As the bridge was created before OpenVPN itself was started, the bridge persists until it is torn down manually. The following commands stop and remove the bridge created with the `movpn-start-bridge` command:

```
# ifconfig br0 down
# brctl delif br0 eth0
# brctl delif br0 tap0
# brctl delbr br0
# openvpn --rmtun --dev tap0
```

Bridging on Windows

Consider the following network layout:

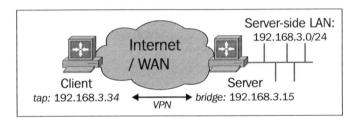

The only difference between the previous network layout and this one is the choice of IP addresses used.

On Windows, the OpenVPN TAP-Win adapter is installed when OpenVPN itself is installed. Usually, the name for the TAP-Win adapter is assigned by the operating system and will be something similar to Local Area Connection 4. Likewise, the name of the Ethernet adapter to which the local area network is attached will also have a name like Local Area Connection 2.

For clarity (and some sanity), we want to rename the VPN (TAP) interface:

1. First we go to the **Network and Sharing Center** and then **Change adapter settings**.

2. Rename the TAP-Win adapter as `tapbridge` by right-clicking on it and selecting **Rename**. On the test computer used, the Ethernet adapter connected to the LAN was renamed to `eth0`. In the **Status** column, note the network group to which the interface belongs. In our case, it belongs to **TheShire**.

3. Select the two adapters that need to be bridged by pressing the control key and clicking on each adapter, then right-clicking and selecting **Bridge Connections**.

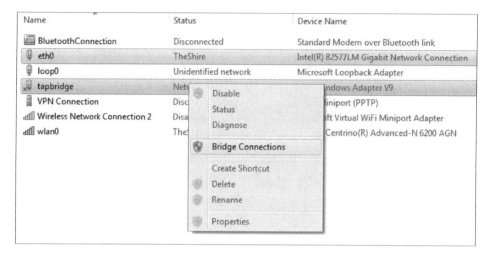

4. Ensure that the newly created **Network Bridge** is part of the same network as the original **eth0** adapter. You can also see that the original LAN adapter now has the label **Bridged** in the **Status** field:

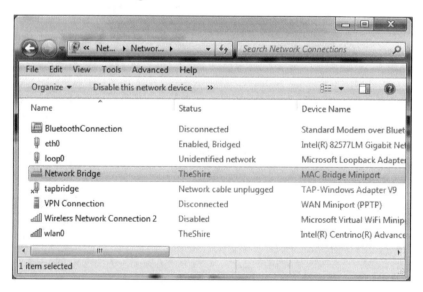

5. There is no need to configure a static IP address for the bridge. The **Network Bridge** has its own (virtual) MAC address (or **Physical Address** in the following screenshot) and hence is assigned its own IP address by the DHCP server on the server-side LAN:

6. Create the OpenVPN server configuration file using a text editor or Notepad:

```
tls-server
proto udp
port 1194

dev tap
dev-node tapbridge   ## == the name of the TAP-Win adapter

server-bridge 192.168.3.15 255.255.255.0 192.168.3.128
192.168.3.250

remote-cert-tls client
tls-auth "c://program files/openvpn/config/ta.key" 0
dh       "c://program files/openvpn/config/dh2048.pem"
ca       "c://program files/openvpn/config/movpn-ca.crt"
cert     "c://program files/openvpn/config/server.crt"
key      "c://program files/openvpn/config/server.key"

persist-key
```

```
persist-tun
keepalive 10 60

verb 3
```

Save the configuration file as `movpn-06-04-server.ovpn` in the OpenVPN configuration directory (usually `C:\Program Files\OpenVPN\config`).

 The server configuration file for the Windows version of OpenVPN is similar to the configuration file for Linux. The major differences are the full paths for the certificate and key files, plus the way the TAP-WIN adapter is specified using the keyword `dev` and `dev-node`. Also note that the `user`/`group` and `daemon`/`logging` options have been removed.

7. Start the OpenVPN server (using elevated privileges):

    ```
    C:> cd \program files\openvpn\config
    C:> ..\bin\openvpn --config movpn-06-04-server.ovpn
    ```

    Notice that the command-line version of OpenVPN on Windows looks and behaves almost exactly the same as the Linux command-line version.

8. The Windows firewall will pop up a security warning when OpenVPN attempts to set up the VPN. Click on **Allow Access** to grant OpenVPN permission to set up the VPN, as shown in the following screenshot:

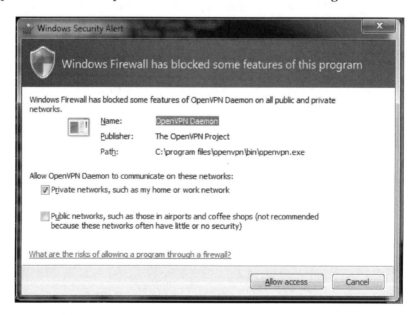

9. If we go back to the **Adapter Settings** screen now, we will see that both the LAN adapter **eth0** and the TAP-Win adapter **tapbridge** are **Enabled** and have the status **Bridged**. This is shown in the following screenshot:

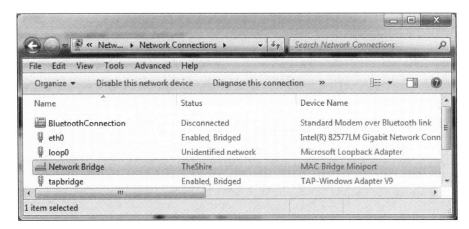

10. Next, connect a Windows client using the `tap-udp-client.ovpn` configuration file created earlier in this chapter. The client will be assigned the first address, `192.168.3.128`, from the pool of available addresses.

11. Finally, we verify that we can reach a host on the server-side LAN:

```
c:\>ping 192.168.3.1

Pinging 192.168.3.1 with 32 bytes of data:
Reply from 192.168.3.1: bytes=32 time=8ms TTL=64
Reply from 192.168.3.1: bytes=32 time=1ms TTL=64
Reply from 192.168.3.1: bytes=32 time=1ms TTL=64
Reply from 192.168.3.1: bytes=32 time=1ms TTL=64

Ping statistics for 192.168.3.1:
    Packets: Sent = 4, Received = 4, Lost = 0 (0% loss),
Approximate round trip times in milli-seconds:
    Minimum = 1ms, Maximum = 8ms, Average = 2ms
```

12. On the server, press the *F4* function key in the command window to stop the OpenVPN server process. For a production-level setup, it is desirable to start and stop OpenVPN using the OpenVPN service that is installed along with OpenVPN.

Using an external DHCP server

In a bridged setup, it is possible to integrate the clients into the server-side network even further. In most networks, a DHCP server is used to assign IP addresses. Normally, OpenVPN assigns IP addresses to its clients using either the following command:

```
server 10.200.0.0 255.255.255.0
```

Or, using the following command:

```
server-bridge 192.168.3.15 255.255.255.0 192.168.3.128 192.168.3.250
```

It is also possible to use an external DHCP server to assign addresses to the OpenVPN clients. To achieve this, simply remove the specification of any IP address ranges after the server-bridge option, as shown in the following (Linux-oriented) configuration file:

```
tls-server
proto udp
port 1194

dev tap0 ## the '0' is extremely important

server-bridge

remote-cert-tls client
tls-auth  /etc/openvpn/movpn/ta.key 0
dh        /etc/openvpn/movpn/dh2048.pem
ca        /etc/openvpn/movpn/movpn-ca.crt
cert      /etc/openvpn/movpn/server.crt
key       /etc/openvpn/movpn/server.key

persist-key
persist-tun
keepalive 10 60

user   nobody
group  nobody

verb 3
daemon
log-append /var/log/openvpn.log
```

Save it as `movpn-06-05-server.conf` and start the OpenVPN server.

When a client connects and requests an IP address using DHCP, the request will be forwarded to the DHCP server on the server-side LAN. The DHCP server assigns an address, which is sent back to the client via the OpenVPN server.

On the OpenVPN client, this can be verified by checking the IP address of the `vpn0` connection:

To verify that this address was assigned by the server-side DHCP server, we check the DHCP clients table on the DHCP server:

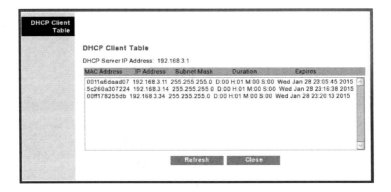

The third entry in the **DHCP Client Table** in the preceding screenshot lists the **MAC Address** of the TAP-Win adapter of the OpenVPN client. This proves that the server-side DHCP server assigned the address to the OpenVPN client.

Checking broadcast and non-IP traffic

The tcpdump and wireshark tools are useful for troubleshooting an "almost-working" OpenVPN setup. Wireshark is available for Linux, Mac OS X, and Windows. It can be used as a command-line tool but most often the GUI-based version is used. On most Unix/Linux-based platforms, the command-line tool tcpdump is also available.

We will now use tcpdump and wireshark to view the flow of packets over a tap-based VPN setup.

Address Resolution Protocol traffic

One of the most basic types of Ethernet traffic present on all networks is **Address Resolution Protocol (ARP)** traffic. ARP is a prime example of an Ethernet protocol that does not travel across point-to-point links (such as tun-based OpenVPN setups). The physical layer (layer 1) is generally an electrical or optical connection between systems. In the case of a VPN, the tunnel takes the place of that physical connection. The next step in the OSI model is the Ethernet layer (layer 2). The ARP protocol is often used to discover other systems at this layer.

> Ethernet is a layer 2 network protocol, whereas a point-to-point link is a layer 3 network protocol. The various protocol layers are defined by the **Open Systems Interconnection (OSI)** model (https://en.wikipedia.org/wiki/OSI_model).

To watch the flow of ARP traffic, we first launch an OpenVPN server using the configuration file movpn-06-01-server.conf created earlier. We then connect two Linux clients to the server. After all connections have been successfully established, we start tcpdump on one of the clients:

```
# tcpdump -nnel -i tap0
```

Now we send a single `ping` packet from one client to the other and look at the `tcpdump` output:

```
⬤ ⬤ ⬤                 ecrist@honeybadger — csh — 76×24
tcpdump: verbose output suppressed, use -v or -vv for full protocol decode
listening on tap0, link-type EN10MB (Ethernet), capture size 65535 bytes
20:00:53.216803 de:c4:8d:29:a4:ee > ff:ff:ff:ff:ff:ff, ethertype ARP (0x0806
), length 42: Request who-has 10.200.0.11 tell 10.200.0.10, length 28
20:00:53.251952 00:bd:48:d9:dc:00 > de:c4:8d:29:a4:ee, ethertype ARP (0x0806
), length 42: Reply 10.200.0.11 is-at 00:bd:48:d9:dc:00, length 28
20:00:53.251995 de:c4:8d:29:a4:ee > 00:bd:48:d9:dc:00, ethertype IPv4 (0x080
0), length 98: 10.200.0.10 > 10.200.0.11: ICMP echo request, id 54985, seq 0
, length 64
20:00:53.287295 00:bd:48:d9:dc:00 > de:c4:8d:29:a4:ee, ethertype IPv4 (0x080
0), length 98: 10.200.0.11 > 10.200.0.10: ICMP echo reply, id 54985, seq 0,
length 64
20:00:54.221075 de:c4:8d:29:a4:ee > 00:bd:48:d9:dc:00, ethertype IPv4 (0x080
0), length 98: 10.200.0.10 > 10.200.0.11: ICMP echo request, id 54985, seq 1
, length 64
20:00:54.257353 00:bd:48:d9:dc:00 > de:c4:8d:29:a4:ee, ethertype IPv4 (0x080
0), length 98: 10.200.0.11 > 10.200.0.10: ICMP echo reply, id 54985, seq 1,
length 64
20:00:55.223086 de:c4:8d:29:a4:ee > 00:bd:48:d9:dc:00, ethertype IPv4 (0x080
0), length 98: 10.200.0.10 > 10.200.0.11: ICMP echo request, id 54985, seq 2
, length 64
20:00:55.258556 00:bd:48:d9:dc:00 > de:c4:8d:29:a4:ee, ethertype IPv4 (0x080
0), length 98: 10.200.0.11 > 10.200.0.10: ICMP echo reply, id 54985, seq 2,
length 64
```

The screenshot shows the ARP traffic between `client1` (10.200.0.10 in this case) and `client2` (10.200.0.11).

- The first packet in the output above is from the client from which the `ping` was initiated. The client needs to know the Ethernet MAC address of the machine we are pinging and hence it sends out an ARP request.

- Because we specified `client-to-client` in the server configuration file `movpn-06-01-server.conf`, the ARP request is forwarded out to all connected clients and the second OpenVPN client responds with its MAC address.

- The second packet is the reply from the second client indicating its own MAC address.

- Now that the address is known, `client1` sends the `ping`. This is captured as an `IPv4 ICMP echo request`.

- An answer is received from the second client. This is the fourth packet (`IPv4 ICMP echo reply`).

NetBIOS traffic

Common Internet File Sharing (CIFS) started out as a proprietary protocol, NetBEUI. Support for sharing files and printers was over Novell's **Internetwork Packet eXchange (IPX)** protocol, and later TCP/IP was added. Nowadays, the Windows file sharing protocol has evolved and is supported only via TCP/IP. Support for the legacy file protocols is still present in older versions of Windows and it is this legacy support which we will use to trigger non-IP traffic.

First we install and enable the NWLink IPX/SPX transport protocol on the TAP-WIN adapter. Then we connect the Windows client to an OpenVPN setup that was launched using the configuration file `movpn-06-01-server.conf`. This configuration has `client-to-client` enabled; thus all connected clients should see all Ethernet broadcast traffic coming from this client.

When the Windows client has successfully connected to the VPN server it will start sending out traffic to announce its name and other Windows file sharing information. It will attempt to do this over TCP/IP, but also using IPX messages.

We use Wireshark on a second VPN client and watch for traffic on the tap interface. The next screenshot shows that the Windows client WINDOWSXP is indeed sending out broadcast NetBIOS traffic over TCP/IP. These are the entries with source address 10.222.0.3 and destination address 10.222.0.255. The latter address is the TCP/IP broadcast address for the VPN we have set up. We also see traffic being broadcast using the IPX protocol. This traffic is selected and highlighted in the screenshot:

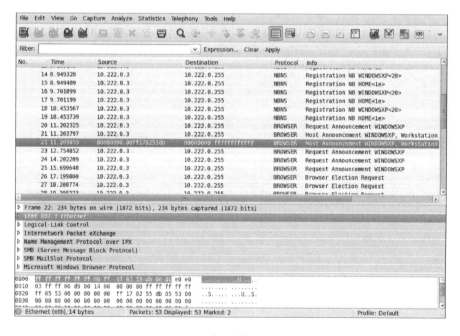

The IPX broadcast messages are *Ethernet* broadcast messages, but they are non-IP-based. This shows that a tap-style OpenVPN setup with `client-to-client` does share all Ethernet traffic, including broadcast traffic, between the connected clients (and the OpenVPN server itself).

Comparing tun mode to tap mode

As we have seen so far in this chapter, there are many similarities, but also some significant differences between a tun-style VPN and a tap-style VPN. In this section, we will discuss those similarities and differences. Most of the differences stem from the single fact that a tun-style VPN is a non-broadcast, point-to-point IP-only network, whereas a tap-style network provides a fully virtual, Ethernet-like network with broadcast support. In short, a tun-style network provides layer 3 network connectivity, whereas a tap-style network provides almost all the functionality of a layer 2 network.

Especially with the `topology subnet` option, a tun-based setup resembles a non-bridged tap-based setup:

- The option `server 10.200.0.0 255.255.255.0` sets up a VPN with a server address of 10.200.1/24. Each client will receive a single /24 IP address, starting at 10.200.0.2/24.
- The way the VPN traffic is encrypted and digitally signed (HMAC) is identical.
- Most scripting capabilities apply to both types of VPN. However, there are some subtle differences in the parameters for the `client-connect` script.
- When properly configured, an end user will not experience any difference between a tun-based setup and a tap-based VPN.

The differences are, of course, much more interesting to discuss. Some differences are obvious, but there are also some subtle differences that can have a major impact when setting up a VPN.

Layer 2 versus layer 3

In a layer 2 network (that is, tap-style), neighboring clients can reach each other by probing the address of a neighbor using ARP broadcasts. The ARP broadcasts allow the clients to discover the MAC address of the other clients. This allows the clients to reach each other over both IP and non-IP protocols.

In a layer 3 network (tun-style), the clients can reach each other only by using IP addresses. The MAC address of the tun adapter is never revealed to the other VPN clients or even to the OpenVPN server itself. Because of this, a layer 3 network packet is slightly shorter than a layer 2 network packet. Under normal circumstances, the longer layer 2 network packets will not have a negative impact on performance.

Routing differences and iroute

Especially when subnet-to-subnet routing is needed, there are some significant differences between tun and tap. In a tun-style network, a client configuration file with an appropriate `iroute` statement is needed to allow the VPN server to reach clients residing on a client-side LAN. As an example, we assume that subnet 192.168.3.0/24 can be reached via the OpenVPN client with the certificate `CN=client1`. On the OpenVPN server, we would add a `client-config-dir` file with the name `client1` containing a statement:

```
iroute 192.168.3.0 255.255.255.0
```

We would add a system route to the server configuration file:

```
route 192.168.3.0 255.255.255.0
```

In a tap-style setup, the `iroute` statement is not valid and will simply be ignored by the server. In order to reach a subnet *behind* a VPN client, a system route must be added on the OpenVPN server with the gateway pointing to the VPN IP address of the client. Let's assume that `client1` from the preceding example is assigned a fixed IP address. This can be achieved using a CCD file:

```
ifconfig-push 10.200.0.99 255.255.255.0
```

In the server configuration file, a route needs to be added to ensure that the system routing tables know that subnet 192.168.3.0/24 can be reached via client 10.200.0.99:

```
route 192.168.3.0 255.255.255.0 10.200.0.99
```

This is far less dynamic than the tun-style `route+iroute` option.

Client-to-client filtering

In a tun-style setup, most traffic can be logged and filtered using firewall or iptables rules. Filtering traffic between OpenVPN clients is much harder to do in a tap-style setup, as was demonstrated earlier in this chapter.

Broadcast traffic and "chattiness" of the network

A layer 3 network does not allow broadcast traffic to be passed over it. This is both an advantage and a disadvantage. Some client/server applications rely on the use of broadcast traffic to communicate between the server and the clients. For such applications, a tap-style network is required.

However, broadcast traffic tends to pollute networks as well. Even if there is no user activity on a client, the operating system will continually send broadcast traffic to discover network resources, neighbors, and so forth. Especially when protocols such as Universal Plug-and-Play or Apple's Bonjour are used, there is a lot of *hidden* broadcast traffic. For clients connected to a VPN over a low-bandwidth network, this can have serious performance implications.

Bridging

The key feature of a tap-style network is the ability to do bridging. Bridging is not possible in a layer 3 network.

In some rare cases, this feature is absolutely required, but a bridged setup should be avoided whenever possible. The main reason for not using a bridged setup is the negative impact on performance. As explained earlier, in a bridged setup *all* traffic from the server-side LAN is forwarded out over the VPN to *all* clients, and vice versa. When many clients are connected over low-bandwidth networks, this can cause the entire network to come to a crawl, on both the client side and even on the server-side LAN. When clients on the server-side LAN are attempting to discover the available resources on the network (for example, file shares or printers in a CIFS-based network), the entire network will be filled with broadcast traffic. The LAN clients will typically wait for responses from all machines connected to the network, both LAN and VPN, before offering access to network shares or printers. This can quickly lead to unacceptable network response times when many VPN clients are connecting and disconnecting.

Summary

In this chapter, we explored the capabilities of a tap-based setup as an alternative deployment model for OpenVPN. We discussed examples highlighting both features and disadvantages of such a setup. Special attention was given to bridged setups, as there are some common misconceptions about bridged mode, as found on OpenVPN Internet support forums.

We also saw that advanced management features, such as filtering traffic between OpenVPN clients, are much harder to achieve in tap mode compared to tun mode.

In the next chapter, we will see how we can use scripts and plugins to influence the way in which an OpenVPN server assigns an IP address to a client, as well as many other features. Scripts and plugins can be used in tap mode as well as tun mode.

7
Scripting and Plugins

Once deployed, a personal or enterprise VPN can be a powerful tool both with regard to security as well as functionality. A well-engineered VPN will allow users to connect to distant resources securely. Sometimes, however, just having a VPN isn't quite enough. A given application may mandate more strict security standards or require better monitoring and control.

Integrating plugins and scripting with OpenVPN can resolve many of these organizational or functional necessities. This chapter will demonstrate how plugins can be used to enhance authentication and how scripting can track connections, generate routing tables, and do much more.

Scripting

Scripting is likely one of the best tools available to an OpenVPN administrator. With the ability to designate both client-side and server-side scripts, OpenVPN can initiate other system responses by opening firewalls, running applications, or even sending a message to an administrator.

One important caveat when writing scripts is the time it takes for a script to complete. OpenVPN is a single-threaded process, which means that while a script is running the entire VPN is blocked to all connected or connecting clients. A slow authentication script can cripple a well-functioning VPN. Plugins are less affected by this, as they do run in a separate thread.

As of Version 2.3.6, OpenVPN supports 13 server-side scripting options and 10 client-side options. The commands with asterisks are setup options, and allow the options that follow to do specific things. The server-side scripts are as follows (in the order of execution):

- `--setenv*`
- `--setenv-safe*`
- `--script-security*`
- `--up-restart*`
- `--up`
- `--route-up`
- `--tls-verify`
- `--auth-user-pass-verify`
- `--client-connect`
- `--learn-address`
- `--client-disconnect`
- `--route-pre-down`
- `--down`

On the client side, the scripts are as follows (in the order of execution):

- `--setenv*`
- `--script-security*`
- `--up-restart*`
- `--tls-verify`
- `--ipchange`
- `--setenv-safe*`
- `--up`
- `--route-up`
- `--route-pre-down`
- `--down`

We will now go through all of these options in brief, explaining their function on both the server side and the client side. Later in this chapter, we will provide a detailed example and discuss the behavior and subtleties of each of these scripts.

Server-side scripts

Let's have a look at the scripts used on the server side.

--setenv and --setenv-safe

The setenv and setenv-safe options are used to set environment variables that can be used by both scripts and plugins. The setenv option allows us to set almost any environment variables, but this option cannot be "pushed" to clients. The setenv-safe option prepends each environment variable with the prefix OPENVPN_, avoiding clashes with system environment variables such as PATH and LD_LIBRARY_PATH. This option can be pushed to clients, allowing for great flexibility.

--script-security

The script-security option determines what types of applications or scripts can be executed from the OpenVPN configuration. There are four options for the security level:

- **0**: This means no external scripts or programs will be allowed. On a Linux/Unix machine, this causes OpenVPN to not function, as OpenVPN always needs to run some external commands to set the IP address. On Windows clients, however, you can OpenVPN in this mode, provided that the default gateway is not altered. For that, an external application needs to be called.

- **1**: This means certain built-in executables are allowed, for example, ip, route, ifconfig, and others. This is the default.

- **2**: This is the most commonly required security level. This allows not only the built-in commands like those listed in the preceding point, but also user-defined scripts.

- **3**: This allows passwords to be passed to the called scripts via environment variables. This could be unsafe, but is useful for certain authentication scripts or even password change operations.

--up-restart

The up-restart option is simply a flag that can be set. If this flag is set, then both the down and up scripts are called (in that order) whenever OpenVPN restarts.

--up

The up script is the first script executed after OpenVPN has performed its initial initialization. Normally, this script is run right after OpenVPN has bound itself to the configured network port and tap TUN or TAP device has been opened. At this point in the startup process, no clients are connected to the server and authorization has not yet taken place. Some folks use up scripts to initialize proxy servers and/or firewall rulesets.

--route-up

After the TUN or TAP device has been opened, the route-up script is executed to setup any system routes on the server side.

--tls-verify

Whenever a client connects to the server, the first script that will be executed on both client and server is the tls-verify script. This script is called several times, once for each certificate that the client presents to the server. At this point, the remote peer is still considered untrusted. This can be used to verify client or server certificate information prior to authentication. If the tls-verify script returns a nonzero exit code the client connection is rejected.

--auth-user-pass-verify

Beyond relatively simply SSL certificate client authentication, OpenVPN supports a rather robust set of tools for username and password authentication. This argument takes two arguments, the command, and its method. The method defines how OpenVPN passes the authentication credentials to the command. The method can be either via-env or via-file. In order to use the via-env option, the script-security option will need to be set to three (3) to support this. If the auth-user-pass-verify script returns a nonzero exit code, the client connection is rejected.

It is important to know that the auth-user-pass-verify script is also executed whenever a client has restarted or needs to renegotiate security parameters with the server. Renegotiation of the security keys normally happens every hour, but can be controlled using the reneg-sec, reneg-pkts, and reneg-bytes options.

--client-connect

This is executed once a client has been authenticated to the VPN server. Most scripts in the wild generally run here. The client-connect script is passed a single argument, which is the name of a temporary file. After the script has finished, the file is processed by OpenVPN and all contents are parsed as extra configuration options. This allows an administrator to add special settings to a particular client, allowing for more flexibility than a CCD file. One of our examples in this chapter utilizes a client-connect script to update a database used to track and trend VPN connection statistics.

--learn-address

The learn-address script allows OpenVPN to help define firewall rules and other address-specific options. It is executed whenever a new client is added, updated, or deleted from OpenVPN's internal address tables. More detailed information is available in the man page. This option supports both IPv4 and IPv6. The learn-address script is actually called separately for IPv4 and IPv6 addresses, once with the IPv4 address as the primary parameter and once with the IPv6 address.

--client-disconnect

As with the client-connect script in the preceding section, the client-disconnect script is the second most commonly used scripting juncture. As mentioned previously, in one of the examples in this chapter, a client-disconnect script will be used to update database records with usage statistics and other information.

--route-pre-down

Once a tunnel shutdown has begun, the route-pre-down script is run. This could be used to automate the shutdown of remote proxy servers, and to close holes in the firewall that were open/established earlier in an --up script.

--down

Inverse to the up option, the down option runs a command after the TUN/TAP device closes. This option takes a command or script as an argument, with additional arguments being passed to the script or command. If you need to run a command before the TUN/TAP device closes, you can use the down-pre option instead.

There is no method to run a script both before and after the TUN/TAP device closes.

Client-side scripts

We will discuss the client-side scripts in this section.

--setenv and --setenv-safe

This is exactly the same as in the preceding *Server-side scripts* section.

--script-security

This is also exactly the same as in the preceding *Server-side scripts* section.

--up-restart

The up-restart option is simply a flag that can be set. If this flag is set, then both the down and up scripts are called (in that order) whenever OpenVPN restarts.

--tls-verify

Whenever a client connects to the server, the first script that will be executed on both client and server is the tls-verify script. This script is called several times, once for each certificate that the server presents to the client. At this point, the remote peer is still considered untrusted. This can be used to verify client or server certificate information prior to authentication. If the tls-verify script returns a nonzero exit code the client connection is rejected.

--ipchange

On the client side, the ipchange script is executed after tls-verify as well as any time the remote (also known as trusted) IP address changes. This can be used to update firewall rules or a proxy server, prior to opening the TUN/TAP adapter.

--up

The up script is the first script that is executed after the client authentication has completed. After the server has successfully authenticated the client, a set of configuration parameters is sent to the client. These parameters include the VPN IP address to use, as well as any other options that are pushed to the client. Some folks use up scripts to initialize proxy servers and/or firewall rulesets.

--route-up

Once authenticated and routes have been established, the `route-up` script is executed. Optionally, this script can be delayed a given number of seconds with the `route-delay` option.

--route-pre-down

Once a tunnel shutdown has begun, the `route-pre-down` script is run. This could be used to close connections to remote proxy servers, other tunnels (SSH) or correct DNS server entries.

--down

Inverse to the `up` option, the `down` option runs a command after the TUN/TAP device closes. This option takes a command or script as an argument, with additional arguments being passed to the script or command. If you need to run a command before the TUN/TAP device closes, you can use the `down-pre` option instead.

 There is no method to run a script both before and after the TUN/TAP device closes.

Examples of server scripts

Server scripting can be used to greatly enhance your OpenVPN deployment. Scripts can be used for authentication, authorization, logging, and more. Coupled with `client-config` options, scripts can be further utilized to generate on-the-fly client configuration directives. For example, authentication can happen via LDAP and authorization rules can be dynamic through that same LDAP directory. Firewall rules can be generated and applied, and the routes can be passed to the client. This section will demonstrate a little of all of these things to aid you in applying those methods.

The most common server-side scripts are the `--client-connect` and `--client-disconnect` scripts. These scripts can be used for many things, including opening firewall rulesets, mounting file systems, and even building client configuration files on the fly.

Coupled with a task scheduler, other scripts can be run outside the direct context of OpenVPN, but can still act on connected clients via the OpenVPN management interface. For example, an administrator can provide allotted time to end users and disconnect users after that allotted time has been exhausted.

Client-connect scripts

Let's now look at the `client-connect` scripts.

Client authentication

Authentication is the definition of who is able to connect. This does not define what those users can do, simply whether they are allowed to connect to the VPN or not. At the most basic level, it is entirely possible to allow a user to connect, but not enable that user to actually do anything. One use for this could be a monitoring script that simply wants to verify your VPN server is running and authenticating users. This pseudo-user shouldn't have the ability to route traffic, since there's no need.

Many variables and authorities can be examined with authentication scripts including smart cards, LDAP or RADIUS servers, certificate information, certificate revocation lists, and more. If you've read this book from the beginning, in *Chapter 5, Advanced Deployment Scenarios in tun Mode*, you should have built a VPN server configuration that already uses LDAP and other backends. With scripting, you can extend support for those backends without a current plugin or you can query additional sources.

The most common server-side script is arguably the `--client-connect` script. This script is executed after all the TLS verification has taken place. In cases where the client-connect script has much to do, this is ideal to prevent a type of **Denial of Server (DoS)** attack caused by your own scripting. Before this script is run, the client has been verified as potentially having the proper `tls-auth` key and a valid certificate. The `client-connect` script can be used as a sort of pre-authentication, as it's executed before the `--auth-user-pass-verify` script. It can also be utilized to dynamically generate a client config.

When using a script, ensure that you have `--script-security` set to 2 or 3 (see definitions earlier in this chapter). Failure to present this option will return an AUTH_FAIL message to clients. As an example, we've created a very simple script that prints the shell environment and exits with zero (0), indicating success to the OpenVPN daemon. In our server configuration, we've added the following two directives:

```
script-security 2
client-connect /usr/local/etc/openvpn/cc.sh
```

There is an environment variable `script_type` that defines the type of script being called. Using this variable, it's possible to have a single, monolithic script to handle all OpenVPN scripting calls.

Here's our example `client-connect` script:

```
#!/bin/sh

printenv > /tmp/movpn
exit 0
```

The exit code is important as anything other than a zero (0) will result in the client being disconnected. With the preceding script and configuration, when there is a new client connection, our script will be executed. This script allows the connection but prints the shell environment to a temporary file. The contents of this file are interesting and will apply to all other scripts:

```
daemon_start_time=1425344172
daemon_pid=4004
local_1=SERVER_IP
trusted_ip=CLIENT_IP
redirect_gateway=0
untrusted_port=1194
tun_mtu=1500
X509_0_ST=Enlightenment
X509_0_CN=client1
X509_0_emailAddress=root@example.org
time_ascii=Mon Mar  2 18:56:17 2015
proto_1=udp
X509_1_emailAddress=root@example.org
tls_id_0=C=ZA, ST=Enlightenment, O=Mastering OpenVPN, CN=client1,
emailAddress=root@example.org
tls_id_1=C=ZA, ST=Enlightenment, L=Overall, O=Mastering OpenVPN,
CN=Mastering OpenVPN, emailAddress=root@example.org
ifconfig_ipv6_local=2001:db8:100::1
untrusted_ip=CLIENT_IP
daemon=1
tls_serial_hex_0=02
trusted_port=1194
dev_type=tun
tls_serial_hex_1=d2:93:32:f0:8e:bc:58:ee
X509_1_ST=Enlightenment
X509_1_CN=Mastering OpenVPN
script_context=init
tls_serial_0=2
PWD=/usr/local/etc/openvpn
daemon_log_redirect=1
tls_serial_1=15173527578309581038
```

```
ifconfig_local=10.200.0.1
dev=tun0
local_port_1=1194
time_unix=1425344177
link_mtu=1541
remote_port_1=1194
X509_0_C=ZA
tls_digest_0=1b:27:a6:b4:5f:7a:9c:3f:17:fb:ff:33:05:61:3f:2a:56:89:16
:d3
tls_digest_1=e4:f1:43:37:34:51:de:99:7a:dc:e3:6d:f2:4c:5b:84:34:4b
:f3:64
script_type=client-connect
X509_1_C=ZA
ifconfig_broadcast=10.200.0.255
ifconfig_pool_remote_ip=10.200.0.2
ifconfig_ipv6_remote=2001:db8:100::2
ifconfig_ipv6_netbits=64
ifconfig_netmask=255.255.255.0
config=/usr/local/etc/openvpn/openvpn.conf
ifconfig_pool_netmask=255.255.255.0
X509_0_O=Mastering OpenVPN
X509_1_L=Overall
verb=4
common_name=client1
X509_1_O=Mastering OpenVPN
```

Using these environment variables, a savvy OpenVPN administrator can customize the configuration in a seemingly simple server setup.

Client authorization

Authorization can occur in a few places, including the `client-config-dir` file, or additions can be made via the `client-connect` script.

> Authentication is proving who you are. Authorization is determining what you are allowed to do.

The first argument passed to the `client-connect` script will be a path to a temporary file that the script can use to pass configuration options for the connecting client to the OpenVPN daemon. This script checks the `common_name` environment variable and if it is `client1`, sets disabled in the client configuration:

```
#!/bin/sh

if [ "$common_name" = "client1" ];
```

```
then
        echo "disable" >> $1
fi

exit 0
```

When `client1` connects, the disable option will be passed to the server, preventing the connection from continuing. Other options can be passed, such as `ifconfig` for static IP addresses, pushing different routes, and more.

Example 1—client-selected routes

Consider a network administrator with two data centers, each with their own pair of OpenVPN servers. There was an occasion where it was necessary to work with one data center while ensuring that if the other was inaccessible, services and systems were still available at the functioning data center.

To aid in testing this, we created some scripts (`client-connect` and `auth-user-pass-verify`) to select which routes were passed to the client.

The following diagram should provide a rough idea of the concept. The VPN client has three configuration options to choose from, full routes (full), routes for **Data Center 1** (dc1), and routes for **Data Center 2** (dc2). Further, the client can connect to either data center and get just the needed routes for any of those three.

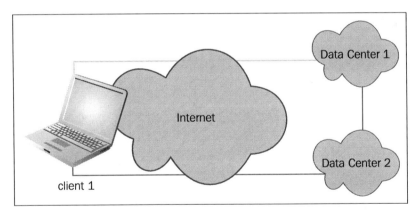

In our scheme, `client1` connects to a data center and will be prompted for their username and password. In reality, we're ignoring the password and reading the username to determine the routes desired.

To capture the route selection, we made use of the `auth-user-pass-verify` script. OpenVPN takes two arguments, a script path and either `via-file` or `via-env` to determine how to pass the credentials to the script. In this example, we selected `via-file`.

The script reads the credentials in from the script and rewrites it to a file that will be accessible by the `client-connect` script:

```
#!/bin/sh
echo 'head -n1 $1' > \
/tmp/openvpn-${untrusted_ip}-${untrusted_port}.tmp
exit 0
```

Next, our `client-connect` script is run and it reads the `.tmp` file created previously. Based on the argument read, it writes the route selection out to the file passed to `client-connect` for configuration arguments:

```
#!/bin/sh
creds="/tmp/openvpn-${untrusted_ip}-${untrusted_port}.tmp"

if [ -f "$creds" ];
then
  selected='head -n1 $creds'
  if [ "$selected" = "dc1" ];
  then
    cat >> $1 <<- EOF
      push "route 10.10.0.0 255.255.255.0"
      push "route 10.10.1.0 255.255.255.0"
    EOF
  elif [ "$selected" = "dc2" ];
then
  cat >> $1 <<- EOF
    push "route 10.20.0.0 255.255.255.0"
    push "route 10.20.1.0 255.255.255.0"
  EOF
else
  cat >> $1 <<- EOF
      push "route 10.10.0.0 255.255.255.0"
      push "route 10.10.1.0 255.255.255.0"
      push "route 10.20.0.0 255.255.255.0"
      push "route 10.20.1.0 255.255.255.0"
    EOF
  fi
fi
exit 0
```

Although this isn't ideal and it's possible to attack this in many ways, it allowed us to have a single OpenVPN configuration for each of the system administrators and gave them some level of dynamic routing based on their tasks.

Example 2—track client connection statistics

Using `client-connect` and `client-disconnect` scripts, it's possible to write client connection statistics to a database or other place. For this example, we just want to track when users connect and how much time they spend connected to the VPN server.

We are assuming you are at least familiar with SQL and so will not focus on the semantics. SQLite 3 is used in the following example to store session information. The schema for our example database is as follows:

```
CREATE TABLE vpn_session (
  session_id  integer   primary key autoincrement not null,
  cn     test      not null,
  connect_time   timestamp   default CURRENT_TIMESTAMP,
  disconnect_time timestamp   default null,
  vpn_ip4    char(15),
  vpn_ip6    char(40),
  remote_ip4    char(40),
  connection_time integer default 0
);
```

The schema can be loaded into a database with the following command:

ecrist@example:~-> sqlite3 movpn.sqlite3 < file.schema

> The directory and file you use for SQLite needs to be readable and writeable by the OpenVPN user. If you have --user or --group defined in your configuration file, that user will need this access. Without it, your `client-connect` and `client-disconnect` scripts will be unable to update the database.

This time, we are going to create a script that will be called for both `client-connect` as well as `client-disconnect`. We will detect and handle the script type within the code. For the `client-connect` type, we are going to insert a new record for the new session. For `client-disconnect`, we will update that record to provide further accounting.

The code is as follows:

```sh
#!/bin/sh

DBFILE="/var/openvpn/movpn.sqlite3"
DBBUFFER="/var/openvpn/buffer.sql"

db_query (){
  SQL="$1"
  /usr/local/bin/sqlite3 $DBFILE "$SQL"
  if [ $? -ne 0 ];
  then
    # There was an error, write the SQL out to a buffer file
    echo "$SQL" | tr -d "\t" | tr -d "\n" | tee -a $DBBUFFER
    echo ";" | tee -a $DBBUFFER
  fi

}

logger "OpenVPN Type: $script_type"
case "$script_type" in
  client-connect)
    # do record insert
    logger "OpenVPN: client-connect"
    SQL="
      INSERT INTO vpn_session (
        cn, connect_time, vpn_ip4,
        vpn_ip6, remote_ip4
      ) VALUES (
        '$common_name', '$time_unix',
        '$ifconfig_pool_remote_ip',
'$ipconfig_ipv6_remote',
        '$untrusted_ip'
      )"
    db_query "$SQL"
    ;;
  client-disconnect)
    # update the record, if it's found
    logger "OpenVPN: client-disconnect"
    SQL="
      UPDATE
```

```
          vpn_session
      SET
          disconnect_time = '$time_unix'
      WHERE
          cn = '$common_name'
          AND disconnect_time IS NULL
          AND session_id = (
             SELECT MAX(session_id)
             FROM vpn_session
             WHERE cn = '$common_name'
             )
      "
      db_query "$SQL"
      ;;
  esac


  exit 0
```

This script makes use of the switch case function to determine what the script type is and behave accordingly. On a new client connection, it will update a database table with connection information and update that database record when the client disconnects. The schema we used here is fairly simple and could easily be extended to support tracking bandwidth usage and multiple client connections.

Using the `sqlite3` command, we can pull the three most recent database entries:

```
ecrist@example:/usr/local/etc/openvpn-> sqlite3 /var/openvpn/movpn.
sqlite3 "SELECT * FROM vpn_session ORDER BY session_id DESC LIMIT 3"
10|client1|1426430834||10.200.0.2||CLIENT_IP|
9|client1|1426430759|1426430759|10.200.0.2||CLIENT_IP|0
8|client1|1426429888|1426429888|10.200.0.2||CLIENT_IP|0
```

Example 3—disconnect user after X minutes

There are a number of ways to handle this scenario. If you provide users a short amount of access, say 30 minutes at a time, a `client-connect` script with a simple sleep can accomplish the disconnect and account lockout. Let's say you sell short, one-time VPN sessions of up to 30 minutes. In this scenario, after the user has reached their 30 minutes of use, a `cron` job will disconnect the user and lock their account using the CCD directory entry.

This example is going to build a bit on the previous one, using the SQLite database we created to track time used. Our script will have a few tasks:

- Calculate VPN connection time used
- Lock out user after allotted connection time
- Disconnect client if currently connected

To accomplish the preceding tasks, we will write a small shell script that will be called by the cron daemon. Here, we will check connection information by querying the management port and the database we created in the previous example. An alternative to querying the management port would be to poll the OpenVPN status log file and act on that data in real time. One serious caveat to polling the management interface is that it is single-threaded and will only allow one connection at a time. If a script hangs or someone is connected to the interface, consecutive polls will also hang. The code is as follows:

```
#!/bin/sh
#
# Determines if user ($1) has been connected more than $2 seconds

if [ $# -lt 2 ];
then
  echo "usage: $0 <user> <time_in_seconds>"
  exit 1
fi

USER=$1
TO=$2

# DB seconds

SQL="SELECT SUM(connection_time) FROM vpn_session WHERE cn='$USER'"
DBTIME='/usr/local/bin/sqlite3 /var/openvpn/movpn.sqlite3 "$SQL"'

if [ "$DBTIME" = "" ];
then
  DBTIME=0
fi

# Check management port
CTIME='echo "status 2" | nc -N localhost 1194 | grep -E "CLIENT_
LIST.*$USER" | cut -f8 -d,'
if [ "$CTIME" != "" ];
```

```
then
  # we have an active connection
  D=`date +"%s"`
  CTIME=`expr "$D - $CTIME"`
else
  CTIME=0
fi


UTIME=`expr $DBTIME + $CTIME`
if [ $UTIME -gt $TO ];
then
  logger "Disconnecting $USER, activity time exceeded ($UTIME/$TO)."
  echo "disable" >> /usr/local/etc/openvpn/ccd/$USER
  cho "kill $USER" | nc localhost 1194
fi
```

Now that we have a script, we can call it:

root@example:~-> timeout.sh client1 1800

This will calculate how many seconds `client1` has been connected to the VPN.
If the time exceeds `1800` (or whatever number you put there), it will disable that
configuration via the `client-config-directory` and kill any active sessions using
the management interface.

> The OpenVPN management interface only allows a single connection
> at a time. Make sure your script handles this limitation correctly.

Examples of client scripts

Many third-party OpenVPN client packages make heavy utilization of client-side
scripting to provide solid integration with various operating systems. Tunnelblick,
originally written by Angelo Laub, uses client-side scripting to integrate OpenVPN
server DNS settings with Mac OS X operating system.

The "client" moniker for client-side scripting can be a bit of a misnomer. In many
cases, the OpenVPN client may, in fact, be another server. Perhaps you have multiple
disparate offices and are using OpenVPN to connect them. The client scripts can be
utilized to start a daemon, backup process, or other services that the local network
depends on the OpenVPN session for.

Client scripts are written similarly to server-side scripts and have a nearly identical
list of environment variables available to them.

Example 4—mount NFS share

A common client connection task is to mount remote shares once connected to a corporate network. Let's consider a web developer who needs the web directory automounted once they've connected to the VPN.

The first task is to write the client-side up and down scripts. The up script will connect the network share and the down script will remove the network share. The up script in this case is pretty straightforward, mounting the webroot folder via NFS from 10.200.0.53. This example is written for a Mac OS X system, utilizing osascript to provide graphical popups to notify the user when the NFS share has been mounted. The code is as follows:

```sh
#!/bin/sh

# make webroot in home if it doesn't exist

mkdir -p ~/remote_shares/webroot
if [ $? -eq 0 ];
then
        mount 192.168.19.53:/webroot ~/remote_shares/webroot
        if [ $? -eq 0 ];
        then
                osascript -e 'tell app "System Events" to display
dialog "~/remote_shares/webroot is mounted"'
        else
                osascript -e 'tell app "System Events" to display
dialog "Unable to mount webroot directory."'
        fi
else
        osascript -e 'tell app "System Events" to display dialog
"Unable to create remote share path."'
fi
```

The following script is fairly simple:

```sh
#!/bin/sh

umount -f ~/remote_shares/webroot
```

Once the scripts are created, the client configuration needs to be updated to allow external scripts by adding the `script-security` directive, along with the `up` directive:

```
script-security 2
up /path/to/script/up.sh
```

 Tunnelblick does quite a bit of its own scripting and will override both of the `--up` and `--down` script calls. To work around this, follow the instructions for script naming and location. These instructions can be found at `https://tunnelblick.net/cUsingScripts.html`.

Example 5—using all scripts at once

In the following example, we will use all scripts on both client and server side at once. While this does not resemble a real-life situation, it does provide some nice insights into the order in which the scripts are executed and into the arguments and environment variables for each of the scripts.

We start out with the following server configuration file:

```
tls-server
proto udp
port 1194
dev tun

server 10.200.0.0 255.255.255.0
server-ipv6 FD00::200:0/112

ca        /etc/openvpn/movpn/movpn-ca.crt
cert      /etc/openvpn/movpn/server.crt
key       /etc/openvpn/movpn/server.key
dh        /etc/openvpn/movpn/dh2048.pem
tls-auth /etc/openvpn/movpn/ta.key 0

persist-key
persist-tun
keepalive 10 60

topology subnet
```

```
user   nobody
group nobody

daemon
log-append /var/log/openvpn.log

route 10.100.0.0 255.255.0.0

route 192.168.0.0 255.255.255.0


ask-pass /etc/openvpn/mopvn/secret
script-security 3
cd /etc/openvpn/movpn
setenv   MASTERING_OPENVPN server
push "setenv-safe SPECIAL hack"
up                      ./movpn-07-01-script.sh
tls-verify              ./movpn-07-01-script.sh
auth-user-pass-verify ./movpn-07-01-script.sh via-env
client-connect          ./movpn-07-01-script.sh
route-up                ./movpn-07-01-script.sh
client-disconnect       ./movpn-07-01-script.sh
learn-address           ./movpn-07-01-script.sh
route-pre-down          ./movpn-07-01-script.sh
down                    ./movpn-07-01-script.sh
```

We save it as `movpn-07-01-server.conf`. Here are some notes about this configuration file:

- The routes that are listed in the server configuration are for demonstration purposes only, as we will see later on.

- In order to work around a bug in OpenVPN 2.3.7, we added the following line:

  ```
  ask-pass /etc/openvpn/movpn/secret
  ```

- In this file, `secret` (the passphrase to decrypt the server private key) is stored in plaintext.

- In this server configuration, we also used the following option to switch to the directory where the script is located:

  ```
  cd /etc/openvpn/movpn
  ```

  This makes the server configuration shorter and easier to read.

> With the `cd` option, it would have been possible to specify the `ca`, `cert`, `key`, `dh`, and `tls-auth` options using a shorter path, for example:
>
>   ca ./movpn-ca.crt
>
> However, it is recommended to always use absolute pathnames or the `--cd` option and relative paths for security-related items to avoid any confusion.

- We also set a server-side environment variable `MASTERING_OPENVPN` with the value of `server` using the following command:

```
setenv MASTERING_OPENVPN server
```

- We push a `safe` environment variable to all clients using the following command:

```
push "setenv-safe SPECIAL hack"
```

- Inside client-side scripts and plugins, this variable should show up as `OPENVPN_SPECIAL`.

Next, we create the following script:

```
#!/bin/bash

exec >> /tmp/movpn-07-01.log 2>&1
date +"%H:%M:%S: START $script_type script ==="
echo "argv = $0 $@"
echo "user = 'id -un'/'id -gn'"
env | sort | sed 's/^/  /'
date +"%H:%M:%S: END $script_type script ==="
```

We save this as `movpn-07-01-script.sh` in the directory `/etc/openvpn/movpn`. Ensure that the script is executable, create an empty log file, and start `openvpn`:

```
# chmod 0755 /etc/openvpn/movpn/mopvn-07-01-script.sh
# touch /tmp/movpn-07-01.log
# chown nobody /tmp/movpn-07-01.log
# openvpn --config /etc/openvpn/movpn/movpn-07-01-server.conf
```

Before we continue, take a look at the `/tmp/movpn-07-01.log` file. When OpenVPN start up, some scripts have already been executed:

```
15:46:57: START up script ===
argv = ./movpn-07-01-script.sh tun0 1500 1541 10.200.0.1
        255.255.255.0 init
```

```
user = root/root
[...]
15:46:57: END up script ===
15:46:57: START route-up script ===
argv = ./movpn-07-01-script.sh
user = root/root
```

The up and `route-up` scripts have been executed. The parameters passed
to the up script provide the name of the TUN/TAP device (`tun0`), the `tun-mtu` (`1500`), and `link-mtu` (`1541`) values, the VPN IP address and netmask
(`10.200.0.1/255.255.255.0`), and the type of invocation (possible values
are `init` or `restart`).

Note that both scripts were executed with "root" privileges. We will go through the
log file output of each script momentarily.

On the client side, we set up a similar configuration. First, create the following
configuration file:

```
client
proto udp

remote openvpnserver.example.com
port 1194
dev tun
nobind

remote-cert-tls server
tls-auth /etc/openvpn/movpn/ta.key 1
ca       /etc/openvpn/movpn/movpn-ca.crt
cert     /etc/openvpn/movpn/client1.crt
key      /etc/openvpn/movpn/client1.key

persist-tun
persist-key

explicit-exit-notify 3
auth-user-pass

script-security 3
cd /etc/openvpn/movpn
setenv  MASTERING_OPENVPN client
```

tls-verify	./movpn-07-01-script.sh
ipchange	./movpn-07-01-script.sh
up	./movpn-07-01-script.sh
up-restart	
route-up	./movpn-07-01-script.sh
route-pre-down	./movpn-07-01-script.sh
down	./movpn-07-01-script.sh

Save it as `movpn-07-01-client.conf` and recreate or copy over the `movpn-07-01-script.sh` file from the server.

Again, we ensure that the script is executable, create an empty log file, and start `openvpn`:

```
# chmod 0755 /etc/openvpn/movpn/mopvn-07-01-script.sh
# openvpn --config /etc/openvpn/movpn/movpn-07-01-client.conf
OpenVPN 2.3.7 x86_64-redhat-linux-gnu [SSL (OpenSSL)] [LZO] [EPOLL]
[PKCS11] [MH] [IPv6] built on Jun  9 2015
library versions: OpenSSL 1.0.1e-fips 11 Feb 2013, LZO 2.08
Enter Auth Username: *****
    ## enter "movpn"
Enter Auth Password: ******
    ## enter "secret"
NOTE: the current --script-security setting may allow this
configuration to call user-defined scripts

Control Channel Authentication: using '/etc/openvpn/movpn/ta.key' as a
OpenVPN static key file
UDPv4 link local: [undef]
UDPv4 link remote: [AF_INET]<IP>:1194
WARNING: this configuration may cache passwords in memory -- use the
auth-nocache option to prevent this
[Mastering OpenVPN Server] Peer Connection Initiated with [AF_
INET]<IP>:1194
TUN/TAP device tun0 opened
do_ifconfig, tt->ipv6=1, tt->did_ifconfig_ipv6_setup=1
/usr/sbin/ip link set dev tun0 up mtu 1500
/usr/sbin/ip addr add dev tun0 10.200.0.2/24 broadcast 10.200.0.255
/usr/sbin/ip -6 addr add fd00::200:1000/112 dev tun0
./movpn-07-01-script.sh tun0 1500 1541 10.200.0.2 255.255.255.0 init
Initialization Sequence Completed
```

You can fill in anything you want for `Auth username` and `Auth password`, as the server-side script will always return success.

After the connection has come up, we verify that the VPN client and server can reach each other using both `ping` and `ping6`.

Next, we restart the VPN connection by sending a special signal to the OpenVPN client:

```
# killall -USR1 openvpn
```

This will trigger a "soft-reset" of the OpenVPN client. After the connection has come back up, we verify once more that the VPN is fully functioning. Soft-resets occur in real-life situations mostly when the `persist-tun` option is used on the client side and an OpenVPN client is on a mobile network with roaming, or whenever the network between the client and the server is not very stable. In this scenario, the server-side scripts are called with slightly different parameters, as we will see in a moment.

Finally, shut down the VPN connection by terminating the client. We will now go through the script logs on both server and client.

The server-side script log

The server-side script log can easily grow to thousands of lines, but fortunately there is some structure in it. Let's first check the order in which the scripts are called:

```
15:46:57: START up script ===
argv = ./movpn-07-01-script.sh tun0 1500 1541 10.200.0.1 255.255.255.0
init
15:46:57: START route-up script ===
argv = ./movpn-07-01-script.sh
15:47:15: START tls-verify script ===
argv = ./movpn-07-01-script.sh 1 C=ZA, ST=Enlightenment,
        L=Overall, O=Mastering OpenVPN, CN=Mastering OpenVPN,
        emailAddress=root@example.org
15:47:15: START tls-verify script ===
argv = ./movpn-07-01-script.sh 0 C=ZA, ST=Enlightenment,
        O=Mastering OpenVPN, CN=client1,
        emailAddress=root@example.org
15:47:15: START user-pass-verify script ===
argv = ./movpn-07-01-script.sh
15:47:15: START client-connect script ===
argv = ./movpn-07-01-script.sh
```

```
                 /tmp/openvpn_cc_5b1f0d25ac0f71c98c44ec128e5c21d6.tmp
15:47:15: START learn-address script ===
argv = ./movpn-07-01-script.sh add 10.200.0.2 client1
15:47:15: START learn-address script ===
argv = ./movpn-07-01-script.sh add fd00::200:1000 client1
17:37:18: START tls-verify script ===
argv = ./movpn-07-01-script.sh 1 C=ZA, ST=Enlightenment,
            L=Overall, O=Mastering OpenVPN, CN=Mastering OpenVPN,
            emailAddress=root@example.org
17:37:18: START tls-verify script ===
argv = ./movpn-07-01-script.sh 0 C=ZA, ST=Enlightenment,
            O=Mastering OpenVPN, CN=client1,
            emailAddress=root@example.org
17:37:18: START user-pass-verify script ===
argv = ./movpn-07-01-script.sh
17:37:18: START client-disconnect script ===
argv = ./movpn-07-01-script.sh
17:37:18: START client-connect script ===
argv = ./movpn-07-01-script.sh
                 /tmp/openvpn_cc_8528c57f838033a03f38ddb72b57ae30.tmp
17:37:18: START learn-address script ===
argv = ./movpn-07-01-script.sh update 10.200.0.2 client1
17:37:18: START learn-address script ===
argv = ./movpn-07-01-script.sh update fd00::200:1000 client1
17:38:50: START client-disconnect script ===
argv = ./movpn-07-01-script.sh
17:38:50: START learn-address script ===
argv = ./movpn-07-01-script.sh delete fd00::200:1000
17:38:50: START learn-address script ===
argv = ./movpn-07-01-script.sh delete 10.200.0.2
17:39:08: START route-pre-down script ===
argv = ./movpn-07-01-script.sh tun0 1500 1541 10.200.0.1 255.255.255.0
init
17:39:09: START down script ===
argv = ./movpn-07-01-script.sh tun0 1500 1541 10.200.0.1 255.255.255.0
init
```

First the up and route-up scripts are called, as we have seen before.

When the first client connects, the tls-verify script is called twice: first for the CA certificate that was used to sign the client certificate and then for the client certificate itself.

Next, the `auth-user-pass-verify` script is executed. When this script returns success (exit code 0) then the client is authenticated and considered *trusted*.

The next script is the `client-connect` script, which is called with a temporary file. This script is often used to set special options for a particular client, or to log client activity in a database. This script can still influence the IP address which is assigned to the client, by printing out an option to the temporary file, for example:

```
echo "ifconfig-push 10.200.0.88 255.255.255.0" > $1
```

The last script that is called when a client connects is the `learn-address` script. This script is called twice, once with the IPv4 address and once with the IPv6 address. This script is actually best suited for updating firewall rules, but most people tend to use `client-connect` scripts for this. The `learn-address` script is needed, especially in a TAP-based setup, in combination with an external DHCP server.

 In a TAP-based setup, the second parameter to the `learn-address` script is the MAC address of the client-side TAP adapter. The client VPN IP address is available as an environment variable.

From the log file, we can see that the OpenVPN client received a `soft-restart` trigger at `17:37:18`. The order of execution of the scripts may seem odd, but it can be explained:

- A new incoming connection is detected. For this, the `tls-verify` and `auth-user-pass-verify` scripts are executed to determine if it is a valid client.

- Once it is determined that this is a valid client and this particular client is already connected, the old client instance is first disconnected. Thus, the `client-disconnect` script is called.

- Next, the `client-connect` script is called for the new client instance. Note that the new client instance may be coming from a new remote IP address.

- Finally, the `learn-address` script is called twice with the action set to `update`, once for the IPv4 address and once for the IPv6 address. If any firewall rules need to be altered, then this would be the best spot to do this.

At `17:38:50`, the client was disconnected. Because we specified `explicit-exit-notify` in the client configuration, the server is notified of this immediately and the `client-disconnect` script is executed.

Note that the `learn-address` scripts are now executed with the action set to `delete`.

At `17:39:08`, the OpenVPN server process itself is stopped, and the `route-pre-down` and `down` scripts are called. Note that the same parameters are passed to this script as to the `up` script.

Environment variables set in the server-side scripts

Now that we understand the order in which the scripts are called, it is time to take a closer look at the environment variables that are available to the scripts.

--up

The environment variables available to the `up` script are as follows:

```
MASTERING_OPENVPN=server
PWD=/etc/openvpn/movpn
SHLVL=1
_=/bin/env
config=movpn-07-01-server.conf
daemon=1
daemon_log_redirect=1
daemon_pid=8070
daemon_start_time=1437659216
dev=tun0
dev_type=tun
ifconfig_broadcast=10.200.0.255
ifconfig_ipv6_local=fd00::200:1
ifconfig_ipv6_netbits=112
ifconfig_ipv6_remote=fd00::200:2
ifconfig_local=10.200.0.1
ifconfig_netmask=255.255.255.0
link_mtu=1541
local_port_1=1194
proto_1=udp
remote_port_1=1194
route_gateway_1=10.200.0.2
route_gateway_2=10.200.0.2
route_net_gateway=<SERVER-IP>
route_netmask_1=255.255.0.0
route_netmask_2=255.255.255.0
route_network_1=10.100.0.0
route_network_2=192.168.0.0
route_vpn_gateway=10.200.0.2
script_context=init
```

```
script_type=up
tun_mtu=1500
verb=1
```

Most of the parameters passed to the `up` script are also present as environment variables. The server-side routing information is also already available here, but it is best to deal with these variables in the `route-up` script.

--route-up

In the `route-up` script, the same environment is available as in the preceding code, with one addition:

```
script_type=route-up
redirect_gateway=0
```

This environment variable is set to `1` if the default gateway also needs to be redirected. All `route` statements that are listed in the server configuration file are presented as environment variables as well. For each route, `route_network`, `route_netmask`, and `route_gateway` are available. Also, note that the OpenVPN keywords `net_gateway` and `vpn_gateway` are represented here as `route_net_gateway` and `route_vpn_gateway`.

--tls-verify

The `tls-verify` script is called with the full certificate name, which is also known as **Distinguished Name (DN)**. Even more certificate information is available as environment variables:

```
X509_0_C=ZA
X509_0_CN=client1
X509_0_O=Mastering OpenVPN
X509_0_ST=Enlightenment
X509_0_emailAddress=root@example.org
X509_1_C=ZA
X509_1_CN=Mastering OpenVPN
X509_1_L=Overall
X509_1_O=Mastering OpenVPN
X509_1_ST=Enlightenment
X509_1_emailAddress=root@example.org
script_type=tls-verify
tls_digest_0=1b:27:a6:b4:5f:7a:9c:3f:17:fb:ff:33:05:61:3f:2a:56:89:16
:d3
tls_digest_1=e4:f1:43:37:34:51:de:99:7a:dc:e3:6d:f2:4c:5b:84:34:4b
:f3:64
```

```
tls_id_0=C=ZA, ST=Enlightenment, O=Mastering OpenVPN, CN=client1,
emailAddress=root@example.org
tls_id_1=C=ZA, ST=Enlightenment, L=Overall, O=Mastering OpenVPN,
CN=Mastering OpenVPN, emailAddress=root@example.org
tls_serial_0=2
tls_serial_1=15173527578309581038
tls_serial_hex_0=02
tls_serial_hex_1=d2:93:32:f0:8e:bc:58:ee
untrusted_ip=<CLIENT-IP>
untrusted_port=46171
```

All of these can be used to determine if this particular client certificate is truly trusted. Note that there are two environment variables, `untrusted_ip=<CLIENT-IP>` and `untrusted_port=46171`, which denote the as-of-yet untrusted client address.

--auth-user-pass-verify

The `auth-user-pass-verify` script has the same environment as the preceding script, with the addition of three new variables:

```
common_name=client1
username=movpn
password=secret
```

The `common_name` is set after successful completion of the `tls-verify` script. The `username` and `password` are passed as environment variables because we set `script-security` to 3 and we added the `via-env` parameter to the `auth-user-pass-verify` option in the configuration file.

--client-connect

The most commonly used script, `client-connect`, has almost the same environment, but the `password` variable has been removed. Furthermore, as the authentication process is now complete, there are two new variables, `trusted_ip=<CLIENT-IP>` and `trusted_port=<port>`, with the exact same values as their untrusted counterparts. Note that the untrusted versions are also still available.

--learn-address

The `learn-address` script has the exact same environment as the `client-connect` script. It requires a command to execute, and a few optional arguments:

* operation: add, update, or delete
* address: The address being learned or unlearned
* common name: The client certificate common name to associate with the address

In a TAP-based setup, the second parameter passed to the script is the MAC address of the client-side TAP adapter. The VPN IP address that was assigned to the client by the server (if so configured) is available in the environment variables `ifconfig_pool_remote_ip` and `ifconfig_pool_netmask`, respectively, as shown here:

```
ifconfig_pool_remote_ip=10.200.0.2
ifconfig_pool_netmask=255.255.255.0
```

--client-disconnect

The `client-disconnect` script has the exact same environment as the `client-connect` script, but it also returns some accounting statistics:

```
bytes_received=7553
bytes_sent=8105
```

This information is mostly interesting for accounting purposes.

--route-pre-down and --down

Finally, the `route-pre-down` and `down` scripts are called with the same parameters as the `up` script. When the `route-pre-down` script is called, the system routes are still present. When the `down` script is called, the system routes will have been removed, provided that OpenVPN had the privileges to do so. The environment variable `signal=sigint` provides information on the type of signal that triggered the shutdown of OpenVPN.

The client-side script log

The client script log has a very similar flow and structure as the server-side log. Again, let's first check the order in which the scripts are called:

```
15:47:15: START tls-verify script ===
argv = ./movpn-07-01-script.sh 1 C=ZA, ST=Enlightenment,
         L=Overall, O=Mastering OpenVPN, CN=Mastering OpenVPN,
         emailAddress=root@example.org
15:47:15: START tls-verify script ===
argv = ./movpn-07-01-script.sh 0 C=ZA, ST=Enlightenment,
         O=Mastering OpenVPN, CN=Mastering OpenVPN Server,
         emailAddress=root@example.org
15:47:15: START ipchange script ===
argv = ./movpn-07-01-script.sh [AF_INET]<SERVER-IP> [AF_INET]1194
15:47:17: START up script ===
argv = ./movpn-07-01-script.sh tun0 1500 1541 10.200.0.2 255.255.255.0
init
```

```
15:47:17: START route-up script ===
argv = ./movpn-07-01-script.sh
17:37:16: START down script ===
argv = ./movpn-07-01-script.sh tun0 1500 1541 10.200.0.2 255.255.255.0
restart
17:37:18: START tls-verify script ===
argv = ./movpn-07-01-script.sh 1 C=ZA, ST=Enlightenment,
         L=Overall, O=Mastering OpenVPN, CN=Mastering OpenVPN,
         emailAddress=root@example.org
17:37:18: START tls-verify script ===
argv = ./movpn-07-01-script.sh 0 C=ZA, ST=Enlightenment,
         O=Mastering OpenVPN, CN=Mastering OpenVPN Server,
         emailAddress=root@example.org
17:37:18: START ipchange script ===
argv = ./movpn-07-01-script.sh [AF_INET]<SERVER-IP> [AF_INET]1194
17:37:20: START up script ===
argv = ./movpn-07-01-script.sh tun0 1500 1541 10.200.0.2 255.255.255.0
restart
17:38:53: START route-pre-down script ===
argv = ./movpn-07-01-script.sh tun0 1500 1541 10.200.0.2 255.255.255.0
init
17:38:53: START down script ===
argv = ./movpn-07-01-script.sh tun0 1500 1541 10.200.0.2 255.255.255.0
init
```

When the client first connects, the `tls-verify` script is called twice, first for the CA certificate that was used to sign the server certificate and then for the server certificate itself. This way, the client can verify that it is connecting to a trusted server.

After that, the little-known `ipchange` script is called. This script does not yet know which client IP address it will be assigned. It is used mostly to adjust firewall settings on the client or to notify another application that a VPN connection setup is in progress.

Once the client is authenticated with the server, a block of information is pushed from the server to the client. This block is then parsed locally as configuration options, after which the `up` and `route-up` scripts are called.

When we sent a USR1 signal to the OpenVPN client, it caused OpenVPN to perform a `soft-restart`. This is seen in the script execution log as well:

- First, the `down` script is called with the last parameter set to `restart` instead of `init`.

- Next, the `tls-verify` and `ipchange` scripts are called, as we need to reauthenticate ourselves with the server again.

- Finally, the `up` script is called once more to set up the VPN IP address. Here, the last parameter to the script is also set to `restart` instead of `init`.

Note that the `route-up` script is not called in this case. This is due to the fact that we included `persist-tun` in the client configuration. As the TUN/TAP interface was not closed or shut down, all client-side routing is still in effect and hence the `route-up` script is not executed.

When the client is shutdown the `route-pre-down` and `down` scripts are called once more, this time with the parameter set to `init`.

Environment variables set in the client-side scripts

Now that we understand the order in which the scripts are called, it is again time to take look at the environment variables.

Most environment variables on the client side resemble the ones on the server side. Some variables are mirrored, such as `common_name` that contains the common name of the server-side certificate, as can be found in the `up` and `ipchange` script environments:

```
common_name=Mastering OpenVPN Server
```

Also present in the `up script` environment is the variable that was pushed from the server to the client:

```
OPENVPN_SPECIAL=hack
```

The OpenVPN client received the `safe` variable `SPECIAL` and created an environment variable for it by prepending `OPENVPN_` to it.

 There is no method for sending information or variables back from the client to the server. In Version 2.4, some system information will be sent back, but this cannot be configured on the client.

When the OpenVPN client is restarted using a `USR1` signal, the `down` and `up` scripts are called with the last parameter set to `restart` instead of `init`. This is also reflected in the environment variables of both scripts:

```
script_context=restart
script_type=down  ## or up
signal=sigusr1
```

When the OpenVPN is terminated, these environment variables contain the following:

```
script_context=init
script_type=down
signal=exit-with-notification
```

Plugins

Due to the ease of scripting, the OpenVPN plugin interface is a relatively underutilized tool available to OpenVPN server administrators. OpenVPN, by default, ships with a pair of plugins, one for PAM authentication and another for executing `--down` scripts with root privileges, regardless of whether the administrator de-escalates privileges.

Down-root

It's a good idea to drop privileges within OpenVPN, and the `down-root` plugin allows you to do that. Applications like firewalls require escalated privileges to add and remove firewall rules. By utilizing the `down-root` plugin, an administrator can provide new firewall rules upon a client connection as well as the ability for the removal of those rules once the client disconnects.

A usage scenario could be a single OpenVPN instance that supports an entire company's staff. Administrative and office staff would not generally need access to lights-out management interfaces and other such systems on a company network. With the addition of firewall rules, OpenVPN can introduce allowed access for specific client connections based on CN or other environmental variables. Once that technician disconnects, removal of the firewall rules prevents another non-technical staff member from gaining that access, even in the event they are on the same subnet or get the same IP as the formerly connected staff member.

The auth-pam plugin

The second plugin OpenVPN ships with is the `auth-pam` plugin. This interfaces with the operating system's **Pluggable Authentication Modules (PAM)** stack. By using PAM, an administrator is able to leverage any backend that can also interface this way. LDAP is an example use case for `auth-pam`.

Many Unix and Linux systems have the ability to authenticate with LDAP. In the case of OpenLDAP, there are a few shared objects such as PADL Software's `pam-ldap` and `nss-ldap`. After configuring these and adding them into the system PAM stack, OpenVPN can be tied in with a few simple configuration parameters.

> The `auth-pam` plugin cannot be used on Windows systems due to the lack of support for PAM.

In its simplest form, the following can be added to the server configuration:

```
plugin openvpn-auth-pam.so login
```

This enables the plugin and instructs it to utilize the login PAM service. Note that this can be any PAM service, including an OpenVPN specific setup defined by the administrator. The third parameter in the preceding code identifies the service. A more complicated configuration could include passed parameters:

```
plugin openvpn-auth-pam.so login login USERNAME password PASSWORD
```

In this instance, we're still using the login PAM service, but it requires two parameters: login and password. OpenVPN will potentially pass three parameters replacing the key words PASSWORD, USERNAME, and COMMONNAME with their obvious counterparts. USERNAME and PASSWORD require that `auth-user-pass` should be set in the client configuration.

To determine the queries made by a PAM service or to debug the `auth-pam` module itself, set OpenVPN logging verbosity to level 7 or higher. Running `auth-pam` along with OpenVPN 2.3.6 gives the following output in the log file:

```
AUTH-PAM: BACKGROUND: received command code: 0
AUTH-PAM: BACKGROUND: USER: ecrist
AUTH-PAM: BACKGROUND: my_conv[0] query='Login:' style=2
AUTH-PAM: BACKGROUND: name match found, query/match-string ['Login:',
'login'] = 'USERNAME'
AUTH-PAM: BACKGROUND: my_conv[0] query='Password:' style=1
AUTH-PAM: BACKGROUND: name match found, query/match-string ['Password:',
'password'] = 'PASSWORD'
```

Looking at the lines with `my_conv`, we can see two query values, `Login:` and `Password:`. Those successfully partially-match `login` and `password`. To demonstrate the partial match, I've changed the `config` line as follows:

```
plugin openvpn-auth-pam.so login log USERNAME password PASSWORD
```

It is evident in the log here that the module was able to successfully match `log` to `Login:` and `password` to `Password:`.

```
AUTH-PAM: BACKGROUND: received command code: 0

AUTH-PAM: BACKGROUND: USER: ecrist

AUTH-PAM: BACKGROUND: my_conv[0] query='Login:' style=2

AUTH-PAM: BACKGROUND: name match found, query/match-string ['Login:',
'log'] = 'USERNAME'

AUTH-PAM: BACKGROUND: my_conv[0] query='Password:' style=1

AUTH-PAM: BACKGROUND: name match found, query/match-string ['Password:',
'password'] = 'PASSWORD'
```

As helpful as this loose matching is, you need to be careful as there is potential for collisions depending upon the PAM plugin that you're using.

A list of projects that provide assorted authentication plugins, as well as various frontends and certificate managers can be found at `https://community.openvpn.net/openvpn/wiki/RelatedProjects`.

Summary

Scripting and plugins are powerful tools to extend OpenVPN. It allows an administrator to integrate OpenVPN better into an existing infrastructure, for example, by enabling authentication against a separate backend system or by recording usage statistics of a client.

Writing OpenVPN scripts can be tricky, as special care needs to be taken about the timing of the scripts. The current version of OpenVPN is monolithic and single-threaded, which means that a lengthy or misbehaving server-side script can block the entire VPN for all users.

It is also important to understand the flow and order in which the scripts are called. In this chapter, we explored how this order works and which environment variables are present to each of the server- and client-side scripts.

In the next chapter, we will see more graphical user interfaces, as we dive into the use of OpenVPN on smart phones, tablets, and other *mobile* devices.

8
Using OpenVPN on Mobile Devices and Home Routers

Nowadays, OpenVPN is available not only on traditional PC-style platforms, but also on smart phones and tablets running Android or Apple iOS, as well as embedded hardware and home routers. For Android, there are two apps: OpenVPN for Android, which is fully open source, and OpenVPN Connect for Android, which is the official app from OpenVPN Technologies, Inc. We will cover both these Android apps, as there are some subtle differences in using them.

In this chapter, we will first explore how to use OpenVPN on Android and iOS, and how to best integrate smart phone use into an existing OpenVPN setup.

Next, we will explore how OpenVPN can be used on small hardware, such as home routers running the popular DD-WRT Linux-based firmware. We will show how to use a home router as both an OpenVPN client and an OpenVPN server.

An important note is that both Android and iOS only support tun mode. This is a limitation of the operating system, not of the OpenVPN app used. Fortunately, most OpenVPN deployments are tun-based, but it will not be possible to build an Ethernet-style VPN or connect to a bridged setup using either iOS or Android.

The following topics will be covered in this chapter:

- Using the OpenVPN for Android app
- Using the OpenVPN Connect app for Android
- Using the OpenVPN Connect app for iOS
- Integrating smart phones into an existing VPN setup

- Setting up DD-WRT with OpenVPN support
- Using a home router as a VPN client
- Using a home router as a VPN server

Using the OpenVPN for an Android app

The OpenVPN for Android app is fully open source and is based on the latest OpenVPN (Git-master) code branch. This means that certain features are available in this version of OpenVPN that have not yet made it into the regular production version of OpenVPN.

For this example, we installed OpenVPN for Android from Google Play on a Samsung Galaxy Note 10.1 2014 tablet running Android 4.3.

For both OpenVPN for Android and OpenVPN Connect, it is handy to set up a special configuration profile. This profile can then be imported into the OpenVPN app with one click. This applies to both the Android and iOS versions of the apps, as we will see later in this chapter.

Note that there are two separate apps, both written by well-known OpenVPN developers. OpenVPN Connect is a product from OpenVPN Technologies, Inc., written by James Yonan. OpenVPN for Android is written by Arne Schwabe.

Creating an OpenVPN app profile

To create an OpenVPN application profile, we will be following the steps given here:

1. We start out with the `basic-udp-client.conf` configuration file, and we replace all references to external files (`tls-auth`, `ca`, `cert` and `key`) with the keyword `[inline]`. We then add inline blobs for these files by copying and pasting in the contents of the `ta.key`, `ca.crt`, `client1.crt`, and `client1.key` files, respectively.

Inline configs are required for the OpenVPN connect app (even the iOS app) due to a need to keep the config and certificates together. These apps support multiple OpenVPN configurations, and this prevents the need to name certificate files uniquely.

2. The resulting configuration profile will look like this:

```
client
proto udp
remote openvpnserver.example.com
port 1194
dev tun
nobind
remote-cert-tls server
tls-auth [inline] 1
ca        [inline]
cert      [inline]
key       [inline]

<ca>
-----BEGIN CERTIFICATE-----
MIIEwTCCA6mgAwIBAgIJANKTMvCOv...
...
-----END CERTIFICATE-----
</ca>

<cert>
-----BEGIN CERTIFICATE-----
MIIDeTCCAmECAQQwDQYJKoZIhvcNAQE...
...
-----END CERTIFICATE-----
</cert>

<key>
-----BEGIN RSA PRIVATE KEY-----
MIIEowIBAAKCAQEA3vzLCSqR3fQF...
...
-----END RSA PRIVATE KEY-----
</key>

<tls-auth>
-----BEGIN OpenVPN Static key V1-----
5f5b2bfff373961654089871b40a39eb
...
-----END OpenVPN Static key V1-----
</tls-auth>
```

3. Save it as `basic-udp-inline.ovpn`.

4. Make the file available on the Android device, either by transferring or by mailing it.

> If you upload the configuration file to a web server, it is very important that the file type and extension remain intact. If the tablet or phone recognizes the OpenVPN profile as a plain text file, then it will usually automatically treat it as a text file. In some cases, it may be desirable to store the `.ovpn` file inside a ZIP file (`.zip`) to avoid such file type mangling.

5. On the OpenVPN server side, launch the server using the `ipv6-udp-server.conf` profile.

6. For the remainder of this example, we use the Android device.

7. Download and install the free app from Google Play on the device.

8. Make sure the `.ovpn` configuration file is available on the device as well.

9. Launch the app for the very first time. An empty list of profiles will appear, as shown here:

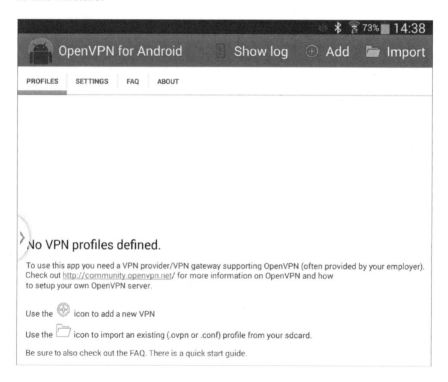

10. Click on the folder icon at the bottom of the screen to import the `.opvn` file. Browse to the location of the `.ovpn` file, select it, and click on **Import**. After a successful import, the log will show:

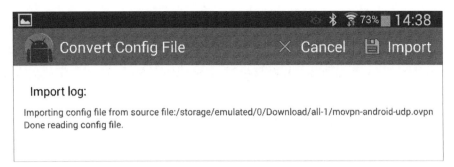

11. Go back to the main OpenVPN app screen. On this screen, you will now see the list of available profiles:

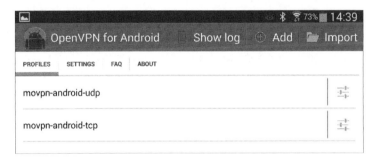

12. On the Android device, click on the profile **movpn-android-udp** once to start the OpenVPN connection. The OpenVPN for Android app will now try to establish the connection. If logging is set to verbose, then the main screen will show an OpenVPN log in a very similar fashion to the desktop OpenVPN client, without timestamps:

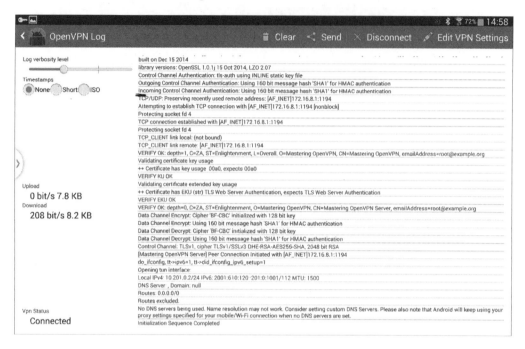

13. OpenVPN will connect. After the connection has been successfully established, the **Vpn Status** in the bottom-left corner will show **Connected**.

 Note from the log file that OpenVPN for Android also supports IPv6 addressing.

14. Next, we verify that the VPN connection is indeed functional.

15. Using an Android Ping app, we ping the VPN server IP address. Start the Ping app and type in the VPN address of the server. As newer versions of Android no longer support ICMP ping messages, a TCP-based ping with destination port 80 is used in this example. Run a tiny web server on the VPN server and make sure that incoming TCP traffic on port 80 is allowed before attempting to ping the VPN server.

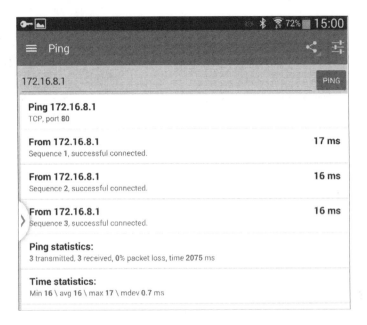

16. Of course, you can also use a regular ICMP ping from the server to the client's VPN IP address to ensure that the VPN connection is functional:

```
[server]$ ping 10.200.0.2
PING 10.200.0.2 (10.200.0.2) 56(84) bytes of data.
64 bytes from 10.200.0.2: icmp_seq=1 ttl=64 time=14.5 ms
64 bytes from 10.200.0.2: icmp_seq=2 ttl=64 time=13.2 ms
```

The Android for OpenVPN app can be used on smart phones and tablets based on either an ARM core or an Intel Atom core. The OpenVPN Connect app, which will be discussed in the next section, is available only for devices based on an ARM chip.

Using the PKCS#12 file

The OpenVPN for Android app can also use an external public certificate/private key pair in the so-called **PKCS#12** format.

You can convert an existing public certificate (.crt) and private key (.key) file to a PKCS#12 (.p12) file using the following commands:

```
$ openssl pkcs12 -export -out client1.p12 \
    -in client1.crt -inkey client1.key -CAfile movpn-ca.crt
Enter Export Password:
Verifying - Enter Export Password:
```

Ensure that you include the CA certificate file as well; otherwise, the ca file must be included in client configuration.

The corresponding client configuration profile is given as follows:

```
client
proto udp
remote openvpnserver.example.com
port 1194
dev tun
nobind

remote-cert-tls server
tls-auth [inline] 1
pkcs12    client1.p12

<tls-auth>
-----BEGIN OpenVPN Static key V1-----
5f5b2bfff373961654089871b40a39eb
...
-----END OpenVPN Static key V1-----
</tls-auth>
```

The advantage of this method is that the OpenVPN configuration is stored separately from the client authentication files. The downside is that this method does not work with the OpenVPN Connect app.

Using the OpenVPN Connect app for Android

The OpenVPN Connect app is the official app from OpenVPN Technologies, Inc. I downloaded and installed the free app from Google Play on the same Samsung Galaxy Note 10.1 2014 tablet as in the previous example.

The OpenVPN Connect app can only be used with profiles that use `[inline]` certificate and key pairs. For this, we use the OpenVPN configuration profile created in the previous example by using the following steps:

1. On the VPN server side, we launch OpenVPN using the standard `ipv6-udp-server.conf` configuration file.

2. After download and installation, launch the app and import the profile:

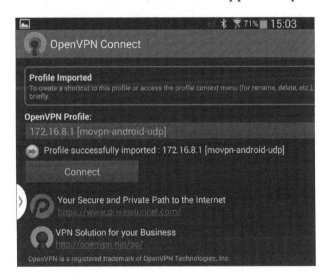

3. Next, select the right profile and click on **Connect**:

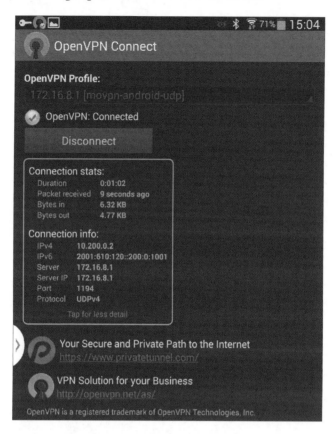

4. After the OpenVPN connection has been established, the client will report **OpenVPN: Connected**.

Note that the OpenVPN Connect client for Android also supports IPv6 addressing, as can be seen in the preceding screenshot.

5. Verifying that the VPN client can be reached from the server and vice versa is left as an exercise to the reader.

Using the OpenVPN Connect app for iOS

For this example, I installed OpenVPN Connect app from Apple's App store on an Apple iPad running iOS 8.1.2, as well as on an iPhone running iOS 8.

 This version of OpenVPN is not open source. A special agreement with Apple was required to gain insight into the Apple iOS networking stack, in order to be able to port OpenVPN to iOS. This negates the need for a jail-broken device.

Similar to the Android version, the OpenVPN Connect app can be best used with profiles that use [inline] certificate and key pairs. Therefore, we again make use of the OpenVPN configuration profile created in the first example of this chapter.

On the VPN server side, we launch OpenVPN using the standard `ipv6-udp-server.conf` configuration file.

Before we can use the OpenVPN profile on iOS, we must transfer it to the device. This can be done via e-mail, or using iTunes. It is a good idea to ensure you're using a secure transfer method. The iTunes connection is secure, but TLS-encrypted e-mail or another transfer method such as Dropbox or Google Drive may also be used.

Here is an example given for OpenVPN in the following steps:

1. After transferring the .ovpn profile, launch the OpenVPN app and scroll
    down to the **File Sharing** section. Click on **OpenVPN** and you will see the
    following screen:

2. Click on the **Add...** button to add a new profile. You can also use drag
    and drop, an OpenVPN configuration (inline mode file, usually with
    extension .ovpn) from a folder or desktop into this window.

3. Select the imported profile and click on **Add** again:

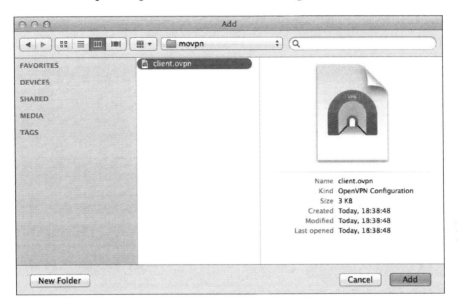

4. The `client.ovpn` file is now available as an OpenVPN Connect profile:

5. When we start the OpenVPN Connect app on a *clean* iPhone or iPad, we will see the following interface:

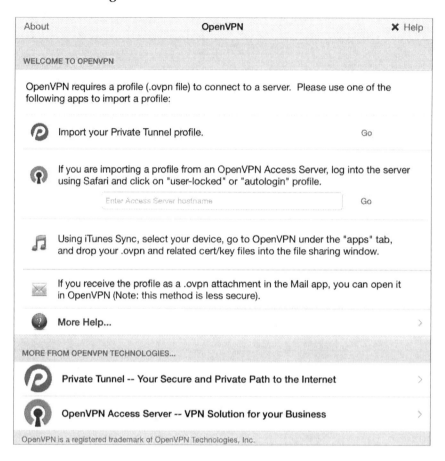

6. After the profile has been imported, an extra section that lists all available profiles becomes available on the screen. The OpenVPN Connect user interface can be a bit tricky at first. For example, when a faulty configuration is imported, the following screen is displayed:

7. The app reports that a profile is available for import, but we can see warning messages stating that there is an error loading this profile. The only available option is to remove the profile by tapping the red **X** mark. When a proper configuration file is imported, the green + button is also available. This is shown in the following screenshot:

8. Click on the + icon to open the OpenVPN connection profile:

9. Finally, use the slider behind the **Connection** entry to start the OpenVPN connection.

10. After the VPN connection has been successfully established, we can see that both IPv4 and IPv6 are supported in the OpenVPN Connect app:

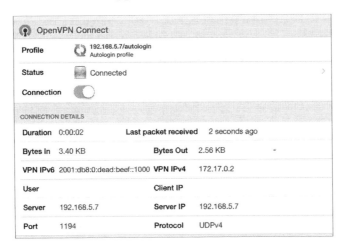

11. You can use the **Connection** slider button again to stop the VPN connection.

Integrating smart phones into an existing VPN setup

OpenVPN on smart phones can only be used as a VPN client, which is the normal usage mode of smart phone anyways. For Android, multiple OpenVPN client apps exist. There are some subtle differences between the different apps, but all of them support only tun-mode setups, as the underlying OS does not support tap devices.

The question of which app to use on Android devices is a difficult one. If you are using a mix of iOS and Android devices then the OpenVPN Connect app is an easier choice, as the user interface is more consistent across the devices. If you use the commercial OpenVPN Access Server, OpenVPN Connect is the only route due to dynamic configuration and some server option differences. If you need some of the special features of the OpenVPN for Android app or if you want to use OpenVPN on non-ARM based phones or tablets, then OpenVPN for Android is the logical choice.

As can be seen from the previous example, some changes are required to use the "app" versions of OpenVPN. Note that we did not make any changes on the server side to support Android or iOS devices, but the server setup used was relatively straightforward. As we saw in the previous examples, the "app" versions support both IPv4 and IPv6, as well as most of the other features of the desktop OpenVPN software. However, especially when routing or file sharing is involved, it can become tricky to generate a single server-side setup to support all platforms. It is also not possible to run client-side scripts, should they be required to set up the VPN connection. It is, of course, possible to use password-protected key files.

If exceptions need to be made for the installed "app" versions, then it is advisable to set up a separate OpenVPN server to serve. So set up a new static IP address and connect.

In the DD-WRT interface, upgrade the firmware again by selecting the "big" version and click on **Upgrade** once more. The upgrade process will again take a few minutes, but afterwards the DD-WRT interface should be available again.

Your router is now ready to be configured as either an OpenVPN client or an OpenVPN server.

Using a home router as a VPN client

You can use the following procedure to configure a DD-WRT router as an OpenVPN client:

1. In the DD-WRT web interface, click on the **Services** tab and then click on **VPN**.

2. Click on the **Enable** radio button next to **Start OpenVPN Client**.

3. Fill in the connection details and enable **Advanced Options**, as shown in the following screenshot:

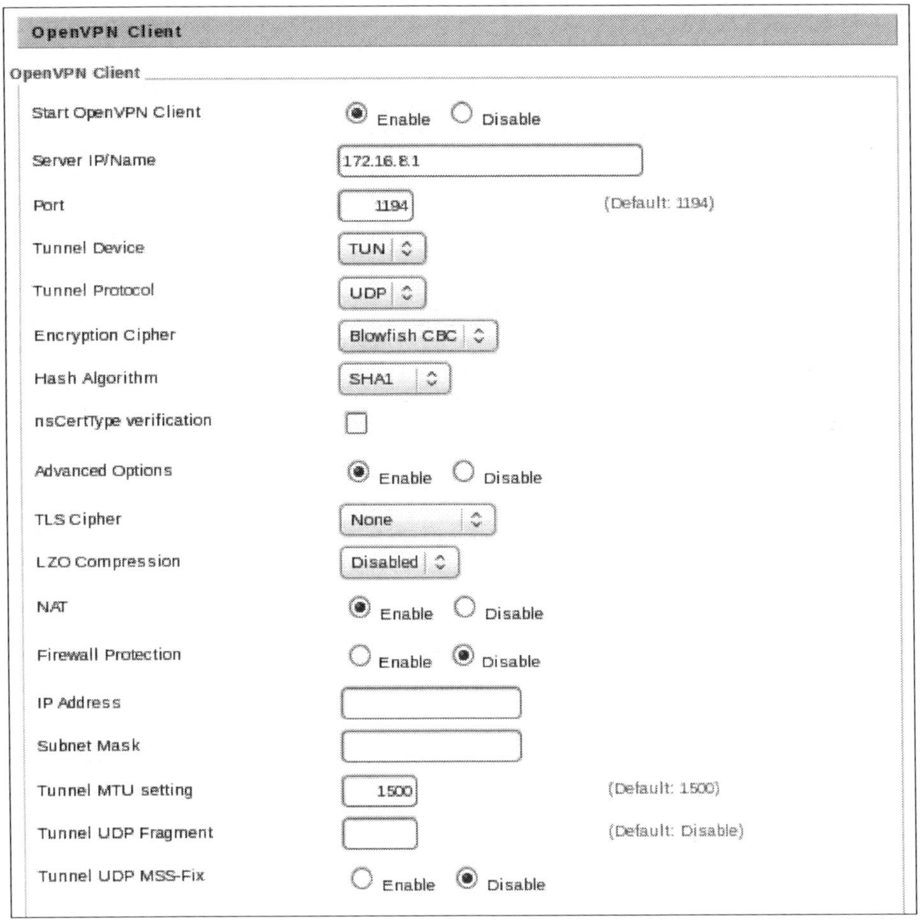

Most settings can be left at their default values, but disable **Firewall Protection** to ensure that the VPN server can reach the client and vice versa, by using the following steps:

1. This is a long web form, so scroll down and fill in the security parameters:
   - ○ TLS auth key
   - ○ CA certificate
   - ○ Client public certificate
   - ○ Client private key

2. The values for these fields are the exact same values as used in the configuration profile for the Android client at the beginning of this chapter:

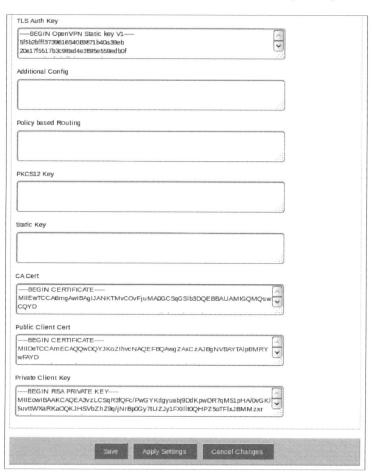

3. After filling in all the security parameters, click on **Save** to save the OpenVPN client configuration. Normally, as soon as a valid profile has been entered, the DD-WRT OpenVPN client will attempt to make a connection with the server. Note that you can normally have only a single profile stored on the DD-WRT device, due to size limitations of the device's NVRAM storage space.

4. After the VPN connection has been established, we can verify that the VPN client can be reached from the server by pinging its VPN IP address:

```
$ ping -c 2 10.200.0.2
PING 10.200.0.2 (10.200.0.2) 56(84) bytes of data.
64 bytes from 10.200.0.2: icmp_seq=1 ttl=64 time=0.591 ms
64 bytes from 10.200.0.2: icmp_seq=2 ttl=64 time=0.659 ms
--- 10.200.0.2 ping statistics ---
2 packets transmitted, 2 received, 0% packet loss, time
  1000ms
rtt min/avg/max/mdev = 0.591/0.625/0.659/0.034 ms
```

The easiest method to troubleshoot any connection problems is by looking at the server side logs; the client-side log can be retrieved using the DD-WRT web interface, but as we will see in the next chapter, the server-side log is usually more informative.

Using a home router as a VPN server

Using OpenVPN on a small wireless router is possible, but it greatly depends on the exact type of the wireless router used. On the DD-WRT and OpenWRT websites, many supported wireless routers are listed, but even most of those have drawbacks. A minimum flash size of 8 MB is required and a sufficiently large NVRAM space is also desirable.

However, even with the right hardware, the performance of OpenVPN on a wireless router will not be very good due to the limited computing power of such devices. For people who want to set up a VPN to their home address, performance is usually fine, unless your home connection is capable of doing more than 100 Mbps upstream.

The following procedure can be used to configure a DD-WRT router as an OpenVPN server:

1. In the DD-WRT web interface, click on the **Services** tab and click on **VPN**.

2. Disable the OpenVPN client first by scrolling down and selecting **Disable** in the **OpenVPN Client** section.

3. In the **OpenVPN Server/Daemon** section, enable **OpenVPN**.

4. Fill in the connection details and compare the details to the lines found in the `basic-udp-server.conf` configuration file:

   1. Select **System** as **Start Type** so that the OpenVPN daemon is launched whenever the DD-WRT router boots.

   2. It is not entirely clear what the exact difference is between **Configure as server** and **Configure as daemon**.

   3. Select **Router (TUN)** as the **Server Mode**, as we want a tun-style OpenVPN setup.

   4. Fill in **10.200.0.0** and **255.255.255.0** as **Network** and **Netmask**. This is the equivalent of the "server" line.

   5. **Port, Tunnel Protocol, Encryption Cipher**, and **Hash Algorithm** can be left at their default values.

   6. Click on **Enable** next to **Advanced Options** to show all available OpenVPN configuration options. We do not need to change any of these options, but it is instructive to see which options are available:

5. Next, we fill in the certificate and public/private key details. For this, we make use of the files from the standard server configuration file `basic-udp-server.conf`.

6. Scroll down in the lengthy web form and paste the contents of the `server.crt`, `ca.crt`, `server.key` and `dh2048.pem` files, respectively:

    ◦   **Public Server Cert**: corresponds to the "cert" line (`server.crt`)

    ◦   **CA Cert**: corresponds to the "ca" line (`movpn-ca.crt`)

    ◦   **Private Server Key**: corresponds to the "key" line (`server.key`)

    ◦   **DH PEM**: corresponds to the "dh" line (`dh2048.pem`)

This terms is shown in the following screenshot:

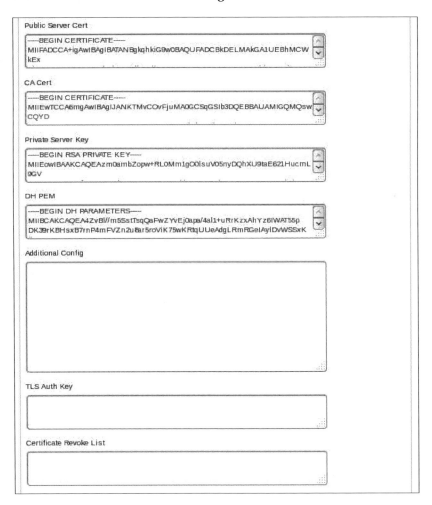

7. Notice that we skipped the **TLS Auth Key** field. If this field is also filled in, then the NVRAM of the DD-WRT device is exhausted and the router will need to be reset. As a result, we will not be able to use the `basic-udp-client.ovpn` client configuration file to connect to this server.

8. Scroll to the bottom of the screen and click on the **Save** button. As soon as the configuration has been stored in NVRAM, the OpenVPN server process will be started.

> Storing all configurations in NVRAM is tricky. Using files might be an alternative choice, but this requires a custom startup script.
>
> If the configuration does not fit into NVRAM, it will most likely crash the DD-WRT device and you will need to manually reset it. The Belkin Playmax router is one example: it was only possible to store the entire configuration in NVRAM by omitting the `tls-auth` key file.

9. Finally, connect a client using the `movpn-04-01-client.conf` configuration file and verify that the VPN connection is working:

```
[client]$ ping -c 4 10.200.0.1
PING 10.200.0.1 (10.200.0.1) 56(84) bytes of data.
64 bytes from 10.200.0.1: icmp_seq=1 ttl=64 time=22.3 ms
64 bytes from 10.200.0.1: icmp_seq=2 ttl=64 time=18.6 ms
64 bytes from 10.200.0.1: icmp_seq=4 ttl=64 time=21.9 ms
64 bytes from 10.200.0.1: icmp_seq=5 ttl=64 time=15.7 ms
```

Summary

OpenVPN is now available on many platforms, including smart phones, tablets, and even certain models of (wireless) routers. The configuration, support, and deployment methods vary across these devices, and those differences should be considered when choosing supported platforms in your environment.

In the next chapter, we will focus on troubleshooting OpenVPN configuration and performance. As both the configuration and the performance of OpenVPN on smart phones as well as wireless routers can be cumbersome, it will be very useful to learn about troubleshooting techniques.

Troubleshooting and Tuning

9

Usually, it is quite easy to set up a VPN using OpenVPN. This is one of the most attractive features of OpenVPN compared to other VPN solutions. However, sometimes it is necessary to troubleshoot a non-working setup or to tune an existing setup to gain performance.

Troubleshooting and tuning OpenVPN are often overlooked topics. The OpenVPN log files on both client and server side provide a lot of information, but you have to know how to read them. There are also quite a few common mistakes to make when setting up the client and server configuration files. In this chapter, you will learn how to interpret the OpenVPN log files and how to detect and fix some of these common mistakes.

Finally, there is a large difference between a working setup and a setup that works well. Your OpenVPN setup may be functioning correctly, yet users may still complain about poor performance. Getting the maximum performance out of an OpenVPN setup can seem like black magic. In this chapter, you will learn some of this black magic.

The following topics will be covered in this chapter:

- How to read the log files
- Fixing common configuration mistakes
- Troubleshooting routing issues
- How to optimize performance using `ping` and `iperf`
- Analyzing OpenVPN traffic using `tcpdump`

How to read the log files

Debugging a non-working setup can seem like a daunting task at first. Where should you begin? Luckily, OpenVPN provides excellent logging and debugging facilities. However, with increased logging verbosity, it also becomes increasingly difficult to read these log files. The default log level of OpenVPN is 1, but it is recommended that you set the verbosity to 3. This often gives the administrator enough information to detect setup issues, while keeping the performance penalty to a minimum.

Setting the verbosity to 5 or higher is recommended only for debugging purposes, as it will severely affect performance.

Every example in this book so far has included the setting verb 3. First, we will go through both client and server log files for a working setup with this verbosity. It is important to understand, and possibly even store, the log files of a working connection. When trying to find a bug in a non-working setup, it is very useful to compare the log files of the non-working case with those of the working setup.

Start the server using the default configuration file `basic-udp-server.conf`:

```
[root@server]# openvpn --config basic-udp-server.conf
```

Do not connect to the client yet. The server log file will now contain the following:

```
1   14:53:27 OpenVPN 2.3.6 x86_64-redhat-linux-gnu
             [SSL (OpenSSL)] [LZO] [EPOLL] [PKCS11] [MH] [IPv6]
             built on Dec  2 2014
2   14:53:27 library versions: OpenSSL 1.0.1e-fips 11 Feb 2013,
             LZO2.03
3   14:53:27 Diffie-Hellman initialized with 2048 bit key
4   14:53:31 WARNING: this configuration may cache passwords in
             memory -- use the auth-nocache option to prevent this
5   14:53:31 Control Channel Authentication: using
             '/etc/openvpn/movpn/ta.key' as a OpenVPN static key
             file
6   14:53:31 Outgoing Control Channel Authentication: Using 160
             bit message hash 'SHA1' for HMAC authentication
7   14:53:31 Incoming Control Channel Authentication: Using 160
             bit message hash 'SHA1' for HMAC authentication
8   14:53:31 Socket Buffers: R=[16777216->131072]
                             S=[16777216->131072]
```

```
9    14:53:31 TUN/TAP device tun0 opened
10   14:53:31 TUN/TAP TX queue length set to 100
11   14:53:31 do_ifconfig, tt->ipv6=0, tt-did_ifconfig_ipv6_setup=0
12   14:53:31 /sbin/ip link set dev tun0 up mtu 1500
13   14:53:31 /sbin/ip addr add dev tun0 10.200.0.1/24
                      broadcast 10.200.0.255
14   14:53:31 GID set to nobody
15   14:53:31 UID set to nobody
16   14:53:31 UDPv4 link local (bound): [undef]
17   14:53:31 UDPv4 link remote: [undef]
18   14:53:31 MULTI: multi_init called, r=256 v=256
19   14:53:31 IFCONFIG POOL: base=10.200.0.2 size=252, ipv6=0
20   14:53:31 Initialization Sequence Completed
```

The timestamps at the front of each line have been abbreviated for the sake of clarity.

Let's go through this log file line by line:

- Lines 1 and 2 indicate the version and build date of OpenVPN itself, as well as the libraries that OpenVPN depends on.

- Line 3 tells us that the server Diffie-Hellman parameters were initialized successfully. The file specified in the server configuration line dh /etc/openvpn/movpn/dh2048.pem was used for this.

- Line 4 is a warning that is almost always printed. There has been discussion among the developers whether this line should be removed or not. In the end, it was decided that, for security reasons, it is best to print out this warning. Unless you are extremely paranoid about security, you can ignore this warning line.

- Line 5 indicates that the control channel is protected using the tls-auth configuration option, and that OpenVPN was able to successfully read the specified file.

- Lines 6 and 7 tell us that two SHA1 keys are derived from the tls-auth file, and are now used to sign (hash) the outgoing traffic and to check the incoming traffic.

- Line 8 shows the size of the Receive (R) and Send (S) buffers that OpenVPN uses. These parameters are useful only when tuning a working setup, as we will see later in this chapter.

- Lines 9 and 10 show that OpenVPN was able to successfully open a `tun` device and was able to set the packet queue depth for this device to `100`.

- Line 11 to line 13 shows the IPv4 settings that are used for this server configuration. They also list that no IPv6 settings were specified. The settings listed here are a translation of the server configuration line `server 10.200.0.0 255.255.255.0`.

- Lines 14 and 15 are the result of specifying `group nobody` and `user nobody` in the server configuration file, respectively.

- Lines 16 and 17 show that OpenVPN is listening for UDP traffic and is bound to an undefined interface (0.0.0.0). This is the result of specifying `proto udp` and `bind` in the server configuration file.

- Line 18 tells us that this is a multi-client setup with real and virtual address table hash sizes of `256`.

- Line 19 lists the range of pool addresses available to OpenVPN clients that can connect to this server. It is also part of the translation of the server configuration line `server 10.200.0.0 255.255.255.0`.

- Line 20 is the magical line that tells us that the server started up successfully and that the initialization has completed. The server is now ready to accept connections from incoming clients.

Next, we launch the client and watch the server-side log file:

```
[root@client]# openvpn --config basic-udp-client.conf
```

After that, we will go through the client-side log file as well:

```
21  15:30:37 <CLIENT-IP>:39086 TLS: Initial packet from
              [AF_INET]<CLIENT-IP>:39086, sid=071ba589 7e9ff2a0
22  15:30:37 <CLIENT-IP>:39086 VERIFY OK: depth=1, C=ZA,
              ST=Enlightenment, L=Overall, O=Mastering OpenVPN,
              CN=Mastering OpenVPN, emailAddress=root@example.org
23  15:30:37 <CLIENT-IP>:39086 VERIFY OK: depth=0, C=ZA,
              ST=Enlightenment, O=Mastering OpenVPN, CN=client3,
              emailAddress=root@example.org
24  15:30:37 <CLIENT-IP>:39086 Data Channel Encrypt: Cipher
              'BF-CBC' initialized with 128 bit key
25  15:30:37 <CLIENT-IP>:39086 Data Channel Encrypt: Using 160 bit
              message hash 'SHA1' for HMAC authentication
```

```
26  15:30:37 <CLIENT-IP>:39086 Data Channel Decrypt: Cipher
             'BF-CBC' initialized with 128 bit key
27  15:30:37 <CLIENT-IP>:39086 Data Channel Decrypt: Using 160 bit
             message hash 'SHA1' for HMAC authentication
28  15:30:37 <CLIENT-IP>:39086 Control Channel: TLSv1, cipher
             TLSv1/SSLv3 DHE-RSA-AES256-SHA, 2048 bit RSA
29  15:30:37 <CLIENT-IP>:39086 [client3] Peer Connection Initiated
             with [AF_INET]<CLIENT-IP>:39086
30  15:30:37 client3/<CLIENT-IP>:39086 MULTI_sva: pool returned
             IPv4=10.200.0.2, IPv6=(Not enabled)
31  15:30:37 client3/<CLIENT-IP>:39086 MULTI: Learn: 10.200.0.2 →
             client3/<CLIENT-IP>:39086
32  15:30:37 client3/<CLIENT-IP>:39086 MULTI: primary virtual IP
             for client3/<CLIENT-IP>:39086: 10.200.0.2
33  15:30:39 client3/<CLIENT-IP>:39086 PUSH: Received control
             message: 'PUSH_REQUEST'
34  15:30:39 client3/<CLIENT-IP>:39086 send_push_reply():
             safe_cap=940
35  15:30:39 client3/<CLIENT-IP>:39086 SENT CONTROL [client3]:
             'PUSH_REPLY,route-gateway 10.200.0.1,topology subnet,
             ping 10,ping-restart 60,
             ifconfig 10.200.0.2 255.255.255.0' (status=1)
```

Let's go through the new log entries:

- Line 21 indicates that an initial packet was received from the client with the IP address <CLIENT-IP>. Normally, a full IPv4 address is listed here.

- Lines 22 and 23 show the verification process of the certificate provided by the OpenVPN client. The important part in these log lines is VERIFY-OK.

- Lines 24 to 27 list the encryption and decryption cipher used, as well as the SHA1 hashes used to hash incoming and outgoing traffic on the data channel. **BF-CBC (Blowfish Cipher Block Chaining)** is the current default cipher for OpenVPN.

- Line 28 shows the TLS cipher used to protect the OpenVPN control channel. The cipher listed here is very similar to the encryption cipher used by a secure web server.

- Line 29 indicates that the client client3 from the IP address <CLIENT-IP> successfully passed the authentication process.

- Lines 30 to 32 list the pool address that will be assigned to this client.

- Lines 33 to 34 show that the client asked for configuration information (PUSH REQUEST), and the reply from the server that it will send a push_reply.

- Line 35 shows the contents of the push_reply message with all the configuration information for this client. This line is extremely useful when debugging an OpenVPN setup, as it shows most of the information that an OpenVPN server has for a particular client, regardless of the configuration file used.

Similarly, here's the client log file (note the timestamps and match them against the timestamps from the server log file):

```
1    15:30:37 OpenVPN 2.3.6 x86_64-redhat-linux-gnu
              [SSL (OpenSSL)] [LZO] [EPOLL] [PKCS11] [MH] [IPv6]
              built on Dec  2 2014
2    15:30:37 library versions: OpenSSL 1.0.1e-fips 11 Feb 2013,
              LZO 2.03
3    15:30:37 Control Channel Authentication: using
              '/etc/openvpn/movpn/ta.key' as a OpenVPN static key
              file
4    15:30:37 UDPv4 link local: [undef]
5    15:30:37 UDPv4 link remote: [AF_INET]<SERVER-IP>:1194
6    15:30:37 [Mastering OpenVPN Server] Peer Connection Initiated
              with [AF_INET]<SERVER-IP>:1194
7    15:30:39 TUN/TAP device tun0 opened
8    15:30:39 do_ifconfig, tt->ipv6=0, tt-did_ifconfig_ipv6_setup=0
9    15:30:39 /sbin/ip link set dev tun0 up mtu 1500
10   15:30:39 /sbin/ip addr add dev tun0 10.200.0.2/24
              broadcast 10.200.0.255
11   15:30:39 Initialization Sequence Completed
```

Let's go through the new log entries:

- Lines 1 and 2 are very similar to the lines from the server log.

- Line 3 indicates that the control channel is protected by using the `tls-auth` configuration option, and that OpenVPN was able to successfully read the specified file.

- Lines 4 and 5 tell us that the client did not bind to a local IP address, and that a UDP connection was established with the server at the IP address `<SERVER-IP>` and port `1194`.

- Line 6 lists that the connection with the OpenVPN server that identifies itself as `Mastering OpenVPN Server` was established successfully. The name of the server is retrieved from the **common name** of the server-side certificate.

- Line 7 tells us that OpenVPN was able to open the TUN device `tun0`.

- Lines 8 to10 list the IPv4 information that the server pushed towards this client, and it shows that the IP address and netmask are set using the standard Linux `/sbin/ip` command.

- Line 11 is again the magical line that tells us that the VPN connection was established successfully, and that we can now securely communicate with the OpenVPN server. However, as we will see later on, the error messages may have yet to occur.

Detecting a non-working setup

An OpenVPN setup can fail for many reasons. In the next section, we will go through a list of common failures. First, let's take a look at what is shown in the log files when a connection attempt fails. Failures can occur very early in the connection attempt, or even after the `Initialization Sequence Completed` line.

If we use the wrong `tls-auth` file, the connection will fail very early on. This is exactly the reason to use a `tls-auth` file, as it will minimize the load on our OpenVPN server when rogue clients attempt access. A client that attempts to connect without specifying a `tls-auth` file will show up in the server logs as follows:

```
16:40:31 Authenticate/Decrypt packet error:
        packet HMAC authentication failed
16:40:31 TLS Error: incoming packet authentication failed from
        [AF_INET]<CLIENT-IP>:49956
16:40:33 Authenticate/Decrypt packet error:
        packet HMAC authentication failed
```

```
16:40:33 TLS Error: incoming packet authentication failed from
         [AF_INET]<CLIENT-IP>:49956
16:40:37 Authenticate/Decrypt packet error:
         packet HMAC authentication failed
16:40:37 TLS Error: incoming packet authentication failed from
         [AF_INET]<CLIENT-IP>:49956
16:40:45 Authenticate/Decrypt packet error:
         packet HMAC authentication failed
16:40:45 TLS Error: incoming packet authentication failed from
         [AF_INET]<CLIENT-IP>:49956
16:41:01 Authenticate/Decrypt packet error:
             packet HMAC authentication failed
16:41:01 TLS Error: incoming packet authentication failed from
         [AF_INET]<CLIENT-IP>:49956
```

Nothing else is reported about this client, as the OpenVPN server rejects the connection attempt immediately. From the timestamps in the log file, we can see that the client is increasing the delay time between connection attempts with every failed connection. If no connection can be made in 60 seconds, then the client will abort:

```
TLS Error: TLS key negotiation failed to occur within 60 seconds (check
your network connectivity)
TLS Error: TLS handshake failed
```

The second connection failure will only become apparent after the connection seems to have been successfully initialized. For this, we specify the use of a different encryption cipher on one side, but forget to do so on the other. The client log file will now show the following:

```
16:56:20 /sbin/ip link set dev tun0 up mtu 1500
16:56:20 /sbin/ip addr add dev tun0 10.200.0.2/24 broadcast 10.200.0.255
16:56:20 Initialization Sequence Completed
16:56:30 Authenticate/Decrypt packet error: cipher final failed
16:56:40 Authenticate/Decrypt packet error: cipher final failed
```

Thus, at first the connection seems to have been established successfully (lines 1 to 3), but after 10 seconds, data channel encryption and decryption is failing.

If the Windows GUI had been used in this case, the GUI icon would have turned green but the VPN itself would not be functional!

Most configuration issues will be reported at either the server or the client end during initialization. Routing issues, which are much more common, will usually not be reported by OpenVPN. Hence, different troubleshooting techniques are required.

Fixing common configuration mistakes

When setting up an OpenVPN configuration, there are a few common mistakes that are easily made. These configuration mistakes can be roughly divided up into four categories:

- Certificate (PKI) errors and mismatches
- Option mismatches, such as `tun` versus `tap`, ciphers, and compression
- Insufficient privileges to run OpenVPN
- Routing mistakes

In this section, we will go through the first three of these categories. Routing mistakes will be discussed later in this chapter.

Wrong CA certificate in the client configuration

The client configuration file will almost always contain three lines like this:

```
ca ca.crt
cert client.crt
key client.key
```

These certificate and private key files were created in *Chapter 3, PKIs and Certificates*, and are used extensively in subsequent chapters.

The CA file, however, does not need to specify the certificate authority that was used to sign the client certificate file. It must be the public certificate of the certificate authority that was used to sign the server certificate. If the server certificate was signed by a different CA, then the client will refuse to connect to the server. This can be seen in the client-side log file:

```
UDPv4 link remote: [AF_INET]<SERVER-IP>:1194

VERIFY ERROR: depth=1, error=self signed certificate in certificate
chain: C=ZA, ST=Enlightenment, L=Overall, O=Mastering OpenVPN,
CN=Mastering OpenVPN, emailAddress=root@example.org

TLS_ERROR: BIO read tls_read_plaintext error: error:14090086:SSL
routines:SSL3_GET_SERVER_CERTIFICATE:certificate verify failed

TLS Error: TLS object -> incoming plaintext read error

TLS Error: TLS handshake failed
```

In this case, no errors are logged on the server side, as the client certificate is considered valid by the server.

The only thing logged on the server is as follows:

```
<CLIENT-IP>:42472 TLS: Initial packet from
    [AF_INET]<CLIENT-IP>:42472, sid=9a1e4a84 cdbb6926

<CLIENT-IP>:51441 TLS: Initial packet from
    [AF_INET]<CLIENT-IP>:51441, sid=17d3c89b 6999ae97

<CLIENT-IP>:43513 TLS: Initial packet from
    [AF_INET]<CLIENT-IP>:43513, sid=4609202f 4c91c23d
```

This shows the successive connection attempts that are made by the OpenVPN client.

How to fix

Ensure that the right CA file is specified in the client configuration file.

Client certificate not recognized by the server

If the client certificate is not recognized by the server, the server will refuse access to it. This can happen if either the wrong (or a rogue) client certificate is used, or if the client's certificate was revoked and the `crl-verify` option is specified in the server configuration file.

The following entries will show up in the server's log file if an unknown client attempts to connect to the OpenVPN server:

```
<CLIENT-IP>:57072 TLS: Initial packet from
    [AF_INET]<CLIENT-IP>:57072, sid=a175f1be 6faed111
<CLIENT-IP>:57072 VERIFY ERROR: depth=0, error=unable to get
    local issuer certificate: C=NL, O=Cookbook, CN=client1,
    name=Cookbook Client, emailAddress=janjust@nikhef.nl
<CLIENT-IP>:57072 TLS_ERROR: BIO read tls_read_plaintext error:
    error:140890B2:SSL routines:SSL3_GET_CLIENT_CERTIFICATE:
    no certificate returned
<CLIENT-IP>:57072 TLS Error: TLS object -> incoming plaintext
    read error
<CLIENT-IP>:57072 TLS Error: TLS handshake failed
```

The server cannot verify the client's certificate, as it does not recognize the CA certificate that was used to sign it. It therefore refuses to allow this client to connect.

On the client side, no messages are printed in the log file for 60 seconds, after which the initial handshake times out and a new connection attempt is made:

```
13:24:23 UDPv4 link local: [undef]
13:24:23 UDPv4 link remote: [AF_INET]<SERVER-IP>:1194
13:25:23 TLS Error: TLS key negotiation failed to occur within
    60 seconds (check your network connectivity)
13:25:23 TLS Error: TLS handshake failed
13:25:23 SIGUSR1[soft,tls-error] received, process restarting
13:25:25 Control Channel Authentication: using
    '/etc/openvpn/movpn/ta.key' as a OpenVPN static key file
13:25:25 UDPv4 link local: [undef]
13:25:25 UDPv4 link remote: [AF_INET]<SERVER-IP>:1194
```

How to fix

Ensure that the client's certificate is recognized by the server. This can be done either by specifying the proper CA certificate in the server configuration file, or by adding the CA certificate to a stacked CA certificate file in the server configuration file:

```
# cat CA1.crt CA2.crt > /etc/openvpn/movpn/ca-stack.pem
```

Next, use the following in the server configuration:

```
ca /etc/openvpn/movpn/ca-stack.pem.
```

This way, client-side certificates that are signed by either `CA1.crt` or `CA2.crt` will be accepted by the server.

Of course, if this is a rogue client that is attempting to connect, then a more appropriate solution might be to blacklist the IP address from which the client is connecting.

Client certificate and private key mismatch

If the certificate and private key on the client do not match, then OpenVPN will not even attempt to connect to the server. The following error will be printed in the log file instead:

```
Cannot load private key file /etc/openvpn/movpn/client1.key:
error:0B080074:x509 certificate routines:
    X509_check_private_key:key values mismatch
Error: private key password verification failed
Exiting due to fatal error
```

This problem can occur especially when the certificate and private key are renewed; it is a common mistake to use the old private key with the new certificate.

How to fix

Ensure that the client's certificate and private key match. Surprisingly, there is no easy-to-use tool for this. To find out if the certificate and private key belong together, we can use the following commands and look for the `modulus` sections:

```
$ openssl x509 -text -noout -in client1.crt
[...]
  Public Key Algorithm: rsaEncryption
  Public-Key: (2048 bit)
```

```
Modulus:
    00:b2:17:bd:31:6d:56:d9:eb:c9:09:98:e2:c1:48:
    c9:6a:e4:4a:6b:54:52:ea:1e:60:94:6b:cb:5e:d5:
    a1:ef:83:05:f8:cf:a4:06:df:06:ee:d6:c8:75:65:
    de:a7:96:68:a1:41:d1:9d:f0:2c:84:3f:ca:b9:d2:
    e8:07:af:37:48:24:69:57:4e:09:70:66:47:6c:47:
    36:4d:c9:29:13:eb:ed:c1:aa:cd:36:84:3c:55:18:
    bc:ce:01:34:b5:89:04:dc:09:c5:ea:f2:57:9f:c2:
    f5:c1:05:dd:66:4d:11:13:05:47:46:26:1a:55:18:
    51:bd:89:65:ba:0d:89:bd:ea:03:58:5e:d3:d9:96:
    a5:5e:2f:5f:b9:c8:88:fc:48:95:cb:4a:b2:12:3b:
    b5:ed:4c:40:4c:50:8d:1d:eb:a5:c9:c0:e6:2c:ec:
    01:0a:56:ac:db:9e:e7:56:f0:06:f7:ba:b6:ac:de:
    41:d4:fb:b3:d6:f5:fe:13:b4:03:81:d9:f7:7c:2e:
    60:2f:9c:5a:81:eb:2e:3a:e1:c4:8b:f8:b6:8d:2d:
    f7:ec:7a:f6:2c:ff:af:1c:d2:7b:58:ca:9e:d1:f4:
    ed:8a:7a:35:00:97:a3:35:dd:79:02:b4:79:9a:66:
    3c:5e:c8:4d:87:eb:68:5d:45:29:73:70:7f:61:28:
    67:b1

$ openssl rsa -text -noout -in client1.key
Private-Key: (2048 bit)
modulus:
    00:b2:17:bd:31:6d:56:d9:eb:c9:09:98:e2:c1:48:
    c9:6a:e4:4a:6b:54:52:ea:1e:60:94:6b:cb:5e:d5:
    a1:ef:83:05:f8:cf:a4:06:df:06:ee:d6:c8:75:65:
    de:a7:96:68:a1:41:d1:9d:f0:2c:84:3f:ca:b9:d2:
    e8:07:af:37:48:24:69:57:4e:09:70:66:47:6c:47:
    36:4d:c9:29:13:eb:ed:c1:aa:cd:36:84:3c:55:18:
    bc:ce:01:34:b5:89:04:dc:09:c5:ea:f2:57:9f:c2:
    f5:c1:05:dd:66:4d:11:13:05:47:46:26:1a:55:18:
    51:bd:89:65:ba:0d:89:bd:ea:03:58:5e:d3:d9:96:
    a5:5e:2f:5f:b9:c8:88:fc:48:95:cb:4a:b2:12:3b:
    b5:ed:4c:40:4c:50:8d:1d:eb:a5:c9:c0:e6:2c:ec:
```

```
01:0a:56:ac:db:9e:e7:56:f0:06:f7:ba:b6:ac:de:
41:d4:fb:b3:d6:f5:fe:13:b4:03:81:d9:f7:7c:2e:
60:2f:9c:5a:81:eb:2e:3a:e1:c4:8b:f8:b6:8d:2d:
f7:ec:7a:f6:2c:ff:af:1c:d2:7b:58:ca:9e:d1:f4:
ed:8a:7a:35:00:97:a3:35:dd:79:02:b4:79:9a:66:
3c:5e:c8:4d:87:eb:68:5d:45:29:73:70:7f:61:28:
67:b1
```

[...]

If we look closely at the modulus from both the public key (certificate) and the private key, we can see that they are equal. Thus, this certificate and private key belong together.

When comparing moduli, it is often sufficient to compare the first few bytes and then the last few bytes.

The auth and tls-auth key mismatch

The `auth` and `tls-auth` options are used to authenticate both control channel and data channel packets using an HMAC signing algorithm. The default value for the `auth` HMAC algorithm is `SHA1`, which uses 160-bit keys. There is no default value for the `tls-auth` option, as it is not required. However, this option is recommended, as it provides an extra layer of protection against DDoS attacks.

If the `auth` algorithm specified in the client and server configurations do not match, then the server will not allow the client to begin the TLS security handshake. Similarly, if the `tls-auth` files on the client and server mismatch, or if the wrong `direction` parameter is given on either side, then the server will also not allow the client to begin the TLS security handshake.

Normally, the following option is specified in the server configuration file:

`tls-auth /etc/openvpn/movpn/ta.key 0`

Correspondingly, on the client we have the following option:

`tls-auth /etc/openvpn/movpn/ta.key 1`

Here, the second parameter defines `direction` of the `tls-auth` keys used. This parameter is not required, but it allows OpenVPN to use different hashing (or HMAC) keys for incoming and outgoing traffic. The key used on the client to sign outgoing traffic must match the key used on the server to verify incoming traffic, and vice versa.

If the wrong `tls-auth` key file is used, or if direction is omitted or not correctly specified, then the following entries will show up in the server log file:

```
Authenticate/Decrypt packet error: packet HMAC
    authentication failed
TLS Error: incoming packet authentication failed from
    [AF_INET]<CLIENT-IP>:54377
```

In the meantime, the client will simply attempt to connect for 60 seconds before a timeout occurs.

How to fix

Make sure that the same `tls-auth` file is used in both client and server configuration files. Also, make sure that the direction parameter is specified correctly on both ends (if used at all).

If you are still unsure of which HMAC keys are used for incoming and outgoing connections, you can increase the log file verbosity to see the actual keys being used by both client and server. Let's add the following to both client and server configuration files:

```
verb 7
```

Now, both sides will print out a large amount of logging information at startup. The lines to look for in the log file are on the server side:

```
Outgoing Control Channel Authentication:
    Using 160 bit message hash 'SHA1' for HMAC authentication
Outgoing Control Channel Authentication:
    HMAC KEY: 4660a714 7f4d33f9 d2f7c61a 9f1d5743 4bf9411e
Outgoing Control Channel Authentication:
    HMAC size=20 block_size=20
Incoming Control Channel Authentication:
    Using 160 bit message hash 'SHA1' for HMAC authentication
```

```
Incoming Control Channel Authentication:
    HMAC KEY: cd1f6d9c 88db5ec7 d7977322 e01d14f1 26ee4e22
Incoming Control Channel Authentication:
    HMAC size=20 block_size=20
```

The HMAC size=20 line corresponds to the fact that 160-bit message hashing using SHA1 is used, as 160 bit is the same as 20 byte.

If the correct tls-auth file and direction parameter are used on the client side, we will find the following:

```
Outgoing Control Channel Authentication:
    Using 160 bit message hash 'SHA1' for HMAC authentication
Outgoing Control Channel Authentication:
    HMAC KEY: cd1f6d9c 88db5ec7 d7977322 e01d14f1 26ee4e22
Outgoing Control Channel Authentication:
    HMAC size=20 block_size=20
Incoming Control Channel Authentication:
    Using 160 bit message hash 'SHA1' for HMAC authentication
Incoming Control Channel Authentication:
    HMAC KEY: 4660a714 7f4d33f9 d2f7c61a 9f1d5743 4bf9411e
Incoming Control Channel Authentication:
    HMAC size=20 block_size=20
```

The incoming and outgoing control channel authentication keys are mirrored on the client versus the server, ensuring proper TLS authentication.

The MTU size mismatch

OpenVPN uses two **Maximum Transfer Unit (MTU)** sizes:

- tun-mtu: This specifies the MTU setting of the tun adapter and specifies the maximum size of each packet inside the VPN tunnel.

- link-mtu: This specifies the maximum size of each packet outside the tunnel. This includes all padding, encryption, and authentication bits, but it is not the actual packet size as it goes over the network. The actual packet size cannot be determined beforehand, as the size of each packet can differ due to compression and encryption algorithms.

The default value of the `tun-mtu` parameter is 1,500 bytes, which is the default MTU size of an Ethernet adapter as well. Under normal circumstances, we can use the following formula to compute the `link-mtu` size from the `tun-mtu` size:

```
link-mtu = tun-mtu + constant
```

Here, `constant` depends on the configuration options used. Among the configuration options that have an influence on this constant, we have the following:

- Compression options such as `comp-lzo` and `comp-noadapt`
- The **initialization vector (IV)** size of the encryption parameter of the `cipher` option
- The `fragment` option that adds an extra byte
- The `no-replay` option that removes a byte

If we see `link-mtu` warning mismatch, this usually points to a misconfiguration elsewhere in our client and server configuration files. As you will see in the subsequent examples, a mismatch in `link-mtu` between the client and the server can occur quite often. Normally, a VPN connection will not function correctly if there is a `link-mtu` mismatch.

> Resist the temptation to fix the `link-mtu` warning itself by explicitly setting it. First, fix the other warnings that may have caused the `link-mtu` warning to appear.

The `link-mtu` parameter is also of great value when tuning a VPN connection. To get the maximum performance out of a VPN connection, we will need to ensure that the packets are not fragmented by the operating system, as this will have a drastic impact on performance. Over satellite-based links in particular, this can decrease performance almost to a stand-still.

If a different MTU size is specified on the server side compared to the client side, the following warning will appear in the log files:

```
WARNING: 'link-mtu' is used inconsistently,
    local='link-mtu 1441', remote='link-mtu 1541'
WARNING: 'tun-mtu' is used inconsistently,
    local='tun-mtu 1400', remote='tun-mtu 1500'
```

This shows that for a fairly `default` configuration, the `link-mtu` overhead is actually 41 bytes. Here, we have added to the client configuration file:

```
tun-mtu 1400
```

At this point, the VPN connection will function. Performance will be limited, however, as packets need to be fragmented and reassembled. It is possible to trigger an error with this setup by sending large ICMP packets with the `do not fragment` flag set. On Linux/FreeBSD, this can be done by using the following command:

```
$ ping -M do -s 1450 10.200.0.2
```

On Windows, we use the following:

```
C:\> ping -f -l 1450 10.200.0.2
```

This will result in 100 percent packet loss for the `ping` command, and it will also show up in the log file:

```
Authenticate/Decrypt packet error:
    packet HMAC authentication failed
```

This error message may appear confusing at first, but it is caused by the fact that the sending party constructed and signed a packet which is larger than 1,400 bytes. The client receives only the first 1,400 bytes of this packet and checks the signature, which fails. It then rejects the packet and prints out the error.

How to fix

Make sure that, if you want to use the `tun-mtu` option that it is specified in both client and server configuration files.

The Cipher mismatch

The encryption cipher that is used for OpenVPN's data channel can be specified by using the following option with a default setting of `BF-CBC`:

```
cipher aes-256-cbc
```

If a different cipher is specified in the client configuration file than in the server configuration file, then the log files on both sides will print out a warning message but the VPN connection will come up. However, as soon as any traffic passes over it, it will fail to decrypt. We can see this in the following excerpt from the client-side log file:

```
WARNING: 'link-mtu' is used inconsistently,
    local='link-mtu 1557', remote='link-mtu 1541'
WARNING: 'cipher' is used inconsistently,
```

```
    local='cipher AES-256-CBC', remote='cipher BF-CBC'
WARNING: 'keysize' is used inconsistently,
    local='keysize 256', remote='keysize 128'
[Mastering OpenVPN Server] Peer Connection Initiated
    with [AF_INET]<SERVER-IP>:1194
TUN/TAP device tun0 opened
do_ifconfig, tt->ipv6=0, tt->did_ifconfig_ipv6_setup=0
/sbin/ip link set dev tun0 up mtu 1500
/sbin/ip addr add dev tun0 10.200.0.2/24 broadcast 10.200.0.255
Initialization Sequence Completed
Authenticate/Decrypt packet error: cipher final failed
```

The three warnings that are printed initially show both the different type and the
different size of the cipher used. The default Blowfish cipher uses 128-bit strength,
whereas the AES-256 cipher uses 256-bit strength, resulting in a slightly larger
encrypted packet (link-mtu of 1,541 bytes for Blowfish versus a link-mtu of 1,557
bytes for AES-256).

How to fix

Make sure that the same cipher is specified in both client and server configuration
files. As both client and server log files print out the expected cipher, it is a relatively
easy error to fix.

 It is currently not possible to push a cipher from the server to the
client. This is on the wish list of the OpenVPN developers, but it
has a substantial impact on the code. It is not going to be added to
OpenVPN before Version 2.4 or even 2.5.

The Compression mismatch

OpenVPN has the ability to compress all VPN traffic that is on-the-fly. For certain
types of traffic, such as plain web traffic, this can improve the performance of the
VPN, but it does add extra overhead to the VPN protocol. For incompressible traffic,
this option actually slightly decreases performance.

The option used to specify compression currently is as follows:

```
comp-lzo [no|yes|adaptive]
```

Note that we do not need to specify the second parameter. The default value is adaptive, if compression is used.

As we will learn in *Chapter 10, Future Directions*, this option will be superseded by a more generic compression option, allowing for different compression mechanisms.

It is possible to push a compression option from the server to the client, but only if a compression option has been specified in the client configuration file itself. If the client configuration file does not contain such an option, then the VPN connection will fail. The client log file will show the following:

```
UDPv4 link remote: [AF_INET]<SERVER-IP>:1194
WARNING: 'link-mtu' is used inconsistently,
    local='link-mtu 1541', remote='link-mtu 1542'
WARNING: 'comp-lzo' is present in remote config but
    missing in local config, remote='comp-lzo'
[Mastering OpenVPN Server] Peer Connection Initiated with
    [AF_INET]<SERVER-IP>:1194
TUN/TAP device tun0 opened
do_ifconfig, tt->ipv6=0, tt->did_ifconfig_ipv6_setup=0
/sbin/ip link set dev tun0 up mtu 1500
/sbin/ip addr add dev tun0 10.200.0.2/24 broadcast 10.200.0.255
Initialization Sequence Completed
write to TUN/TAP : Invalid argument (code=22)
```

The server log file will list the same WARNING messages, and it will also show decompression warnings:

```
client3/<CLIENT-IP>:45113 Bad LZO decompression header byte: 42
```

Odd but true: if we wait long enough, the client will restart due to the compression errors and will attempt to reconnect. This time, however, the connection will succeed, as the comp-lzo option still resides in memory.

How to fix

Make sure that, if you want to use compression, the `comp-lzo` option is specified in both client and server configuration files. With the `comp-lzo` option in the client-side configuration file, we can now control the type of compression used at the server side using a `push` option. Use the following:

```
comp-lzo no
push "comp-lzo no"
```

This will turn off compression, but unfortunately this is not the same as not specifying any compression method at all. This will hopefully be addressed in a future release.

The fragment mismatch

One of the most commonly used tuning parameters is the `fragment` option. You will learn more about this option in the section *How to optimize performance by using ping and iperf* later in this chapter.

Like the `comp-lzo` option, the `fragment` option does not need to be specified on either side. However, we cannot specify it only on one side; it must be configured on both. If it is specified only on one side, then it must also be specified on the other. Technically speaking, it is not even necessary to use the same value for the `fragment` option on both sides, but it is recommended.

If the `fragment` option is not specified on the client side but it is used on the server side, then the VPN connection will not function properly, as can be seen in the client's log:

```
WARNING: 'link-mtu' is used inconsistently,
   local='link-mtu 1541', remote='link-mtu 1545'
WARNING: 'mtu-dynamic' is present in remote config but
   missing in local config, remote='mtu-dynamic'
[Mastering OpenVPN Server] Peer Connection Initiated with
   [AF_INET]194.171.96.101:1194
TUN/TAP device tun0 opened
do_ifconfig, tt->ipv6=0, tt->did_ifconfig_ipv6_setup=0
/sbin/ip link set dev tun0 up mtu 1500
/sbin/ip addr add dev tun0 10.200.0.2/24 broadcast 10.200.0.255
Initialization Sequence Completed
write to TUN/TAP : Invalid argument (code=22)
```

Again, it will appear as if the VPN has come up (Initialization sequence completed), but the log file will fill up with code=22 error messages.

Note that the warning actually lists mtu-dynamic, which is the deprecated name of this feature.

How to fix

Make sure that, if you want to use the fragment option, then it is specified in both client and server configuration files.

Note that, unlike the comp-lzo option, this feature cannot be pushed from the server to the client.

The tun versus tap mismatch

The most common use case for using a tap style network is a bridged setup, as we have learned in *Chapter 6, Client/Server Mode with Tap Devices*. Not all devices, however, support a tap-style network. Most notably, all Android and iOS devices lack this capability. Hence, if we connect such a device to a tap style OpenVPN server, the server log file will list warnings from these clients:

```
<CLIENT-IP>:39959 WARNING: 'dev-type' is used inconsistently,
    local='dev-type tap', remote='dev-type tun'
<CLIENT-IP>:39959 WARNING: 'link-mtu' is used inconsistently,
    local='link-mtu 1573', remote='link-mtu 1541'
<CLIENT-IP>:39959 WARNING: 'tun-mtu' is used inconsistently,
    local='tun-mtu 1532', remote='tun-mtu 1500'
```

Apart from these warnings, the server will not detect anything about the connecting clients. On the client, similar warnings will be listed, along with this one:

```
WARNING: Since you are using --dev tun with a point-to-point topology,
the second argument to --ifconfig must be an IP address.  You are using
something (255.255.255.0) that looks more like a netmask. (silence this
warning with --ifconfig-nowarn)
```

As we cannot push the subnet topology in a tap-style setup, the client falls back to a default Net30-style network. This type of network is inherently incompatible with a tap-style network, but apart from that, the client does not list any warnings or errors.

Even if we were to (erroneously) add a topology subnet to suppress this warning on the client, the VPN would still not function correctly.

How to fix

Make sure that the same type of network (tun or tap) is used on both sides. If you must use Android or iOS devices, then you must set up a tun-style server configuration, as these operating systems do not support a tap-style network.

The client-config-dir issues

In *Chapter 4, Client/Server Mode with tun Devices*, we learned about CCD files and their uses in the section *Client-specific configuration – CCD files*. CCD files are generally used to connect a client-side LAN to the server network by using an `iroute` statement.

Experience on the OpenVPN mailing lists and forums has shown that the `client-config-dir` option is susceptible to error and misconfiguration. The three main reasons for this are as follows:

- The CCD file or the directory in which it resides, cannot be read by OpenVPN after it switches to a `safe` user, such as `nobody`.
- The `client-config-dir` option was specified without an absolute path.
- The name of the CCD file is not listed correctly. Normally, the name of a CCD file is the same as the name from `/CN= field` of the client certificate, without `/CN= part` and without any extension!

With the `normal` log level, OpenVPN does not complain if it cannot find or read a CCD file. It simply treats the incoming connection as a standard connection, and thus the required `iroute` statement is never reached.

The easiest way to debug this is to temporarily add an extra option to the server configuration:

```
ccd-exclusive
```

Restart the server and have the client try to reconnect. If the server cannot read the appropriate CCD file for a connecting client, it will refuse access. If this happens, we know that the CCD file has not been read. If the client can connect, then there is a different issue—most likely a routing issue.

Another way to see what the OpenVPN server does with CCD files is to increase the log level to 4 and reconnect a client for which a CCD file is listed. The contents of this CCD file for the client with the certificate `/CN=client1` are as follows:

```
ifconfig-push 10.200.0.99 255.255.255.0
iroute 192.168.4.0 255.255.255.0
```

This instructs the OpenVPN server to assign the VPN IP address 10.200.0.99 to this client, and to route the subnet 192.168.4.0./24 via this client. The server log file now lists the following:

```
<CLIENT-IP>:38876 [client1] Peer Connection Initiated with [AF_
INET]<CLIENT-IP>:38876
```

```
client1/<CLIENT-IP>:38876 OPTIONS IMPORT: reading client specific options
from: /etc/openvpn/movpn/clients/client1
```

```
client1/<CLIENT-IP>:38876 MULTI: Learn: 10.200.0.99 -> client1/<CLIENT-
IP>:38876
```

```
client1/<CLIENT-IP>:38876 MULTI: primary virtual IP for client1/<CLIENT-
IP>:38876: 10.200.0.99
```

```
client1/<CLIENT-IP>:38876 MULTI: internal route 192.168.4.0/24 ->
client1/<CLIENT-IP>:38876
```

```
client1/<CLIENT-IP>:38876 MULTI: Learn: 192.168.4.0/24 ->
client1/<CLIENT-IP>:38876
```

If the highlighted line is not present, then the CCD file is not read. Also, the next lines starting with MULTI: show how the OpenVPN server interprets the lines found in the CCD file. This can be important to further debug any iroute issues.

How to fix

If the server process cannot read the CCD file, then check the permissions of the full path to the file, including all subdirectories leading to it. Make sure the user specified with the user option has permission to read all directories and the CCD file itself.

Make sure that the client-config-dir option lists an absolute path instead of a relative one. Also, if we are using the chroot option (see the manual page for details), then make sure the client-config-dir directory is visible inside chroot-jail.

Use the ccd-exclusive option to quickly determine if OpenVPN can read the CCD file. If it can, then increase the log level on the server side to see how OpenVPN interprets the statements found in the CCD file.

No access to the tun device in Linux

If OpenVPN is started with insufficient privileges, or if OpenVPN is set to drop root privileges and switch to another `userid` (for example, `nobody`), then access to the `tun` device can be lost. This can also occur if OpenVPN is used in a virtualized environment, such as OpenVZ or **Virtual Private Server (VPS)**.

If OpenVPN is started with insufficient privileges, the VPN connection will not come up at all:

```
UDPv4 link local: [undef]
UDPv4 link remote: [AF_INET]<SERVER-IP>:1194
[Mastering OpenVPN Server] Peer Connection Initiated with
    [AF_INET]<SERVER-IP>:1194
ERROR: Cannot ioctl TUNSETIFF tun: Operation not permitted
    (errno=1)
Exiting due to fatal error
```

Check `userid` or use `sudo` to switch to a privileged user before starting OpenVPN.

The more common scenario when insufficient privileges are available is after an automatic restart of the VPN connection. Consider the following client configuration file:

```
client
proto udp
remote openvpnserver.example.com
port 1194
dev tun
nobind

remote-cert-tls server
tls-auth /etc/openvpn/movpn/ta.key 1
ca       /etc/openvpn/movpn/movpn-ca.crt
cert     /etc/openvpn/movpn/client3.crt
key      /etc/openvpn/movpn/client3.key

user    nobody
group nobody
```

This is the basic configuration file with two lines added at the bottom. When we launch the VPN connection using this configuration file, the connection comes up properly, but a warning is printed:

```
WARNING: you are using user/group/chroot/setcon without persist-tun --
this may cause restarts to fail
```

Indeed, after the VPN connection needs to be restarted (for example, due to a bad network connection), the restart will fail:

```
[Mastering OpenVPN Server] Inactivity timeout (--ping-restart),
    restarting
Mon Jun  1 16:51:50 2015 /sbin/ip addr del dev tun0 10.200.0.2/24
RTNETLINK answers: Operation not permitted
Linux ip addr del failed: external program exited with error
    status: 2
SIGUSR1[soft,ping-restart] received, process restarting
WARNING: you are using user/group/chroot/setcon without
    persist-key -- this may cause restarts to fail
Error: private key password verification failed
Exiting due to fatal error
```

Here, we see that OpenVPN failed to restart as the user nobody was not allowed to read the private key that was used for this connection. If we had specified a user that did have the right permissions, we would have seen a different error:

```
ERROR: Cannot ioctl TUNSETIFF tun: Operation not permitted
    (errno=1)
Exiting due to fatal error
```

Note that, during the restart, OpenVPN cannot shut down the existing tun device or delete any system routes. This will also be the case if persist-tun is used, but in that case it would be harmless.

How to fix

Add the following options to the client configuration file if you are using the `user` and/or `group` options as well:

`persist-tun`

`persist-key`

Make sure you start OpenVPN with sufficient privileges.

Also, make sure that OpenVPN has the right SELinux security context, or try running OpenVPN with SELinux set to permissive or disabled mode:

`# setenforcing permissive`

Missing elevated privileges in Windows

With some older versions of the OpenVPN installer program for Windows, the right privileges were not set for the OpenVPN GUI application.

For this particular example, a single route was pushed from the OpenVPN server to all clients:

`push "route 192.168.122.0 255.255.255.0"`

On Windows Vista and higher, OpenVPN needs elevated privileges to be able to add or remove system routes. If these privileges are not present, the VPN will usually be initialized correctly and the GUI-icon will turn green:

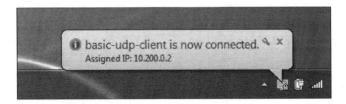

We can even ping the OpenVPN server on its VPN server IP address. However, the log file in the OpenVPN GUI will show some errors:

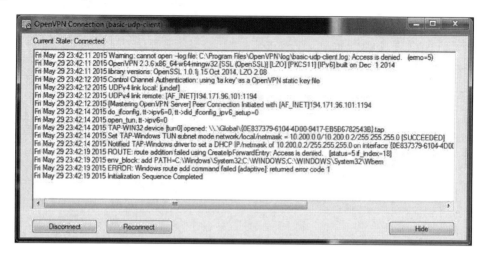

The first line is actually tricky:

```
Warning: cannot open -log file: .....: Access is denied
```

The tricky part is that as soon as we click on the **Disconnect** button, the log is gone, as it could not be written to disk! This is caused by the fact that the default log directory `C:\Program Files\OpenVPN\log` is accessible only to a user with elevated privileges.

The last few lines in the log file tell us that OpenVPN was unable to add the route that was pushed by the server. Again, this is caused by the fact that the OpenVPN program was run with insufficient privileges.

How to fix

After restarting the OpenVPN GUI with elevated privileges (turn on **Run as Administrator**), the route is added correctly. This can be seen from the routing table:

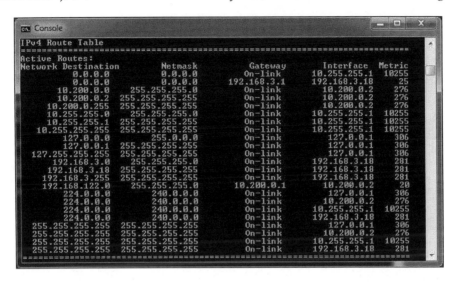

The pushed route, `192.168.122.0/24`, is now present in the routing table, using the server's VPN IP address `10.200.0.1` as the gateway.

Troubleshooting routing issues

Most of the questions asked on the OpenVPN e-mail lists and user forums are actually routing questions. Setting up a VPN connection is one thing, but integrating it into your existing network is quite another. To a novice, the difficult part is to see where OpenVPN stops and where routing begins. This section is intended as a step-by-step guide to troubleshoot routing issues in a fairly basic OpenVPN setup.

Consider the following network plan:

- The network at the main office location needs to be made accessible to a secondary office and to people working from home
- The servers in the secondary office needs to be made accessible to the IT department of the main office
- The people working from home only need to access the computer resources at the main office

For this, an OpenVPN server is set up at the main office, with the employees connecting as regular VPN clients, and with the secondary office connecting as a special client, disclosing its own network.

Drawing a detailed picture

Before creating the configuration files for OpenVPN, draw a detailed picture of the network layout, including all subnets, IP addresses, gateway IP addresses, interface names, and more.

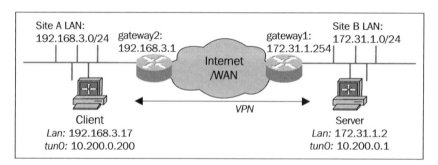

The public IP addresses used are not listed in this picture, but it is recommended to do so. Also, the connections from people working from home are not included, but they will connect to the public IP address of gateway1 in the preceding picture.

On gateway1, a port forwarding rule is added, so incoming and outgoing UDP traffic on port 1194 is forwarded to the OpenVPN server at 172.31.1.2:1194.

As we need to disclose the network in the secondary office, we will also need to use a client-config-dir file with the appropriate iroute statement.

The server and client configuration files for this setup are already listed in *Chapter 4, Client/Server Mode with tun Devices,* with some minor IP address changes. The new set of configuration files is as follows:

```
proto udp
port 1194
dev tun


server 10.200.0.0 255.255.255.0


tls-auth /etc/openvpn/movpn/ta.key 0
dh       /etc/openvpn/movpn/dh2048.pem
ca       /etc/openvpn/movpn/movpn-ca.crt
cert     /etc/openvpn/movpn/server.crt
key      /etc/openvpn/movpn/server.key


persist-key
persist-tun
keepalive 10 60


topology subnet


user   nobody
group nobody


verb 3
daemon
log-append /var/log/openvpn.log


push "route 172.31.1.0 255.255.255.0"
client-config-dir /etc/openvpn/movpn/clients
route 192.168.3.0 255.255.255.0 10.200.0.1
```

This file is saved as `movpn-09-01-server.conf`. For the OpenVPN client in the secondary office, a special certificate is created with the name `/CN=SecondaryOffice`. The corresponding CCD file, therefore has the name `/etc/openvpn/movpn/clients/SecondaryOffice`. Its contents are as follows:

```
ifconfig-push 10.200.0.200 255.255.255.0
iroute 192.168.3.0 255.255.255.0
```

For all clients, the `basic-udp-client.conf` or `basic-udp-client.ovpn` configuration file can be used. This, by the way, shows the flexibility of OpenVPN's configuration files. In most cases, there is no need to change the client configuration files, even if the network layout on the server side is modified, or a secondary network is brought into the VPN.

Next, we start the OpenVPN server and the secondary office client, and we make sure that the CCD file is picked up. The VPN client in the secondary office can `ping` the OpenVPN server at its VPN IP address, and so can a test user at home.

 At this point, the VPN is working, but routing is not.

Start in the middle and work your way outward

The most efficient method to troubleshoot this setup is to consider the VPN link as the middle, and then work outwards step-by-step until all parts of the network are connected. First, there are some tests to perform on the OpenVPN client in the secondary office. For almost all tests, a simple `ping` command will suffice.

Note that it does not make sense to move on to the second test if the first test is failing, and similarly, to the third test, if the second test is not yet working:

- Can the client reach the server's VPN IP address?

  This should function; otherwise, there is a problem with our VPN. It could be a very restrictive firewall/iptables setup on the server. The VPN server IP should be private (RFC1918, typically) and, thus, won't be routable across the general internet.

- Can the client reach the server's LAN IP address?

  If this is not functioning, then most likely there is a firewall or iptables rule that is blocking access. Check the inbound rules or try disabling the firewall rules for debugging.

- Can the client reach the server-side gateway IP address?

  If not, then check the answers to the following questions:

  - Is IP forwarding enabled on the server?
  - Is there a firewall/iptables rule blocking forwarding access to the server from a particular IP range?
  - Is there a firewall rule on the server-side gateway blocking access from non-LAN IP addresses? (This would be a good security policy.) If so, then it needs to be adjusted to allow traffic coming from the VPN IP 10.200.0.0/24.
  - Is there a return route on the gateway to tell it where packets originating from the VPN should go back to? Packets with destination address in the 10.200.0.0/24 range should be forwarded to the OpenVPN server at IP `172.31.1.2` on the router `gateway1`. Note that this is usually not the case. The actual syntax for adding such a route to the gateway depends on the model and firmware of the router used.

- Can the client reach another server on the server-side LAN?

  If not, then check the answers to the following questions:

  - Does this server on the server-side LAN have the proper gateway as the default gateway?
  - Is there a firewall rule on the server blocking access from non-LAN-IP addresses? (This would actually be a good security policy!)

After making sure that the client can reach all machines on the server-side LAN, it is time to make sure that the reverse is also true. Ensure that the OpenVPN server can reach all machines on the LAN behind the secondary client. The tests to perform are very similar:

- Can the server reach the client's VPN IP address?

  This should function; otherwise, there is a problem with our VPN. It could be a very restrictive firewall/iptables setup on the client. However, at this point it is highly unlikely to be a problem. Better safe than sorry, though, so let's test this.

- Can the server reach the client's LAN IP address?

  If this is not functioning, then most likely there is a firewall/iptables rule that is blocking access. Check the inbound rules.

- Can the server reach the client-side gateway IP address?

  If not, then check the answers to the following questions:

  - Is IP forwarding enabled on the secondary office client?

    Is there a firewall/iptables rule blocking forwarding access on the client from a particular IP range?

  - Is there a firewall rule on the client-side gateway blocking access from non-LAN IP addresses? (This would be a good security policy.) If so, then it needs to be adjusted to allow traffic coming from the VPN IP 10.200.0.1.

  - Is there a return route on the gateway in the secondary office to tell it where packets originating from the VPN should go back to? Packets with the source address 10.200.0.1 should be forwarded to the OpenVPN client at IP 192.168.3.17 on the router gateway2. Note that this is usually not the case. The actual syntax for adding such a route to the gateway depends on the model and firmware of the router used. Also, note that we only allow packets from the OpenVPN server itself to pass through, as all other clients do not require access to this network.

- Can the OpenVPN server reach another machine on the client-side LAN?

  If not, then check the answers to the following questions:

  - Does this server on the client-side LAN have the proper gateway as the default gateway?

  - Is there a firewall rule on the server blocking access from non-LAN-IP addresses? (This would actually be a good security policy!)

At this point, the OpenVPN client in the secondary office should be able to reach all machines in the server-side LAN, and the OpenVPN server in the main office should be able to reach all machines in the client-side LAN. There is only one more step: make sure that the servers on the server-side LAN can reach the servers on the client-side LAN and vice versa. Again, there are four tests to perform, starting on a machine on the server-side LAN:

- Can this machine reach the OpenVPN client's VPN IP address?

  This should function, as the client can reach this machine, as a result of the fourth test. However, better safe than sorry, so let's test this.

- Can this machine reach the client's LAN IP address?

  If this is not functioning, then most likely there is a firewall or iptables rule that is blocking access. Check the inbound rules on the OpenVPN client.

- Can the server-side LAN machine reach the client-side gateway IP address?

  If not, then check the answers to the following questions:

  - Is IP forwarding enabled on the secondary office client? Is there a firewall/iptables rule blocking forwarding access on the client for a particular IP range? Note that packets coming from the machine on the server-side LAN will have a different source address (172.31.1.X) to that of the OpenVPN server itself (10.200.0.1).

  - Is there a firewall rule on the client-side gateway blocking access from non-LAN-IP addresses? (This would be a good security policy.) If so, then it needs to be adjusted to allow traffic coming from the server-side LAN IP range 172.31.1.0/24. Similarly, a firewall rule may need to be added on the server-side gateway to allow traffic coming from the client-side LAN IP range 192.168.3.0/24.

  - Is there a return route on the gateway in the secondary office to tell it where packets originating from the VPN should go back to? Packets with source address 172.31.1.0/24 should be forwarded to the OpenVPN client at IP 192.168.3.17 on the router gateway2. Note that this is usually not the case.

- Can the server-side LAN machine reach another machine on the client-side LAN?

  If not, then check the answers to the following questions:

  - Does the server on the client-side LAN have the proper gateway as the default gateway?

  - Is there a firewall rule on the client-side machine blocking access from non-LAN-IP addresses? (This would actually be a good security policy!)

By methodically working through all of these steps, we can resolve almost all routing issues. In some cases, more advanced debugging techniques may be required. This may require us to temporarily disable firewall rules, so special care should be taken before attempting this.

Find a time to temporarily disable firewall

There have been too many cases on the OpenVPN mailing lists of people not being able to get routing to work, where it turned out to be a firewall or iptables rule that was too restrictive. There is no need to disable all firewall rules, but if you get stuck at one of the twelve steps listed previously, then try disabling the firewall related to the device that you cannot reach or that you are sending traffic from.

 If you need to make use of a NATted setup then make sure that you do not disable the NATting rules.

If all else fails, use tcpdump

The low-level networking tool `tcpdump` is a great tool for testing connectivity. In order to debug routing issues, we can use `tcpdump` to see if any traffic is arriving at or leaving a particular network interface, and we can check the source and destination addresses of this traffic. On a Windows client or server, it might be easier to run Wireshark (`http://www.wireshark.org`), which provides similar functionality, including a GUI.

In the twelve steps listed previously, the following `tcpdump` statements can help:

1. Run `tcpdump -nnel -i tun0` on the server to see if any traffic is coming in over the VPN at all.

2. Run `tcpdump -nnel -i eth0` on the server (where `eth0` is the LAN interface of the server in use) to see if any traffic is coming in on the LAN interface at all. If not, then most likely a firewall rule is dropping inbound traffic on the tunnel interface.

3. Run `tcpdump -nnel -i eth0` on the server to see if any traffic is leaving the LAN interface with the following:
   ```
   source address      = 10.200.0.200
   destination address = 172.31.1.254
   ```

   Also, check whether we can see return traffic from the server-side gateway with the source and destination addresses reversed.

4. Again, run `tcpdump -nnel -i eth0` on the server to see if any traffic is leaving the LAN interface with the following packet headers:

```
source address     = 10.200.0.200
destination address = 172.31.1.XXX
```

Here, `172.31.1.XXX` is the IP address of the machine we are trying to reach on the server-side LAN. Is there any return traffic seen?

And so on and so on for the remaining steps!

How to optimize performance by using ping and iperf

Getting maximum performance out of an OpenVPN setup can be difficult to achieve. On a clean Ethernet network, the default settings of OpenVPN are fairly good. However, some tuning is required on gigabit-speed networks.

When an ADSL or cable-modem connection is used, performance is also usually pretty good. However, under certain circumstances, the performance of our OpenVPN tunnel can fall way behind the performance of the normal network. These circumstances are almost always ISP-dependent, but nevertheless, it is worthwhile exploring how to increase performance.

The key to optimizing performance is to have good tools for measuring performance in the first place. Two basic, yet invaluable, tools for measuring network performance are `ping` and `iperf`. The `iperf` tool is readily available on Linux, FreeBSD, and Mac OS. There are ports available for Windows and even Android.

Using ping

Using `ping`, we can determine the optimal MTU size for our network. Most network operators now provide their customers with an Ethernet-style MTU of 1,500 bytes. This leads to an effective packet payload of 1,472 byes. The remaining 28 bytes are the TCP/IP overhead for things like the source and destination address.

However, if there is a network between the client and the server that has a lower MTU, then it can greatly increase performance to reduce the size of the OpenVPN packets to just below that size. To find out what the maximum transfer size is for our network, we use the following:

```
$ ping -M do -s 1472 www.example.org
```

On Windows, we use the following:

```
C:\> ping -f -l 1472 www.example.org
```

This will send ICMP packets to a remote server of our choice, with the do not fragment flag set, instructing the network routers not to break up this packet into smaller bits. If there is a network between the client and the server with a smaller MTU, then the ping command will fail:

```
$ ping -M do -s 1472 www.example.org
PING www.example.org (IP) 1472(1500) bytes of data.


ping: local error: Message too long, mtu=1480
```

This tells us that performance will most likely improve if we use either a fragment size of 1,480 or an MTU size that is 1,480 bytes instead of the default value of 1500. Note that this is not a guarantee—only by measuring the actual VPN performance we will know what the impact actually is.

Using iperf

By using iperf, we can measure the performance of a network, both inside and outside a VPN tunnel. This will give us valuable insight into how much bandwidth we are wasting by using a VPN tunnel.

Before measuring the performance of the VPN tunnel itself, always try to measure the performance of the normal network. It will be quite hard to make the VPN perform better than the underlying network.

First, launch iperf on the server with the following command:

```
$ iperf -s
```

Next, launch iperf on the client with the following command:

```
$ iperf -c openvpn.example.org
```

On the cable network that was used for testing, the result is as follows:

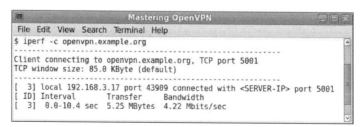

This is actually the upload speed of the cable connection used. We can now test the performance of the VPN tunnel over the same network:

```
[  3]   0.0-10.8 sec   5.25 MBytes   4.09 Mbits/sec
```

Repeating the measurement yields very similar numbers, so it is fair to state that the performance of the VPN tunnel is a few percent below that of the underlying network. This actually makes sense, as the use of a VPN does introduce some overhead for the encapsulation, encryption, and authentication (signing) of the original data. It will be hard to further optimize this network.

Similarly, for the download speed of the cable connection used, we find that the performance of the VPN tunnel is a few percent lower:

Performance of the underlying network is shown as follows:

```
[  4]   0.0-10.6 sec   51.6 MBytes   40.7 Mbits/sec
```

Now, compare this to the VPN tunnel:

```
[  4]   0.0-10.7 sec   49.5 MBytes   39.0 Mbits/sec
```

Again, we see a 4.5 percent drop in performance.

We can now use the `fragment` and `mssfix` parameters to see if we can increase performance. There will be a little bit trial-and-error work in order to find the sweet spot for a particular setup. It is not known what the exact sweet spot will be in advance, but the method for finding it is always the same. Now, add the options to both client and server configuration files:

```
fragment X
mssfix
```

By doing this and by varying X, we get the following results:

X (bytes)	Download (Mbps)	Upload (Mbps)
1200	37.9	3.94
1300	38.1	4.01
1400	38.4	4.04
1472	38.8	4.06
1500	37.6	3.98
<none>	39.0	4.09

We can conclude that OpenVPN's default settings are actually the sweet spot for this network. We could repeat this exercise by varying the `tun-mtu` parameter, but we would find the same result. However, it is advisable to first tune performance by using the `fragment` parameter, as this parameter has less influence on the forwarding of packets.

Gigabit networking

We will now perform the same procedure on a non-utilized gigabit Ethernet network. The `iperf` performance of the underlying network is 950 Mbps up and down.

When we launch the OpenVPN server using the `basic-udp-server.conf` configuration and attach a client to it by using the `basic-udp-client.conf` configuration file, we achieve the following `iperf` performance:

```
[ ID] Interval          Transfer       Bandwidth
[  5] 0.0-10.0 sec    193 MBytes     161 Mbits/sec
[  4] 0.0-10.0 sec    242 MBytes     203 Mbits/sec
```

There is now a clear drop in performance. Unfortunately, lowering the `fragment` parameter does not help us here. With `fragment 1200`, we achieve 149 Mbps and 115 Mbps, respectively.

On high-speed networks, it also makes sense to experiment with the encryption cipher. The servers used in this example are both capable of fast AES instructions, thanks to the AES-NI extension that is present on the CPUs (a 2 GHz Xeon E5 2620 and a 3.5 GHz (turbo) Xeon E5 2643, respectively). Let's add the following:

```
cipher aes-256-cbc
```

We now get the following result:

```
[  5] 0.0-10.0 sec    316 MBytes     265 Mbits/sec
[  4] 0.0-10.0 sec    266 MBytes     223 Mbits/sec
```

On a capable CPU, the cipher has a large impact on performance. As OpenVPN is a monolithic program, a high number of cores do not help at all. The clock speed of the CPU is a dominant factor. By connecting a 3.8 GHz (turbo) Core i7 laptop to the 3.5 GHz Xeon E5-2643 server, we achieve a much higher throughput using the exact same configuration:

```
[  5] 0.0-10.0 sec    707 MBytes     593 Mbits/sec
[  4] 0.0-10.0 sec    529 MBytes     443 Mbits/sec
```

Thus, if you want to set up an OpenVPN tunnel across a high-speed network, then the best advice is to use high clock speed CPUs that have support for the AES-NI instruction set. With such a setup, it is possible to achieve network speeds of over 500 Mbps in both directions.

Analyzing OpenVPN traffic by using tcpdump

The low-level networking tool `tcpdump`, or its GUI equivalent Wireshark, is a last resort tool for troubleshooting network issues and network performance. In this section, we will walk through the process of capturing and analyzing the encrypted network traffic produced by OpenVPN.

First, we set up our standard OpenVPN network using the `basic-udp` configuration files. On the client, there is also a web server running. We will use the `wget` command on the server side to retrieve a file from the web server so that we can look at the resulting network traffic.

We run `tcpdump` on the Ethernet interface and capture the network traffic while doing a `wget` outside the tunnel:

```
wget -O /dev/null https://CLIENT-IP/test1
```

The resulting `tcpdump` output is as follows (modified for the sake of clarity):

```
# tcpdump -nnel -i eth1 tcp port 80
tcpdump: verbose output suppressed, use -v or -vv for full protocol decode
listening on eth1, link-type EN10MB (Ethernet), capture size 65535 bytes
17:28:35.499618 1:1:1:1:1:1 > 2:2:2:2:2:2, IPv4, length 66:   <SERVER-IP>.40310  >  <CLIENT-IP>.80
17:28:35.499672 2:2:2:2:2:2 > 1:1:1:1:1:1, IPv4, length 66:   <CLIENT-IP>.80     >  <SERVER-IP>.40310
17:28:35.499877 1:1:1:1:1:1 > 2:2:2:2:2:2, IPv4, length 60:   <SERVER-IP>.40310  >  <CLIENT-IP>.80
17:28:35.499905 1:1:1:1:1:1 > 2:2:2:2:2:2, IPv4, length 164:  <SERVER-IP>.40310  >  <CLIENT-IP>.80
17:28:35.499937 2:2:2:2:2:2 > 1:1:1:1:1:1, IPv4, length 54:   <CLIENT-IP>.80     >  <SERVER-IP>.40310
17:28:35.500616 2:2:2:2:2:2 > 1:1:1:1:1:1, IPv4, length 1514: <CLIENT-IP>.80     >  <SERVER-IP>.40310
17:28:35.500636 2:2:2:2:2:2 > 1:1:1:1:1:1, IPv4, length 1514: <CLIENT-IP>.80     >  <SERVER-IP>.40310
17:28:35.500646 2:2:2:2:2:2 > 1:1:1:1:1:1, IPv4, length 1514: <CLIENT-IP>.80     >  <SERVER-IP>.40310
17:28:35.500656 2:2:2:2:2:2 > 1:1:1:1:1:1, IPv4, length 1353: <CLIENT-IP>.80     >  <SERVER-IP>.40310
17:28:35.500744 2:2:2:2:2:2 > 1:1:1:1:1:1, IPv4, length 54:   <CLIENT-IP>.80     >  <SERVER-IP>.40310
17:28:35.500844 1:1:1:1:1:1 > 2:2:2:2:2:2, IPv4, length 60:   <SERVER-IP>.40310  >  <CLIENT-IP>.80
17:28:35.500891 1:1:1:1:1:1 > 2:2:2:2:2:2, IPv4, length 60:   <SERVER-IP>.40310  >  <CLIENT-IP>.80
17:28:35.501037 1:1:1:1:1:1 > 2:2:2:2:2:2, IPv4, length 60:   <SERVER-IP>.40310  >  <CLIENT-IP>.80
17:28:35.501057 2:2:2:2:2:2 > 1:1:1:1:1:1, IPv4, length 54:   <CLIENT-IP>.80     >  <SERVER-IP>.40310
^C
13 packets captured
13 packets received by filter
0 packets dropped by kernel
```

As we can see, there are 13 packets to transfer a 5 KB text file. Most of these packets were used to set up and tear down the connection, but there are four large packets that were used to actually transfer the data. The first three of the four packets are 1,514 bytes in size, which is the maximum size of an Ethernet packet.

Next, we run the same `wget` command inside the tunnel. We now observe the encrypted traffic on the Ethernet adapter:

```
# tcpdump -nnel -i eth1 udp port 1194
tcpdump: verbose output suppressed, use -v or -vv for full protocol decode
listening on eth1, link-type EN10MB (Ethernet), capture size 65535 bytes
17:23:44.224950 1:1:1:1:1:1 > 2:2:2:2:2:2, IPv4, length 95:    <SERVER-IP>.1194   > <CLIENT-IP>.48693: UDP, length 53
17:23:44.225061 2:2:2:2:2:2 > 1:1:1:1:1:1, IPv4, length 95:    <CLIENT-IP>.48693  > <SERVER-IP>.1194: UDP, length 53

17:23:46.798604 1:1:1:1:1:1 > 2:2:2:2:2:2, IPv4, length 135:   <SERVER-IP>.1194   > <CLIENT-IP>.48693: UDP, length 93
17:23:46.798792 2:2:2:2:2:2 > 1:1:1:1:1:1, IPv4, length 135:   <CLIENT-IP>.48693  > <SERVER-IP>.1194: UDP, length 93
17:23:46.799099 1:1:1:1:1:1 > 2:2:2:2:2:2, IPv4, length 119:   <SERVER-IP>.1194   > <CLIENT-IP>.48693: UDP, length 77
17:23:46.799112 1:1:1:1:1:1 > 2:2:2:2:2:2, IPv4, length 231:   <SERVER-IP>.1194   > <CLIENT-IP>.48693: UDP, length 189
17:23:46.799238 2:2:2:2:2:2 > 1:1:1:1:1:1, IPv4, length 119:   <CLIENT-IP>.48693  > <SERVER-IP>.1194: UDP, length 77
17:23:46.800221 2:2:2:2:2:2 > 1:1:1:1:1:1, IPv4, length 1487:  <CLIENT-IP>.48693  > <SERVER-IP>.1194: UDP, length 1445
17:23:46.800316 2:2:2:2:2:2 > 1:1:1:1:1:1, IPv4, length 1487:  <CLIENT-IP>.48693  > <SERVER-IP>.1194: UDP, length 1445
17:23:46.800403 2:2:2:2:2:2 > 1:1:1:1:1:1, IPv4, length 1487:  <CLIENT-IP>.48693  > <SERVER-IP>.1194: UDP, length 1445
17:23:46.800492 2:2:2:2:2:2 > 1:1:1:1:1:1, IPv4, length 1487:  <CLIENT-IP>.48693  > <SERVER-IP>.1194: UDP, length 1445
17:23:46.800539 2:2:2:2:2:2 > 1:1:1:1:1:1, IPv4, length 319:   <CLIENT-IP>.48693  > <SERVER-IP>.1194: UDP, length 277
17:23:46.800580 2:2:2:2:2:2 > 1:1:1:1:1:1, IPv4, length 119:   <CLIENT-IP>.48693  > <SERVER-IP>.1194: UDP, length 77
17:23:46.800864 1:1:1:1:1:1 > 2:2:2:2:2:2, IPv4, length 119:   <SERVER-IP>.1194   > <CLIENT-IP>.48693: UDP, length 77
17:23:46.800886 1:1:1:1:1:1 > 2:2:2:2:2:2, IPv4, length 119:   <SERVER-IP>.1194   > <CLIENT-IP>.48693: UDP, length 77
17:23:46.800890 1:1:1:1:1:1 > 2:2:2:2:2:2, IPv4, length 119:   <SERVER-IP>.1194   > <CLIENT-IP>.48693: UDP, length 77
17:23:46.800895 1:1:1:1:1:1 > 2:2:2:2:2:2, IPv4, length 119:   <SERVER-IP>.1194   > <CLIENT-IP>.48693: UDP, length 77
17:23:46.800899 1:1:1:1:1:1 > 2:2:2:2:2:2, IPv4, length 119:   <SERVER-IP>.1194   > <CLIENT-IP>.48693: UDP, length 77
17:23:46.800903 1:1:1:1:1:1 > 2:2:2:2:2:2, IPv4, length 119:   <SERVER-IP>.1194   > <CLIENT-IP>.48693: UDP, length 77
17:23:46.801122 2:2:2:2:2:2 > 1:1:1:1:1:1, IPv4, length 119:   <CLIENT-IP>.48693  > <SERVER-IP>.1194: UDP, length 77

17:23:56.410192 2:2:2:2:2:2 > 1:1:1:1:1:1, IPv4, length 95:    <CLIENT-IP>.48693  > <SERVER-IP>.1194: UDP, length 53
17:23:56.410540 1:1:1:1:1:1 > 2:2:2:2:2:2, IPv4, length 95:    <SERVER-IP>.1194   > <CLIENT-IP>.48693: UDP, length 53
^C
22 packets captured
22 packets received by filter
0 packets dropped by kernel
```

Here, we see 22 packets being captured. The first and last two packets are OpenVPN `heartbeat` packets and can be ignored. The remaining 18 packets are the encrypted equivalent of the packets shown in the first `tcpdump` output. As we can see here, the length of the packet is slightly smaller, and especially the `payload` of each packet is quite a bit smaller: the largest UDP `payload` packet is 1,445 bytes. These 1,445 bytes contain the encrypted and signed data from the `wget` command. In our setup, we did not specify a `fragment` parameter, which means that OpenVPN 2.3 will default to an internal fragmentation of 1,450 bytes.

The total size of each packet never exceeds 1,487 bytes, which is fairly close to optimal: normally, packets should not exceed the MTU size, which is 1,500 bytes.

This `tcpdump` screen dump also shows that there is no fragmentation occurring other than within OpenVPN. This is good, as we want to avoid packet fragmentation by the operating system, or the network, for maximum performance. If we had seen packet fragmentation here, then this would have been an excellent indication that we needed to add extra fragmentation in our OpenVPN configuration.

Let's take a look at what happens if we add `fragment 1400` to our setup. We restart the server and client and rerun the `wget` command:

```
                          Mastering OpenVPN: tcpdump
 File  Edit  View  Search  Terminal  Help
# tcpdump -nnel -i eth1 udp port 1194
tcpdump: verbose output suppressed, use -v or -vv for full protocol decode
listening on eth1, link-type EN10MB (Ethernet), capture size 65535 bytes
17:25:57.335410 1:1:1:1:1:1 > 2:2:2:2:2:2, IPv4, length 103:  <SERVER-IP>.1194   > <CLIENT-IP>.54570: UDP, length 61
17:25:58.429775 2:2:2:2:2:2 > 1:1:1:1:1:1, IPv4, length 103:  <CLIENT-IP>.54570  > <SERVER-IP>.1194:  UDP, length 61

17:25:59.639719 1:1:1:1:1:1 > 2:2:2:2:2:2, IPv4, length 135:  <SERVER-IP>.1194   > <CLIENT-IP>.54570: UDP, length 93
17:25:59.639906 2:2:2:2:2:2 > 1:1:1:1:1:1, IPv4, length 135:  <CLIENT-IP>.54570  > <SERVER-IP>.1194:  UDP, length 93
17:25:59.640271 1:1:1:1:1:1 > 2:2:2:2:2:2, IPv4, length 127:  <SERVER-IP>.1194   > <CLIENT-IP>.54570: UDP, length 85
17:25:59.640291 1:1:1:1:1:1 > 2:2:2:2:2:2, IPv4, length 239:  <SERVER-IP>.1194   > <CLIENT-IP>.54570: UDP, length 197
17:25:59.640452 2:2:2:2:2:2 > 1:1:1:1:1:1, IPv4, length 127:  <CLIENT-IP>.54570  > <SERVER-IP>.1194:  UDP, length 85
17:25:59.641499 2:2:2:2:2:2 > 1:1:1:1:1:1, IPv4, length 1439: <CLIENT-IP>.54570  > <SERVER-IP>.1194:  UDP, length 1397
17:25:59.641595 2:2:2:2:2:2 > 1:1:1:1:1:1, IPv4, length 1439: <CLIENT-IP>.54570  > <SERVER-IP>.1194:  UDP, length 1397
17:25:59.641696 2:2:2:2:2:2 > 1:1:1:1:1:1, IPv4, length 1439: <CLIENT-IP>.54570  > <SERVER-IP>.1194:  UDP, length 1397
17:25:59.641777 2:2:2:2:2:2 > 1:1:1:1:1:1, IPv4, length 1439: <CLIENT-IP>.54570  > <SERVER-IP>.1194:  UDP, length 1397
17:25:59.641833 2:2:2:2:2:2 > 1:1:1:1:1:1, IPv4, length 543:  <CLIENT-IP>.54570  > <SERVER-IP>.1194:  UDP, length 501
17:25:59.641874 2:2:2:2:2:2 > 1:1:1:1:1:1, IPv4, length 127:  <CLIENT-IP>.54570  > <SERVER-IP>.1194:  UDP, length 85
17:25:59.642059 1:1:1:1:1:1 > 2:2:2:2:2:2, IPv4, length 127:  <SERVER-IP>.1194   > <CLIENT-IP>.54570: UDP, length 85
17:25:59.642137 1:1:1:1:1:1 > 2:2:2:2:2:2, IPv4, length 127:  <SERVER-IP>.1194   > <CLIENT-IP>.54570: UDP, length 85
17:25:59.642144 1:1:1:1:1:1 > 2:2:2:2:2:2, IPv4, length 127:  <SERVER-IP>.1194   > <CLIENT-IP>.54570: UDP, length 85
17:25:59.642147 1:1:1:1:1:1 > 2:2:2:2:2:2, IPv4, length 127:  <SERVER-IP>.1194   > <CLIENT-IP>.54570: UDP, length 85
17:25:59.642181 1:1:1:1:1:1 > 2:2:2:2:2:2, IPv4, length 127:  <SERVER-IP>.1194   > <CLIENT-IP>.54570: UDP, length 85
17:25:59.642224 1:1:1:1:1:1 > 2:2:2:2:2:2, IPv4, length 127:  <SERVER-IP>.1194   > <CLIENT-IP>.54570: UDP, length 85
17:25:59.642324 2:2:2:2:2:2 > 1:1:1:1:1:1, IPv4, length 127:  <CLIENT-IP>.54570  > <SERVER-IP>.1194:  UDP, length 85

17:26:09.117163 2:2:2:2:2:2 > 1:1:1:1:1:1, IPv4, length 103:  <CLIENT-IP>.54570  > <SERVER-IP>.1194:  UDP, length 61
17:26:09.117517 1:1:1:1:1:1 > 2:2:2:2:2:2, IPv4, length 103:  <SERVER-IP>.1194   > <CLIENT-IP>.54570: UDP, length 61
^C
22 packets captured
22 packets received by filter
0 packets dropped by kernel
```

With `fragment 1400` added to our setup, we can see in the `tcpdump` output that the packet payload is now 1,397 bytes in size, which is very close to the limit of 1,400. We can also see that more packets are now needed to transfer the 5 KB text file over the tunnel, which means a decrease in performance. From this screenshot, we can conclude that we should remove the parameter again.

From the preceding screenshot and the previous one, we can also deduce that each OpenVPN packets incurs a 42-byte overhead. This overhead partly contributes to the overhead incurred by using any VPN solution. It does comprise the entire overhead, as all network packets need to contain overhead information about the source address, destination address, packet type, checksums, flags, and many more.

Finally, let's take a look at the contents of an actual encrypted OpenVPN packet. For this, it is handy to use the Wireshark tool (`http://www.wireshark.org`). Wireshark basically provides a GUI on top of the low-level `tcpdump` tool. It can decode the contents of most types of network traffic, as we can see in the following screenshot (the screenshot has been anonymized for privacy reasons):

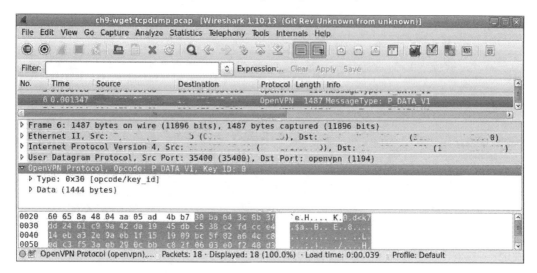

This screenshot tells us the following things:

* The actual packet size is 1487 bytes.

* It contains Ethernet and IPv4 headers, like any network packet on an Ethernet network.

* This is an OpenVPN packet with source port 35400 and destination port 1194, which means that it is travelling from the client to the server. It actually is one of the encrypted packets of the 5 KB file transfer from the client to the server.

* The `payload` of the packet is an OpenVPN data packet (format version 1), with a payload size of 1,487 bytes. Note that `tcpdump` reported 1,488 bytes earlier, but Wireshark can decode the payload and see that the first byte is an OpenVPN opcode.

This packet will be received by OpenVPN, checked for authentication, decrypted, and decompressed (if we had specified). The resulting unencrypted packet is then forwarded to the operating system's routing tables, which decide where to route the packet to. In our case, the packet will remain on the server and will be given to the `wget` process.

Summary

In this chapter, you learned some basic techniques for troubleshooting and tuning OpenVPN. You also got an insight into reading the client and server log files. You learned how to detect and fix some of the most often-made mistakes. Most questions on the OpenVPN e-mail list are about routing issues, therefore we discussed detecting and fixing routing problems. Finally, there is a large difference between a working setup and a well-working setup, so we looked at examples on how to detect and address performance issues.

Of course, OpenVPN is not perfect, and therefore your non-working setup could also be caused by a bug in OpenVPN itself. There are several channels for reporting bugs, including an e-mail list (`openvpn-users@lists.sourceforge.net`), an IRC channel (`#openvpn` on freenode.net IRC), and a forum website (`https://forums.openvpn.net`). You can also report feature requests or wish lists to these channels, some of which might make it into a future version of OpenVPN.

In the next chapter, you will learn what is new in the upcoming OpenVPN releases. You will also learn what are the currently known issues with the OpenVPN codebase and you will learn about the plans in place to address these issues.

10
Future Directions

The history of OpenVPN has been bumpy — ranging from a fledgling starter, to widely used, to nearly dead, and back again. The gap in development from 2006 to roughly 2009 was significant, but the hard work and dedication of developers such as David Sommerseth (dazo), Gert Doering (cron2), Steffan Karger, and Samuli Seppänen has given the project a successful recent past and a bright future.

OpenVPN is available on nearly every platform available. Snom (an IP phone manufacturer), for example, includes a version of their VOIP phone firmware with an OpenVPN client included. pfSense, OpenWRT, and other WAP/firewall operating systems include OpenVPN and (usually) a web interface to manage deployment.

In recent years, OpenVPN has been available on many mobile phones as well. The first was available for Android, *OpenVPN for Android* by *Arne Schwabe*. This utilized a ported tun driver and did not support tap mode (bridged) VPNs.

The OpenVPN application for iOS (Apple) didn't come until much later, however. It took OpenVPN Technologies, Inc. nearly a year to negotiate with Apple to support an external VPN API and grant access to that API for their use. On Android, the OpenVPN source could be ported to the platform, with some omissions for tap, since the tap driver was not available on the platform. Due to the development environment on iOS, the client had to be written from the ground up. James Yonen wrote a nearly feature-complete client in a few months in C++ and *OpenVPN Connect* was published to the App Store®.

Current strengths

OpenVPN 2.3 is light years ahead of where we stood in the recent past. A quick glance at the change list from around 2008 until now shows quite a significant number of important updates, bug fixes, and enhancements.

There are a number of things OpenVPN does well. OpenVPN is extensible, pluggable, and dynamic. It has functional support for IPv6, push default gateway (even in broken networks), and floating across public IPs while maintaining connections.

Cross-platform support is unbeatable across the various VPN implementations.

Current weaknesses

There are notable weaknesses in the current version of OpenVPN. First, the entire application is written as a single, monolithic application. The same binary that is used for client connections is also used as the server instance. This isn't too much of a problem, but there is no modularization of code, so all of the logic needs to be handled regardless of the context in which the application is executed.

Working through the monolithic design woes, developers will have an easier time implementing features such as IPv6, additional compression algorithms, and so on. Also, changes to improve the network stack need to be updated in many places within the code, rather than a single library or component. This is the reason the IPv6 and IPv4 stacks are handled separately today.

Scaling at gigabit speeds and above

Typically, on modern hardware, OpenVPN is able to support a couple of hundred client connections before kernel limitations reduce performance to unfavorable levels. This limit hasn't been a problem until more recently when higher speed internet connections have become available. In the past, a single OpenVPN server on a good uplink could easily keep pace with many client connections on a typical home Internet connection.

Today, however, gigabit connections at home aren't rare, and even where they are unavailable now, these high-speed uplinks will be available in the very near future. With the right high-clock speed processor, OpenVPN is capable of (nearly) saturating a gigabit Ethernet link.

This requires the AES encryption instructions (known as AES-NI) found in modern processors, such as Intel's Core i7 and Xeon E5 processors, as well as modern AMD processors. It also requires the encryption cipher to be set to AES, for example, by using `--cipher aes-256-cbc` in both server and client configurations.

 It is not possible to push the encryption cipher from the server to the client. This is a limitation of the current design of OpenVPN, and it will hopefully be addressed in a future version.

The operating system and encryption library also play a role here. Most server setups use the OpenSSL libraries for encryption and decryption. Support for the AES-NI instruction set was included only in OpenSSL 1.0.0. CentOS 5, for example, still uses OpenSSL library (0.9.8e-fips), which does not have support for these instructions. It is quite easy to verify whether a processor and the operating system make use of the AES-NI instructions. Using the `openssl speed` command, you can quickly determine encryption performance for both OpenVPN's default cipher (BlowFish or `bf-cbc`) and the AES cipher (`aes-256-cbc`):

```
$ openssl speed -evp bf-cbc
[...]
type          ...    256 bytes   1024 bytes   8192 bytes
bf-cbc        ...    137977.26k  138565.97k   137470.47k


$ openssl speed -evp aes-256-cbc
type          ...    256 bytes   1024 bytes   8192 bytes
aes-256-cbc          566760.53k  588199.94k   591250.12k
```

This test was run on an Intel Core i7-4810MQ processor running Fedora 20 and clearly, AES is much faster than BlowFish. We can safely conclude that AES-NI is supported by both the CPU and the operating system. If we disable OpenSSL's support for AES-NI instructions, the effect on performance is quite dramatic:

```
$ OPENSSL_ia32cap=0 openssl speed -evp aes-256-cbc
type          ...    256 bytes   1024 bytes   8192 bytes
aes-256-cbc          120009.39k  264001.19k   262821.68k
```

Using a processor such as the Core i7, it is possible to achieve performance of over 500 Mbps in both directions, as was shown in *Chapter 9, Troubleshooting and Tuning*.

Additional improvements can be found utilizing `--mssfix`, `--tun-mtu`, and `--fragment`. When used together, speed increase of up to 400 percent can be achieved.

Other factors can contribute to performance problems outside of OpenVPN. Scaling beyond gigabit speeds will require an extensive redesign of OpenVPN, as it requires an entirely different approach to handling such high levels of traffic. Keep in mind that network traffic is usually processed in chunks of 1500 bytes (referred to as **Maximum Transmission Unit (MTU)**). For a gigabit link, this means that the operating system kernel and the OpenVPN process need to handle roughly 80,000 packets per second. On a 10-gigabit link, this increases to well over 800,000 packets, which even the most modern processors cannot easily handle. Increasing the MTU from 1500 bytes to 9000 bytes, also known as jumbo frames, reduces the packet count while not reducing the amount of bandwidth. Jumbo frames need to be supported by all nodes on the network, or packet fragmentation can occur.

Where we are going

Starting in 2010, the open source developers began discussions about ways to improve the OpenVPN server process and improve efficiency. A number of areas that could be improved were identified. Fortunately, the beginnings of this endeavor were completed with James' client code rewrite for the iOS application. The official road maps for the coming v2.4 and the future v3.0 releases can be found on the OpenVPN community wiki in the following locations:

- `http://community.openvpn.net/openvpn/wiki/OpenVPN2.4`
- `http://community.openvpn.net/openvpn/wiki/RoadMap`

More specifically, modularization for plugins, even making the OpenSSL and PolarSSL support modules, has been discussed. This will allow for easier integration of other libraries as they become available, and even support for something entirely different from SSL could be achieved with this approach. Better threading and process offloading is also being considered to improve the client connection volume and bandwidth utilization.

Despite the great advancements we've already made, there's much room for improvement. A key issue, with no solution in sight, is support for the development team. There are only a very small number of developers active and devoted to the project. The end result is a slow development cycle and new features are rare.

Some items currently being worked on include better IPv6 support, proper Windows privilege separation, and TLS roaming.

A full list of current bugs is available on the OpenVPN community bug tracker. Patches are always welcome on the mailing list and well-written and tested patches are certain to get quick approval. The link `http://community.openvpn.net/openvpn/report/1` takes you directly to the open bug reports.

Improved compression support

Starting with Version 2.4, OpenVPN will support different mechanisms for compressing the VPN traffic. Currently, only LZO2 compression is supported, but in Version 2.4 you can also compile in support for the Snappy and LZ4 compression algorithms. This can improve performance quite a bit, depending on the type of traffic that is flowing over the VPN. Plain web server traffic will see a nice performance boost, while hard-to-compress traffic such as images or video files will likely see a small performance *decrease* due to the extra overhead of compressing and decompressing each packet.

Per-client compression

In Version 2.3 and below, if compression is enabled at the server, it must also be enabled at the client. This has proven difficult to identify from client logs in the past, as the tunnel just appeared to fail passing traffic. On the v2.4 roadmap, there is compression negotiation. This would allow per-client compression, and even compression protocol/algorithm negotiation.

New cryptographic routines

In Version 2.4 support for Elliptic Curve authentication algorithms is included for the first time. It will not yet be possible to use Elliptic Curves for all traffic, but it does allow the use of ECDSA based certificates.

Hopefully, we will also see support for GCM-based encryption in Version 2.4. **GCM (Galois/Counter Mode)** encryption, is more efficient and performant than the currently used **CBC (Cipher Block Chain)** encryption routines.

Authenticated Encryption with Associated Data (AEAD) will also debut in v2.4.

Mixed certificate/username authentication

Currently, OpenVPN supports authentication using certificates and/or a username and password, but either/or is not possible. The option `--client-cert-not-required` actually turns off certificate verification altogether.

In Version 2.4, it will be possible to support clients that connect using either a certificate, or a username and password, or both. This allows for greater flexibility when granting users different levels of access to your VPN setup. For this, a new option is added.

- `verify-client-cert none`: This is effectively the same as `--client-cert-not-required`.

- `verify-client-cert optional`: This will verify the certificate supplied by the client, but it will not reject the connection if verification fails.

- `verify-client-cert require`: This will verify the certificate supplied by the client and reject the connection if verification fails. This will be the default setting, as it effectively is the default in OpenVPN Version 2.3 and older.

The `--client-cert-not-required` option will be deprecated in the near future and is mentioned in the v3.0 roadmap.

IPv6 support

The networking code within OpenVPN uses separate functions for IPv4 and IPv6 code paths. A couple of years ago, there was a major overhaul of how IPv4 was handled, but the work was never done for the IPv6 functions. OpenVPN 2.3 does support a completely native IPv6 transport as well as encapsulated traffic. Using IPv6 DNS servers and garnering that information from DHCP isn't supported, but is on the roadmap for v2.4.

`push "redirect-gateway ipv6"` is also on the list. You can still imitate a default route with IPv6 by pushing the special routes manually:

```
push "route-ipv6 ::/0 2600:dead:beef::1"
```

Windows privilege separation

OpenVPN currently requires administrative privileges on all client workstations. Users with standalone workstations should have the ability to update configuration without administrative privileges, and the client application should have the ability to accept valid server configuration assertions.

Two approaches have been presented to accomplish this. One of them is Windows-centric and the other one offers principles that can be deployed or implemented on other platforms.

The first of the two is accomplished by providing an OpenVPN interactive service. Heiko Hund first suggested the approach in February 2012 (`http://thread.gmane.org/gmane.network.openvpn.devel/5685/focus=5728`). The concept includes a centralized service that acts as a wrapper around another OpenVPN process. A client connection from an interactive user would start OpenVPN or the OpenVPN GUI and that process would then connect to this service. The service would then take the arguments from the client and create the actual VPN tunnel, establishing routes and other options.

Proper implementation has requirements not previously implemented or really considered. First, the private key needs to be properly protected:

> *To be complete, the wrapper [=interactive service] must also own the OpenVPN private key – otherwise the configuration would be copyable by a non-privileged user, something that the enterprise model is determined to prevent. Protecting the private key can be accomplished by storing the key in the system certificate/key store, and accessing the key through a Cryptographic Provider API such as Crypto API on Windows, PKCS#11 on Linux, or Keychain on Mac.*

> *James Yonan*

Second, the interactive service must not allow access from other processes (non-OpenVPN) running as the same (current) user:

> *The pipe/socket to the privileged process [=interactive service] needs to be access-controlled so that only openvpn can use it. You don't want to introduce a privilege escalation vulnerability where operations that would normally be privileged (like changing the default route) can now be done by any process in user space just by leveraging on the OpenVPN pipe/socket.*

> *James Yonan*

Third:

> *Other non-privileged software might be able to access the APIs for these wrappers [=interactive service], for example by pushing routes into the API. Malware that would normally be confined to user space can now perform privileged operations such as modifying the default route. The end user can now connect to any VPN server of their choice (a major violation of enterprise model). What you've essentially done with this model is introduce a privilege escalation vulnerability because operations that would normally require privilege, such as adding routes, can now be done by a non-privileged user.*

> *James Yonan*

The second approach utilizes two or three separate COM+ objects, as suggested by Alon Bar-Lev in March 2012 (`http://thread.gmane.org/gmane.network.openvpn. devel/5755/focus=5869`). With this approach, three components are needed: the OpenVPN GUI, the OpenVPN service, and the OpenVPN network handler.

The OpenVPN GUI would not change much from what it is today. It would continue to hand tasks and updates to a backend process. As there is no current privilege separation, the current GUI does not need to handle any authorization. With the use of COM+ and the network OpenVPN module, the GUI can be completely unprivileged.

Summary

After spending years in the OpenVPN IRC channel and on the OpenVPN support forum, there are some recurring difficulties among the server administration user base: basic networking and routing, X.509 certificate management, and user or client authentication. Having now read this book, you should have a solid grasp of these concepts and understand the underlying mechanisms. The differences between the tun and tap virtual network adapters have been discussed as well.

OpenVPN is a very active open source project and is ever evolving. The techniques and examples within Mastering OpenVPN will likely not go stale in the near future. Inefficiencies within the code are anticipated, however, so we *strongly* recommend that you read the manual (man page) available at `https://openvpn.net/index. php/open-source/documentation/manuals.html`.

Like most open source projects, OpenVPN needs more help—more volunteers to help moderate the forum and help on IRC, and additional developers to help increase the speed of development are all needed. There are aspirations to build a bounty system to aid in this effort. The community is strong and the protocol is widely recognized.

There is a lot of work to do, but the feature set of OpenVPN compared to other VPN applications puts it right in line with expectations. If you would like to get involved with the OpenVPN project, look through the following resources to identify interesting work and contact someone to help you get started:

- IRC: `https://freenode.net` #openvpn and #openvpn-devel
- Web forum: `https://forums.openvpn.net`
- Mailing list: `http://sourceforge.net/p/openvpn/mailman/`
- Bug tracker: `http://community.openvpn.net/openvpn/report/1`
- Man pages: `https://openvpn.net/index.php/open-source/documentation/manuals.html`

Index

E

K

Thank you for buying
Mastering OpenVPN

About Packt Publishing

Packt, pronounced 'packed', published its first book, *Mastering phpMyAdmin for Effective MySQL Management*, in April 2004, and subsequently continued to specialize in publishing highly focused books on specific technologies and solutions.

Our books and publications share the experiences of your fellow IT professionals in adapting and customizing today's systems, applications, and frameworks. Our solution-based books give you the knowledge and power to customize the software and technologies you're using to get the job done. Packt books are more specific and less general than the IT books you have seen in the past. Our unique business model allows us to bring you more focused information, giving you more of what you need to know, and less of what you don't.

Packt is a modern yet unique publishing company that focuses on producing quality, cutting-edge books for communities of developers, administrators, and newbies alike. For more information, please visit our website at www.packtpub.com.

About Packt Open Source

In 2010, Packt launched two new brands, Packt Open Source and Packt Enterprise, in order to continue its focus on specialization. This book is part of the Packt Open Source brand, home to books published on software built around open source licenses, and offering information to anybody from advanced developers to budding web designers. The Open Source brand also runs Packt's Open Source Royalty Scheme, by which Packt gives a royalty to each open source project about whose software a book is sold.

Writing for Packt

We welcome all inquiries from people who are interested in authoring. Book proposals should be sent to author@packtpub.com. If your book idea is still at an early stage and you would like to discuss it first before writing a formal book proposal, then please contact us; one of our commissioning editors will get in touch with you.

We're not just looking for published authors; if you have strong technical skills but no writing experience, our experienced editors can help you develop a writing career, or simply get some additional reward for your expertise.

OpenVPN 2 Cookbook

ISBN: 978-1-84951-010-3   Paperback: 356 pages

100 simple and incredibly effective recipes for harnessing the power of the OpenVPN 2 network

1. Set of recipes covering the whole range of tasks for working with OpenVPN.

2. The quickest way to solve your OpenVPN problems!

3. Set up, configure, troubleshoot and tune OpenVPN.

4. Uncover advanced features of OpenVPN and even some undocumented options.

Beginning OpenVPN 2.0.9

ISBN: 978-1-84719-706-1   Paperback: 356 pages

Build and integrate Virtual Private Networks using OpenVPN

1. A practical guide to using OpenVPN for building both basic and complex Virtual Private Networks (VPNs).

2. Learn how to make use of OpenVPNs modules, high-end-encryption and how to combine it with servers for your individual privacy.

3. Advanced management of security certificates.

4. Get to know the new features of the forthcoming version 2.1 of OpenVPN.

Please check **www.PacktPub.com** for information on our titles

OpenVPN
Building and Integrating Virtual Private Networks

ISBN: 978-1-90481-185-5   Paperback: 272 pages

Learn how to build secure VPNs using this powerful
Open Source application

1. Learn how to install, configure, and create
   tunnels with OpenVPN on Linux, Windows,
   and MacOSX.

2. Use OpenVPN with DHCP, routers, firewall,
   and HTTP proxy servers.

3. Advanced management of security certificates.

Understanding SSL VPN

ISBN: 978-1-90481-107-7   Paperback: 212 pages

Business and Technical Benefits of Web-Based
Remote Access to Private Networks

1. Understand how SSL VPN technology works.

2. Evaluate how SSL VPN could fit into your
   organisation?s security strategy.

3. Practical advice on educating users,
   integrating legacy systems, and eliminating
   security loopholes.

4. Written by experienced SSL VPN and data
   security professionals.

Please check **www.PacktPub.com** for information on our titles